Candide
and Related Texts

Voltaire

Candide
and Related Texts

Translated, with an Introduction, by
David Wootton

Hackett Publishing Company, Inc.
Indianapolis/Cambridge

Copyright © 2000 by Hackett Publishing Company, Inc.

05 04 03 02 01 00   1   2   3   4   5   6   7   8   9

For further information, please address

Hackett Publishing Company, Inc.
P.O. Box 44937
Indianapolis, IN 46244-0937

www.hackettpublishing.com

Cover design by Abigail Coyle and Brian Rak
Text design by Abigail Coyle and Meera Dash

Cover art: engraving, Moreau Le Jeune (Jean-Michel Moreau), "*Candide s'enfuit au plus vite dans un autre village,*" in *Romans et Contes de M. de Voltaire* (1778).

Library of Congress Cataloging-in-Publication Data

Voltaire, 1694–1778.
   [Candide. English]
   Candide and related texts / Voltaire ; translated, with an introduction, by David Wootton.
     p. cm.
   Includes bibliographical references.
   ISBN 0-87220-547-9 (cloth) — ISBN 0-87220-546-0 (paper)
   1. Voltaire, 1694–1778. Candide. I. Wootton, David, 1952– II. Title.
PQ2082.C3 E5 2000
843'.5—dc21   00-040874

CONTENTS

ABBREVIATIONS

SV = *Studies on Voltaire and the Eighteenth Century*
D = number of a letter in Voltaire, *Correspondence*, ed. Theodore Besterman, *Complete Works*, vols. 85–135 (Oxford: The Voltaire Foundation,
1968–1977)

John Cage tells the story somewhere of going to a concert of music composed by a friend of his. The composer had also written the program notes for the music in which he said, among other things, that he hoped his music might go some way to diminishing the suffering in the world. After the concert his friend asked him what he thought of the event and Cage answered, "I loved the music but I hated the program notes." "But don't you think there's too much suffering in the world?" the friend asked, obviously put out. "No," Cage replied, "I think there's just the right amount."

The opening words of Adam Phillips, *Darwin's Worms*
(London: Faber and Faber, 1999)

Whereof one cannot speak, thereof one must be silent.

The final words of Ludwig Wittgenstein,
Tractatus Logico-Philosophicus
(London: Routledge and Kegan Paul, 1922)

Introduction

What can one expect from a man [Voltaire] who is almost always at odds with himself, and whose heart is always being led astray by his head. . . . Of all the people in existence the one he understands the least is himself. . . . He laid claim to more happiness than he had a right to expect. . . . The flattery and praise of his admirers completed what his excessive pretensions had begun, and having thought he was the master of his admirers he became their slave, with his happiness depending on their approval. This false foundation covered over an immense void . . . and what's the result? The fear of death—for the prospect of death makes one tremble—doesn't prevent one from complaining about life; and, not knowing who to blame, one ends up blaming Providence, when one's only quarrel is with oneself.

—Théodore Tronchin, Voltaire's doctor, to Jean-Jacques Rousseau, 1 September 1756[1]

From Arouet to Voltaire

Candide was published early in 1759: Voltaire (1694–1778), who had suffered a lifetime of ill-health, was sixty-four. No one, least of all Voltaire, would have guessed that he would live almost another twenty years, and that much of his very best work and his years of greatest influence lay ahead of him. We should read *Candide* as an old man's attempt to tell us what he has learned from life.

Voltaire was born François-Marie Arouet, the son of a successful lawyer and banker, though he would later claim his true father was a nobleman, officer, and poet, and would change his name to Voltaire at the age of twenty-three, thus cutting his ties with his family. From his earliest years Voltaire's ambition was to be a famous playwright and epic poet, and he achieved enormous success early on with his tragedy, *Oedipus* (1718), and his epic poem, *La Henriade*, about Henry IV of France (1728). In 1731 he published his first major history, *The History of Charles XII*, conquering a third field of literature. It was as epic poet, as playwright, and as historian that Voltaire expected to be remembered. He regarded the novel as an insignificant literary form, and *Candide* in any case is a mere novella or *conte*, a short story or tale. At the same time he pursued an extraordinarily successful career as a financial investor and moneylender, a career that—far more than his earnings from publishing—meant that by 1759 he was extremely wealthy.

---

1. D6985.

In 1759 Voltaire was perhaps the most famous and successful, and—after Helvétius, who had been a tax farmer before he became an author—the wealthiest literary figure in Europe, but nothing about his life had been straightforward. At nineteen he was fired from his first job, on a diplomatic embassy to The Hague, because he had tried to elope with a young noblewoman. At twenty-one he was sent out of Paris into provincial exile for some satirical verses against the regent who ruled in place of the young Louis XVI. He then spent a year (1717–18) in the Bastille prison for a second offense. In 1726 he had a falling out with a great nobleman, the chevalier de Rohan. As a mark of contempt, Rohan had his servants administer a thrashing to Voltaire. Voltaire, to reassert his status, sought to fight a duel against Rohan. He was thrown in the Bastille, and then spent two and a half years (1726–28) in exile in England. When he left England it was rumored that he had escaped just ahead of arrest and execution for forgery. In 1732 he caused offence by dedicating a play not to a French nobleman but to an English merchant. In 1734 his *Letters Concerning the English Nation* or *Philosophical Letters* (a volume in praise of Shakespeare, inoculation against smallpox, and political and economic freedom) was banned and burned, and he had to flee Paris and the court at Versailles, taking refuge in the château at Cirey (in Lorraine) of his mistress, the philosopher Mme. du Châtelet. In 1736 his poem *Le Mondain*, in praise of luxury, so outraged the authorities he had to flee temporarily to Holland.

Briefly, between 1743 and 1747, Voltaire was in favor at court: appointed royal historiographer, elected to the Académie Française, and appointed gentleman-in-waiting to the king. But there was soon a falling out (partly because Mme. du Châtelet was the victim of cheating at cards), and in 1750 (after the death of Mme. du Châtelet in childbirth), Voltaire went to live in Berlin at the court of Frederick the Great, ruler of Prussia. Frederick was a homosexual and was keen to attract other homosexuals to his court. His efforts to seduce Voltaire had begun in 1736 (Voltaire already had a reputation for bisexuality), and the two had exchanged love poetry and endearments. Voltaire seems to have thought that he and Frederick would be in effect a married couple; but conflicts soon developed. Frederick said of Voltaire that one throws away the orange peel once one has sucked the orange dry. Voltaire and his niece (and lover), Mme. Denis, fled Berlin, only to be arrested, threatened, and imprisoned in Frankfurt. Between March 1753 and January 1755 Voltaire was in effect stateless and homeless. He did not dare entrust himself once more to Frederick, and he could not obtain permission to return to France, where the French government regarded his association with Frederick as an alliance with a hostile foreign power.

Only in January 1755 did he obtain leave to settle in Geneva, where (since a foreigner could not own land) he purchased a life interest in a

house that he renamed *Les Délices*, "The Delights." Voltaire was successful and wealthy, but the kings of France and Prussia had tossed him aside.
His greatest ambition, to establish himself as the leading literary figure in
a glittering court, where his plays would be performed to universal ac-
claim, would now never be realized. In these circumstances it would not be
surprising if Voltaire blamed providence when his only quarrel was with
himself, for he had lost his audience and his status, and was reduced to
living with himself, with whom he had always been at odds. Tronchin's
diagnosis seems entirely persuasive. Is it not natural that this old man,
afraid of death and complaining about life, should have been the author of
Candide, a book responsible for the invention of the word "pessimism"?
Yet there is nothing in our story so far to prepare us for the life, the
laughter, the happiness that bubble through every crack and crevice of
Candide's story.

OPTIMISM

Einstein apparently once said that the most important question is, "Is the
universe friendly?" An orthodox Christian should already know the answer to this question, and the first person to address it with any serious-
ness for well over a thousand years was Pierre Bayle (1647–1706), who
published his *Dictionnaire historique et critique* in 1697.[2] The dictionary
was more of a philosophical encyclopedia than the biographical dictionary
it claimed to be. Bayle was a French Protestant, who had fled from
persecution in France and was writing in exile in Holland. But even in
Holland there were limits to what one could say and publish. By quoting
authors long dead, Bayle was able to pretend that the questions he chose to
discuss were merely questions of fact. Thus in an article superficially
devoted to clarifying the beliefs of an obscure ancient Greek philosopher,
Xenophanes, Bayle marshaled a range of pagan authors to demonstrate
that the universe was anything but friendly. This, and a number of related
articles, were to spark an intellectual debate that was still flourishing when
Candide was published.

   Nothing could have been more simple than Bayle's arguments (or
rather the arguments that he collected from respectable authorities such as
Cicero and Erasmus). Bayle claimed that we all experience more misery
than happiness in our lives. He maintained that painful experiences are
usually much more intense than pleasurable ones—an hour of toothache

---

2. Was Bayle a Christian? The question is vexed. See Gianluca Mori, *Bayle
philosophe* (Paris: Honoré Champion, 1999) and David Wootton, "Pierre Bayle,
Libertine?" in *Oxford Studies in the History of Philosophy*, vol. II, ed. M. A. Stewart
(Oxford: Oxford University Press, 1997), 197–226.

can outweigh the pleasures of a week's holiday. He said that almost no one would choose to live their life over again if they had the choice. Bayle implied that if we do not commit suicide it is because we cling unreasonably to life. He asked how a good God could have allowed evil to enter the world. He dismissed traditional arguments that Adam and Eve, not God, were responsible for the entry of sin and death into the world, by maintaining that God could not escape the responsibilities attached to his own foreknowledge—God, permitting Eve to be tempted, was like a parent allowing a teenage child to drive while drunk (Bayle's example, of course, was different: he said it was like a father allowing a young daughter to go to a ball where he knew she would be seduced). He pointed out that orthodox Christians believe that many more people will be damned than saved— which means that the Devil recruits more successfully than Christ does. If one looks at the evidence impartially, he concluded, everything suggests that the universe is not under the control of a good God. Rather, one might imagine that there was a struggle going on between good and evil gods, neither of whom is fully in control, though the evil god has the upper hand. Philosophy and experience, for Bayle, were compatible only with the beliefs of the ancient Manicheans, who were dualists.

Gottfried Leibniz (1646–1716) devoted much of his intellectual life to addressing Bayle's arguments, publishing his *Théodicée* in French in 1710 (Leibniz was German but wrote in Latin and French). Leibniz's approach to the problem of evil was deductive. He believed one could prove God existed because the very idea of God required that he must exist. God, he believed, was obliged to create a universe that was as large and diverse as possible, and that was governed by as few general principles as possible. Such a universe must be constructed to be as favorable as possible to intelligent and sentient beings. Leibniz thought God would create no universe other than the best of all possible universes, and that one of the features of this universe would be that it would be good for us. He thought it inevitable that there would be things in the universe that would seem painful or evil, but he claimed pain and evil would only exist in order to make possible a greater good (a baby teething experiences pain, but the pain is a necessary part of acquiring adult teeth; the rape of Lucretia, Leibniz's supporters maintained, had been the precondition for centuries of Roman liberty), and consequently evil would always be outweighed by good. He thus had to deny Bayle's claim that misery outweighs happiness.

But his theory posed a number of problems. First, Leibniz's God is committed to diversity, so even if this is the best of all possible universes, it is quite possible that we inhabit the worst of all existing worlds, or live in the worst of all centuries. The indigenous peoples of the Americas may die in untold numbers of smallpox, and syphilis may ravage Europe, but this must still be the best of all possible universes. Second, Leibniz's universe is tightly structured—every event is preordained, part of an inflexible chain of causation. If there was room for uncertainty about what will happen next, then the best universe might degrade into the second best or worse. This leaves no scope for free will or accident, and no scope for making things better than they would otherwise have been. Third, Leibniz's universe seems likely to be stable and therefore static—it seems hard to imagine how Paradise, if once possible, should be destroyed, and how sin and death could take over the best of all possible worlds. It is therefore hard to reconcile Leibniz's philosophy with a Christian eschatology of Fall, Incarnation, and Redemption, although Leibniz certainly intended that this reconciliation should take place.

From the mid-1730s Voltaire was probably aware of Leibniz's arguments as Mme. du Châtelet was an admirer of his work; and from 1736 Voltaire was discussing the philosophy of Leibniz and his disciple Johann Christian Wolff in correspondence with Frederick. Indeed the works of Leibniz and Wolff were widely discussed at the time. Voltaire was hostile to key aspects of Leibniz's theories, such as his denial of free will (though he was to change his mind on this question in 1740)[3] and his insistence that the universe is a tightly knit structure—Voltaire, following Newton, believed that the universe contained vast empty spaces, which implied that one could change one planet without significant effects on other planets— for example, inhabitants of distant stars would not have been adversely affected if Columbus had not discovered the New World. Where Leibniz's theory appeared to imply that the smallest event in history might be crucial to everything that had happened since, Voltaire insisted that much of what had happened in the past had had no consequences, and therefore could have happened differently. But, despite his consistent opposition to Leibniz's deductive system, Voltaire was already committed to what was soon to be called "optimism," that is, the doctrine that this is the best of all possible worlds or universes—the terminology one chooses depends on whether or not one imagines there are other inhabited worlds.

In 1733 Pope had published the first part of his *Essay on Man*, in which he sought to explain man's place in nature, the principles of morality, and the foundations of society. Voltaire read Pope in 1734, when letter 25 of his own *Letters Concerning the English Nation*, a letter added to the first French edition, was on its way through the press, so it seems there can be no doubt that Pope's *Essay* and Voltaire's letter were written independently of each other. Nevertheless, Voltaire was soon to stress that the two works had exactly the same argument.[4] Pope's essay reached a conclusion that was similar to Leibniz's, but it started from the empirical fact that the

---

3. E. D. James, "Voltaire on Free Will," *SV* 249 (1987), 1–18.

4. 20 Sept. 1735 (D915).

universe showed every indication of having been constructed according to a plan—which appeared to prove the existence of an all-powerful God. Like Leibniz, Pope believed God was committed to a principle of diversity, or a great chain of being—the universe contained not only angels and flies as well as human beings, but every conceivable creature in between. And, like Leibniz, he asserted that evil only exists for the sake of a greater good. Consequently, where Leibniz had claimed this is the best of all possible universes, Pope claimed that "Whatever is, is right" (which was translated into French as *tout est bien,* or "all is well," and which Voltaire thought meant "all is for the best" or "nothing could be better").

It would thus appear that Leibniz, Pope, and Voltaire were all, quite independently, committed to similar views. Pope, who was nominally a Catholic, wanted to give expression to views expounded to him by his friend Bolingbroke, a skeptic and deist. Voltaire was later to insist repeatedly that the arguments of Pope and Bolingbroke were taken from Shaftesbury's *Characteristics* (1711). This was evidently a matter of importance to him: Shaftesbury had been taught by Locke, and Voltaire was throughout his life a great admirer of Locke's philosophy. Voltaire, when he wrote letter 25 of the *Letters,* may himself have been writing under the influence of Shaftesbury, but his primary purpose was to attack Pascal, and, in the person of Pascal, orthodox Christianity. Pascal had argued that sin has made human beings miserable and that human life is profoundly unattractive. Voltaire insisted that human beings are happy; that the world they live in is well suited to them and they to the world ("to conclude that the earth, that mankind, and the brutes are just what they ought to be, is, in my opinion, thinking like a wise man"), and that the fact that we cannot get everything we want is fine, because human beings live in hope and are thereby driven to hard work. Where Pascal had insisted that we should look into ourselves and take the measure of our own inadequacy, Voltaire insisted that we should look outward, look to the future, and aspire to success. In place of guilt and self-examination, he advocated hope and ambition.

Leibniz (the best of all possible worlds), Pope (all is well), and Voltaire (the earth is just what it ought to be) had reached similar conclusions for very different reasons and by very different means. Leibniz favored deduction and was hostile to Locke and Newton; Pope and Voltaire favored induction and supported Locke and Newton. Leibniz intended to defend the Christian God against Bayle's hypothetical Manicheism; Voltaire intended to defend Shaftesbury's deism against Christianity; and Pope intended to defend both deism and Christianity against atheism. Voltaire could therefore only be expected to agree with Leibniz or Pope when their very different purposes coincided.

The theme of optimism is one that Voltaire returned to again and again throughout his life. In 1747, for example, before he had to flee from Versailles, he published *Zadig*, a story in which terrible things happen, but in which we are asked to believe that (as in Leibnizian discussions of the rape of Lucretia) evil happens only to prevent a greater evil or make possible a greater good. Zadig himself does not seem convinced that every individual event can be shown to be for the best, but this does not mean that Voltaire was no longer an optimist. No good may come of my dying of smallpox, but death and disease may still be a necessary part of the divine plan.

However, when on 1 November 1755 much of Lisbon was destroyed by an earthquake, Voltaire wrote a poem directly attacking not only Leibniz but also Pope. It now seemed to him ridiculous to maintain that all is well. The first version of his poem was savagely criticized by almost all who heard or read it—Tronchin told Voltaire to burn it—because it contained no reference to hope in a life after death. Voltaire added extensively to the poem to make it more palatable, but he had now taken a public position as an outright opponent of optimism.

In *Candide* Voltaire was to address the whole range of issues raised by the debate on optimism, which had been fueled in France by translations of Wolff and Pope. Voltaire's character Pangloss is a disciple of Leibniz, while Martin speaks for Bayle's Manicheism. The old woman, too, clearly voices Bayle's view that everyone's life contains far more misery than happiness, and Candide discovers by empirical enquiry that she is right (Voltaire even strengthens Bayle's argument by pointing out that boredom can be as intolerable as physical pain—there is no evidence that Bayle was tortured by boredom, as Voltaire certainly was).

Moreover, Voltaire constructs the story so that at every step (at least until we reach the end) optimism is undermined. It is not merely that all sorts of dreadful things happen. Voltaire quite deliberately exploits each of the three weaknesses I have pointed to in Leibniz's theodicy. First, the Fall. In attacking optimism Voltaire insisted he was defending Christian orthodoxy against Socinians (who denied the doctrine of original sin). Since Voltaire was in most of his work a bitter enemy of orthodox Christianity, this claim (like his description of the "Poem on the Lisbon Disaster" as a "sermon") was intended to puzzle his readers. Candide, like Adam and Eve, is kicked out of Paradise and condemned to hard work. His universe superficially replicates that of Christianity—except for the fact that Candide is redeemed by work, not by faith.

Second, fatalism. Candide's universe appears to be loosely, not tightly structured. Chance, not fate, determines who lives and who drowns when one's ship goes down. Moreover, within this loosely structured universe, individuals have some power to determine their fate. Candide's story would have ended unhappily had he not listened, first to the old woman, who tells him to buy a farm, and then to the old man, who shows him how to make the most of it. Voltaire, it has been argued, had replaced optimism (the claim that everything is already as good as it could be) with meliorism (the claim that things can be made better).

Third, diversity. Candide travels from world to world, from the Old World to the New. Which, he wants to know, is the best? What if my world is much worse than the best? Perhaps El Dorado exists somewhere, even if we cannot get to it.

Hard work; a flexibility that makes improvement possible; a critical analysis of alternatives—every time Voltaire attacks Leibniz he appears to suggest that the world can be made better. On the one hand, Voltaire wants to prove that the optimists (his younger self perhaps included, though even his younger self believed in the transforming power of hope and ambition) are mistaken, for there is a great deal wrong with the world. On the other hand, Voltaire does not seem convinced that there is bound to be more pain than pleasure in life (despite all the evidence, one might say). Bayle's arguments (soon to be called "pessimism") are equally misleading, and Martin does not prove a reliable guide. Life is often dreadful, but can be delightful.

The story of *Candide*'s composition is often told as follows.[5] Voltaire was an optimist until 1747. After that he was struck by a series of dreadful blows. He was driven from Versailles; Mme. du Châtelet was taken from him, first by a younger lover and then by death; his escape to Berlin rapidly turned from idyll to nightmare; just as Candide's love for Cunégonde turns sour when Cunégonde becomes ugly, so Voltaire's companion, Mme. Denis, had become "fat as a pig." The Lisbon earthquake was all that was needed to confirm that there was something dreadfully wrong with the world. When he wrote *Candide,* Voltaire was an enemy of optimism because life had disappointed him. This story has a dramatic structure that Tronchin's claim that Voltaire had never found happiness because he had never known where to look for it lacks, but it shares with

---

5. E.g., W. H. Barber, *Leibniz in France* (Oxford: Clarendon Press, 1955), 223–30; Ira O. Wade, *Voltaire and "Candide"* (Princeton: Princeton University Press, 1959), 138–41; W. H. Barber, *Voltaire: Candide* (London: Edward Arnold, 1960), 54–7; Voltaire, *Candide,* ed. J. H. Brumfitt (Oxford: Oxford University Press, 1968), 22–7; Voltaire, *Candide,* ed. Daniel Gordon (Boston: Bedford/St. Martin's, 1999), 15–8. The problem with this approach is summarized in Roger Pearson, *The Fables of Reason: A Study of Voltaire's 'Contes Philosophiques'* (Oxford: Clarendon Press, 1993), 112: "Why *Candide*? The less satisfactory answers to this perennial question have insisted too greatly on the misfortunes of Voltaire's own life as the spur to his onslaught on Optimism. . . . Yet by 1758 Voltaire had already . . . found relative contentment. . . ."

Tronchin's analysis the conviction that Voltaire would not have turned against optimism if his own life had turned out well.

Later I will offer an alternative account, but first we need to identify a central problem with this conventional account, which depends on identifying a turning point in Voltaire's life (the Lisbon earthquake), and stressing the extent to which Voltaire after that turning point was different from Voltaire before.[6] For one can tell the story very differently, so as to emphasize continuity rather than change. First, the Voltaire of 1734 and the Voltaire of *Candide* both believe in hard work and hope. It is hard to explain the enormous impact of the *Letters Concerning the English Nation* unless one reads it as a meliorist tract that argues that England is better than France, but France could make itself much more like England.

Second, Voltaire had seen the key objections to optimism from the beginning. Proponents of the discontinuity thesis usually avoid mentioning the fact that, as early as 1736, Voltaire rejected the Leibniz-Wolff position by making exactly the same point that the dervish makes in the last chapter of *Candide*.[7] Far from the world having been made to ensure human happiness, it looks very much, he argued, as if God was thinking of other things. The optimists make the same mistake that mice on a ship would be making if they said the captain of the ship was concerned to ensure their welfare.

Similarly, the conventional interpretation plays down or ignores the fact that in later life Voltaire was perfectly prepared to revert to optimistic arguments. The essay on "All is well" in the *Portable Philosophical Dictionary* (1764) sticks very closely to the antioptimistic position, but Voltaire's later essay on whether humankind is a child of the devil (1768), while

---

6. Theodore Besterman, *Voltaire* (3rd ed., Oxford: Blackwell, 1976), 365–74; an approach criticized in Geoffrey Murray, *Voltaire's "Candide": The Protean Gardener, 1755–1762* (*SV* 69 [1970]), 161–86. See also 312–5 on another supposed turning point in the autumn of 1758.

7. D1139 (26 Aug. 1736): "It doesn't seem likely that the first principles of things will ever be well understood. The mice who live in some tiny holes of an immense building do not know whether the building is eternal, nor do they know who designed it, nor do they know why it was built. They try their best to stay alive, to populate their holes, and to escape from the carnivorous animals who hunt them. We are the mice. . . ." This letter is discussed in Barber, *Leibniz in France*, 179; but not, for example, in William H. Barber, *Voltaire: "Candide"* (London: Arnold, 1960), or in Voltaire, *Candide*, ed. Brumfitt, both of which find the first pre-echo of *Candide* in the letter to Kahle of 1744 (D2495: Barber, *Voltaire: Candide*, 51; *Candide*, ed. Brumfitt, 22). It is to Thiriot (9 Sept. 1757; D7456) that we owe the image of a boat in place of a building. In later life Voltaire was fond of a rather different image, that we are all turkeys waiting for Christmas (D1187; D1558; D19116; see below, p. 142).

ostensibly an attack on Hobbes, is also a critique of Bayle, and concludes that if everything is not good, everything is at least tolerable.[8] And crucially, in his novel *Histoire de Jenni* (1775), Voltaire (or at least his character Friend) relies on a series of optimistic arguments to refute atheism, arguments that Barber finds strikingly similar to those of Leibniz.[9] Any account of the place of *Candide* in Voltaire's life needs to allow for such continuities. If the Lisbon earthquake was, as Besterman claims, "the death of optimism," then optimism, like Pangloss, seems to have been capable of returning from the dead.[10]

ART AND LIFE

The debate about optimism was first and foremost a debate between Bayle and Leibniz; by structuring his story around the contrast between Pangloss and Martin, Voltaire reproduced the two-sidedness of the debate itself. But there is more doubling than just this contrast between two philosophies, for every character seems to have a pair.[11] Candide is paired with Cunégonde through sexual attraction. The old woman is paired with Cacambo, for both are faithful and reliable servants. Jacques the Anabaptist, the good Dutch merchant, is paired with Vanderdendur, the evil Dutch merchant. And then these pairings overlap. At the end of the novel Pangloss, the heterosexual, is paired with Cunégonde's brother, the homosexual; although he is still Martin's polar opposite. Moreover, characters exchange roles: Cunégonde rescues Candide and later Candide rescues Cunégonde. New patterns emerge: Cunégonde and the old woman have similar stories; young Candide models himself on an old man.

Candide is doubled through and through: the story itself falls into two halves—the journey to and from El Dorado. The outward journey passes through Amsterdam and Lisbon; the return journey through Paris and Venice. A detailed analysis shows that individual chapters consist of two halves that mirror each other; groups of chapters also mirror each other;

---

8. "On Whether Man Was Born Wicked and the Child of the Devil," from *L'A B C;* translated in *Political Writings*, ed. David Williams (Cambridge: Cambridge University Press, 1994), 106–14.

9. Barber, *Leibniz in France*, 241.

10. Besterman, *Voltaire*, 365. Voltaire scholars are clearly uncomfortable with Voltaire's failure to take sufficiently seriously his own refutation of optimism: e.g., Haydn Mason writes of "the modified kind of optimism into which he *relapsed* in later years" (my emphasis), "Voltaire and Manichean Dualism," *SV* 26 (1963), 1143–60, at 1159.

11. I am grateful to Stuart Warner for discussing this with me.

the beginning reflects the end.[12] The more closely one looks the more doubled the world of *Candide* appears to be. The very tight and careful patterning of the story reminds us that this is a world created by Voltaire, and, in creating a world of pleasure and pain and good and evil, he is imitating God. If the story of *Candide* seems to show that Leibniz was wrong to think of the world as governed by necessity not chance, one might say that the structure of *Candide* seems to show that Leibniz is right: there will be nothing random or arbitrary in a well-designed universe.

Any account of *Candide* needs to focus on pairing, doubling, and mirroring. These enact an internal dialectic: between optimism and pessimism, male and female, homosexuality and heterosexuality, fatalism and meliorism, language (Pangloss) and silence (the dervish). The novel adopts a complex attitude to these dualities. On the one hand they appear to be fundamental and inescapable. But on the other, each pairing proves to be misleading. Neither the optimist nor the pessimist can foresee a happy ending. Both homosexuals and heterosexuals are alike in their experience of sexual attraction, but sexual attraction, which has so long seemed an irresistible force, disappears from the story at the end. The novel may appear to give the last word to the dervish and Candide, who want all the talking to stop—but it is itself a system of words, proof that Voltaire has not fallen silent.

This might appear to point to a fundamental duality: on the one hand there is the world we live in, on the other Voltaire's novel, which is a representation of the world. Voltaire himself raises the issue of representation when Pococurante criticizes Raphael, claiming his paintings do not look real. What sort of representation of the "real" world is *Candide*? As a system of representation, *Candide* is as puzzlingly doubled as it is in every other respect. Nobody reading it could imagine for a moment that it was a "true" story, that Candide was a real person. Voltaire (who loved puppet and magic lantern shows) seems to make the characters deliberately two-dimensional.[13] The story depends on every tired convention of contemporary romances—shipwrecks and pirates, women raped and sold into slavery, sudden deaths and improbable resurrections—so that one can never forget that this is first and foremost a fiction. The continuous doubling and pairing itself draws attention to the presence of an author who has designed and structured the whole.

And yet at the same time much of *Candide* is drawn directly from

---

12. C. J. Betts, "Exploring Narrative Structures in *Candide*," *SV* 314 (1993), 1–131.

13. Indeed reading the proofs of *Candide* made Voltaire think of magic lantern shows: Voltaire, *Candide,* ed. René Pomeau (Oxford: Voltaire Foundation, 1980), 55, commenting on D8004.

disciplines that claim to represent the "real" world: journalism, history, geography. The story is set in historical time (Candide is in Lisbon on 1 November 1755 when the earthquake occurs) and geographical space (it is easy to trace all the voyages on a map; even when Candide goes somewhere Voltaire knows does not exist, El Dorado, it is a place that has long been shown on maps); some of the characters are real people—the actress, for example, to whom Candide is attracted in Paris. All of it is improbable, yet none of it is impossible. *Candide* simultaneously presents itself as only a story and at the same time it has all the trappings of a true history.

Thus two types of doubling may be said to characterize Candide. On the one hand, there are pairings and mirrorings within the text. On the other, there is a constant oscillation between the realistic and the fantastical. These two doublings are fundamentally different, and it is remarkable to see Voltaire experimenting with each separately as he works his way toward *Candide*. "Scarmentado" is, like *Candide*, a voyage in which everything goes wrong. It is set in historical time (the early seventeenth century, which Voltaire had just been describing in his *Essai sur les moeurs* [1756] or *Universal History*), and can be traced on a map. But Scarmentado travels on his own. Everything goes wrong, nothing goes right (except insofar as is necessary for him to survive and keep traveling). He ends up back where he began. "Scarmentado" oscillates between history and fiction (though it lacks the clichés of romantic literature that are so important in *Candide*), but it has no internal pairings or mirrorings.

"The Comforter Comforted" is the other element in the equation. This story is located in neither time nor space. Real people and historical events are referred to, but they exist outside the world of the story; the two are not intermingled. But it contains two characters, "Comforter" and "Comforted," who are opposites (male and female, princess and philosopher), but who exchange roles. And these two characters tell stories within Voltaire's story, as Cunégonde, the old woman, and Martin tell stories within *Candide*, stories intended to educate one for life. *Candide*, one might say, is quite straightforwardly an attempt to write simultaneously a story that, like "Scarmentado," intermingles fiction and fact, and one that, like "The Comforter Comforted," pairs and exchanges roles and has two halves that mirror each other. All three stories are about education. Scarmentado learns to make the best of things; the princess cannot learn from her philosopher how to be philosophical; Candide learns to work the land. But in *Candide* something happens that does not happen in either of its predecessors. Scarmentado ends up where he began; the comforter ends up, in a simple reversal of the starting position, being comforted. Candide ends up somewhere quite different from where he began. *Candide* is much more dynamic, and puts the case for meliorism much more powerfully than either of its predecessors. It is—to use the word not in the sense in which Voltaire and his contemporaries use it, but in the sense in which we commonly use it—a much more optimistic work.

What makes for change in the world of *Candide?* Voltaire admired Locke, and Locke argued that all knowledge comes from experience. It is thus tempting to read *Candide* as a story in which Candide learns from experience, to read Candide's journeys as a metaphor for experience.[14] But this does not, I would suggest, correspond to what happens, for Candide is almost as impervious to experience as Pangloss, and what he experiences (romantic love, for example) is entirely shaped by his assumptions about the world. What changes Candide's life is the stories people tell. Crucially, he learns from the old woman that everyone's experience of life is rather like his own (and rather like Bayle's), and this eventually enables him to found a community in which everyone contributes to the welfare of everyone else.

On this account, the key moment in *Candide* occurs in chapter 10, when the old woman insists on telling her story. At this moment roles shift, lessons are learned. The old woman becomes Cunégonde's social equal, putting the whole notion of an established social hierarchy into doubt, and she rescues Candide and Cunégonde from the solipsism that had led them to think of their own stories as exceptional and peculiar. The old woman's story (Scarmentado's story would have served equally well, for the two are very similar) serves the function of the comforter's story—it is a remedy against despair, even though it is a story of misery. Indeed it has the paradoxical effect of helping Cunégonde overcome despair, while teaching Candide to abandon dogmatic optimism. Thanks to the old woman's story Candide and Cunégonde discover what they have in common with their fellow passengers.

If *Candide* is more about storytelling than traveling, why are journeys so important in the stories of Candide, the old woman, and Scarmentado? These journeys are extraordinarily long and involve an almost unending series of disasters. One is bound to think that their purpose is to show that the world is the same—and just as awful—wherever one goes. Only a journey through the whole world can test Leibniz's claim that this is the best of all possible worlds (and one can imagine a sequel to *Candide* involving space travel, a theme Voltaire had explored in *Micromégas*). But we may add that the world had also changed since the days of Bayle and Leibniz. The Seven Years War (1756–63) was the first war to be fought by the European powers in the New World and in Asia, as well as in Europe. Where Scarmentado, notionally traveling in the early seventeenth century, travels through a whole series of distinct and independent societies, Can-

---

14. E.g., Pearson, *Fables of Reason*, 115–9.

dide, a hundred and fifty years later, is never far from a French or an English battleship. European power has been globalized and as a result the world has shrunk; it has become a mere "globule" rather than a "globe."[15]

The story of *Candide* reaches out to the furthest corners of the globe, but it starts on the eve of a war in Germany. For Voltaire, the Seven Years War was not simply one war among many, each equally futile and destructive. This war had been deliberately started by Frederick, his former intimate friend. In the first year the war had gone very badly for Frederick, and he had written to Voltaire predicting his own defeat and death, but then the tide of battle turned, and his army appeared invincible. It is Frederick's army that Candide is pressganged into joining, Frederick's battle that he fights, Frederick's military training that wins him a Spanish commission. *Candide* is in part an indictment of what Frederick has done to Europe and the wider world. And, of course, just as Voltaire followed Frederick's career with close attention after their parting, so Frederick followed Voltaire's. He read *Candide*, he claimed, seven times, praising it as the only novel ever written that was worth reading more than once.[16]

One might think that a story about disaster would make one's own life worse, more unbearable: Rousseau had claimed that this was the effect on him of Voltaire's poem about the Lisbon earthquake. But for some reason this is not the impact of the old woman's story on Candide, on Cunégonde, or on us—on her audience. The right story, it seems, can bring about change; and the right story, it seems, is a story of disaster. There is thus a third respect in which *Candide* is not unitary. Like a Russian doll, it contains stories within stories, and the stories within it are strikingly similar to *Candide* itself. We can describe the story of the old woman as a mini-*Candide* within *Candide*. Both are stories about optimism and pessimism, but they are also devices for bringing about change in a world full of misery. Like the old woman's story, *Candide* is not a mere tale, but an education.

On 18 August 1756 Rousseau wrote a long letter to Voltaire attacking his poem on the Lisbon earthquake and defending optimism. Rousseau pointed out that Voltaire was successful, wealthy, and free. It might be too much to say that he was healthy, but at least he had the services of the finest doctor. Rousseau described himself, by contrast, as insignificant, poor, and sick. The difference between them, Rousseau believed, was that while Voltaire saw pain and suffering everywhere, he for his part lived in hope and was an optimist, for he believed that in the end all would be well.

---

15. Murray, *Voltaire's "Candide,"* ch. 3, esp. 215–22. Voltaire was busy buying maps of the globe as he finished *Candide:* D7912, D7940, D7965.

16. Though he could also be sharply critical: see Richard A. Brooks, *Voltaire and Leibniz* (Geneva: Droz, 1964), 101.

Voltaire, he implied, did not realize the value of what he had; indeed happiness consisted not in having things but in living in hope.

Tronchin's letter to Rousseau two weeks later was written after he had read Rousseau's letter to Voltaire, which he had been asked to forward to its addressee. Like Rousseau, Tronchin found Voltaire's rejection of optimism psychologically puzzling, but he seems to have been persuaded by Rousseau's explanation. They both agreed that Voltaire had been spoiled by his own success. Where modern critics tell us that Voltaire abandoned optimism because too many things had gone wrong for him, Rousseau and Tronchin thought he did so because too many things had gone right.

Later Rousseau was to say that *Candide* was Voltaire's reply to his letter, but at the same time he claimed never to have read the book, which conveniently meant that he never had to explain what sort of reply he thought it was.[17] Two things are surely obvious. First, Voltaire, speaking through the old woman, is claiming that we all have a story of pain and suffering to tell. Rousseau and Tronchin, preoccupied with Voltaire's success, have failed to realize that Voltaire too is a victim, a victim (as we now know) not just of recent disasters, but of childhood sexual abuse.[18] Unable to bring himself to tell his real story, Voltaire tells a fiction full of stories comparable to his own. We might say that he tells his story of rape compulsively, over and over again in the persons of Cunégonde, the old woman, and (most closely resembling his own story of abuse by the Jesuits) Cunégonde's brother. It is not success that has turned Voltaire away from optimism, he appears to be telling us, but a new willingness to acknowledge the world as it is and to recognize that there is nothing exceptional about his own story.

If *Candide* is not so much a book about travel-as-education as a book about the educative and therapeutic power of storytelling, then we need to see that it has a double purpose. First, it is a device that enables Voltaire to tell a version of his own story—generations of scholars who have sought for Voltaire "in his story" have not been entirely mistaken. Second, it invites us to rethink the story we might tell of our own lives, to find a way of telling our own story so that it helps us discover a reasonably happy ending. Both purposes require us to rethink the dervish's advice to be silent. Conventional talk about metaphysics, even about politics, is dismissed at the end of *Candide* as worthless; but there are other things to

---

17. See R. A. Leigh, "From the *Inégalité* to *Candide:* Notes on a Desultory Dialogue between Rousseau and Voltaire (1755–1759)," in *The Age of Enlightenment: Studies Presented to Theodore Besterman,* ed. W. H. Barber et al. (Edinburgh: Edinburgh University Press, 1967), 66–92.

18. See David Wootton, "Unhappy Voltaire, or 'I Shall Never Get Over It As Long As I Live'," *History Workshop Journal* No. 50 (2000), 141–59.

talk about, such as happiness. Indeed such conversations might even lead to a new way of talking about both philosophy and politics.

HAPPINESS

When Théodore Tronchin wrote to Rousseau they were both convinced, on the evidence of the "Poem on the Lisbon Disaster," that Voltaire was unhappy. Tronchin thought it was a sufficient refutation of Voltaire's poem to say that his own life was a happy one, and that he expected his children to be happy in their turn. The advocates of what I have called the discontinuity thesis agree: Voltaire must have been unhappy or distressed to abandon optimism.[19] It would thus seem natural, if we turn to the letters that Voltaire was writing at this very time, to discover some evidence of this unhappiness.

Let us take August and September 1756, the period of Rousseau's and Tronchin's letters, as a test (a period for which there are forty surviving letters from Voltaire). There is plenty of evidence of Voltaire's being ill (he is close to death; he "lives without digesting"; he is "an old sick man who plants cabbages"—one variation among many others on the theme of cultivating one's garden or working one's land), and for much of the period Voltaire is afraid that his niece Mme. de Fontaines, Mme. Denis's sister, is actually going to die.

Nevertheless, on 9 August:

> I will not go to Vienna. I am too happy in my retreat at Les Délices. Happiness is living in your own house with your nieces, your books, your gardens, your vines, your horses, your cows, your eagle, your fox, and your rabbits, who cover their noses with their paws. I have all that, and the Alps beyond them, which make an astonishing sight. I prefer telling off my gardeners to paying my court to kings.

On 21 August, to the Duchess of Saxe-Gotha, "I know no unhappiness, other than that of being far from your most serene highness." On 3 September, Les Délices "would deserve the name, if only I enjoyed some good health." (On 12 September, it would deserve the name if Rousseau would visit.) On 6 September, "it is a shame to be ill at such a fine time of year and in so beautiful a place." On 10 September news has reached him that war has begun and Frederick has seized Leipzig. "My thoughts are fixed on ripening my grapes and my peaches. I wander along paths bordered by flowers in a garden that I have designed, and I take little interest

---

19. Where (e.g., *Candide,* ed. Brumfitt, 25) mention is made of Voltaire's "newly found contentment" this is not seen as integral to the mindset of the author of *Candide.*

in the affairs of the Vandals and the Saxons." He writes an undated letter to the philosopher Condillac (a fellow Lockean) to say that if he will come and write a book at Les Délices, "I will add to your book a chapter on happiness." On 20 September, "Meanwhile I must stay in my very pretty, very peaceful, and very free retreat. Monsieur the count of Gramont . . . said yesterday on seeing my terrace, my gardens, my surroundings, that he could not imagine how I could ever leave." On 26 September, "I still dare hope that there are some people more powerful than I am who will be less happy than I am."

On just two occasions in these two months Voltaire's letters speak of unhappiness, not happiness (4 August, in the context of events in Paris; 17 September in the context of war and ill health), but the overall impression is very straightforward: Voltaire is either very happy, or he wants only good health or good company to be perfectly contented. He stands prepared to write a chapter on happiness.

One might reply that we should turn instead to the period of *Candide*'s composition. Voltaire appears to have written his book in three phases: at the very beginning of 1758, when we find what appear to be echoes of *Candide* in his correspondence; during a period of six weeks in July and August when he was visiting the elector Palatine, to whom he is supposed to have read aloud from his unfinished story; and in October, when he locked himself in his room for several days to finish the book. Were we to accept the thesis of Van den Heuvel, for example, then we would expect to find Voltaire at his most miserable in early 1758, when he is at work on the opening chapters of the book.[20] And indeed Voltaire has troubles enough. Frederick has defeated the French, putting paid to Voltaire's hopes of revenge. The countess Bentinck appears indifferent to his declarations of devotion. The Genevans are angered by the article on Geneva in d'Alembert's and Diderot's *Encyclopédie,* and are proving themselves to be less tolerant and broad-minded than Voltaire had hoped and believed. There is snow as far as the eye can see.

But Voltaire, now not at Les Délices but in his winter residence in Lausanne, is both warm and happy: "I have only been happy in my retreat [from court]," he writes on 5 January; in two other letters the same day he calls it his "sweet retreat." He is living *"une vie douce"* (10 January). His view of the lake and Alps (which sparkle in the sunlight) delights him—it is the best prospect he has ever seen (23 January). He puts on plays: "This

---

20. Jacques van den Heuvel, *Voltaire dans ses contes* (Paris: Colin, 1967), ch. 4: "L'hiver infernal." But see René Pomeau and Christiane Mervaude, *Voltaire en son temps,* vol. 3 (Oxford: Voltaire Foundation, 1991), 335–6, who stress that Voltaire was working on the end at the same time as he was working on the beginning of his story.

is how we forget the quarrels of kings and those of authors: the first horrific, the second ridiculous" (8 January). There is a war going on, but "happy is he who watches with a tranquil eye all these great events in the best of all possible worlds." "One could hardly pass one's life more sweetly, far from the horrors of war and the literary infighting of Paris" (21 January). Forty-four of Voltaire's letters survive from January 1758, and not one speaks of personal unhappiness or distress; indeed this is the month in which he submitted his article "Heureux" (happy) to the *Encyclopédie*.[21] The origins of *Candide* are to be found rather in Voltaire's happiness than his despair.

Only one commentator, Geoffrey Murray, has sought to read *Candide* in this context.[22] Throughout Voltaire's correspondence, his happiness is defined in terms of what he variously calls his garden, his hermitage, his retreat. And just as a hermitage and a retreat are defined by the world that has been left behind, so, as Murray remarks, "the very thing which defines the garden, which gives it its meaning, is its being continuously paired with that other world which is to be found somewhere, if not everywhere, beyond the garden walls," the world of kings, of courts, of literary infighting, of battlefields, and of earthquakes.[23] Voltaire, in his retreat, can never forget the world outside, or, to put it rather differently, forgetting that world becomes his full-time occupation. And it is this constant struggle to forget, this inability to forget, which defines the character of Voltaire's happiness, for it is always tinged with shame, fear, and relief, each of which indicates the continuing presence of the outside world.

Thus, shortly after the Lisbon earthquake, Voltaire writes to Jean-Robert Tronchin (Théodore's cousin, a banker and Voltaire's financial agent) thanking him for some perfume: "it is shameful for us to be sybarites when a province of Europe has been destroyed." And to Nicolas-Claude Thiriot: "I have once more become a sybarite, and have made a delightful home for myself. . . . When I spoke in verse about the miseries of my fellow human beings I did so out of pure generosity, for, having made allowances for my uncertain good health, I am so happy that it makes me feel ashamed." And to J.-R. Tronchin again, "one must try to be quiet in one's retreat while the earth trembles, or while it stands on the brink of being destroyed"; or again, after a minor earthquake had shaken Lausanne, "It cost us only a bottle of Muscat wine which fell from a table,

21. Voltaire, *Oeuvres alphabétiques*, vol. 1, ed. Jeroom Vercruysse (Oxford: Voltaire Foundation, 1987), 158–63; an essay remarkable for its fatalism.

22. Though one may note D. J. Adams, *La femme dans les contes et les romans de Voltaire* (Paris: A. G. Nizet, 1974), 184–5.

23. Murray, *Voltaire's "Candide,"* 100.

and which has paid for the whole district. We're lucky to get off so cheaply."[24]

War inspires exactly the same range of emotions, which are not new to Voltaire. In the *Essai sur les moeurs* he had quoted the following four lines of poetry, translated from Arabic, on the downfall of a court favorite:

Mortel, faible mortel, à qui le sort prospère
Fait goûter de ses dons les charmes dangereux,
Connais quelle est des rois la faveur passagère;
Contemple Barmécide, et tremble d'être heureux.

"This last line," Voltaire writes, "in particular is translated word for word. Nothing seems to me more beautiful than *tremble to be happy.*"[25] We are not told that Candide trembled in his garden in Constantinople, but from his window he watched the boatloads of courtiers being sent into exile, and the stuffed heads of those who had been executed in the provinces being shipped to court. Although his role model, the old man (and surely, if anyone in the story can be said to be Voltaire himself, it is this old man), who teaches him how to cultivate his land, says he knows nothing about what takes place in Constantinople, he still knows enough to acknowledge that those who engage in politics come to a bad end. He too has seen the severed heads, and without this knowledge his oranges would not taste as sweet.

In the light of this evidence we need to rethink the relationship between Voltaire's attack on optimism and his own life. It would seem that it was only when Voltaire acquired a retreat, an escape from the world, when he gave up his obsession with success at court, his attempt to become the social equal of men like the duc de Rohan, that he discovered happiness. Rousseau was right to think that Voltaire was actually enjoying something to which he, Rousseau, only aspired but wrong to think that Voltaire did not appreciate the value of what he had. Crucially, becoming happy freed Voltaire to admit that he had not been happy in the past and that most human beings live lives that are painful and miserable. It was happiness, not misery, that led Voltaire to abandon optimism. There is a profound paradox here, which I leave to your consideration.

Enlightenment moral philosophy is couched in terms of the impartial spectator who identifies with others and feels sympathy for their suffer-

---

24. Idem, 172–6.

25. "Mortal, feeble mortal, whom kindly fate / allows to taste the dangerous delights of her gifts / know how passing is the favor of kings; / think of Barmécide, and tremble to be happy." Voltaire, *Essai sur les moeurs,* ed. René Pomeau (2 vols., Paris: Garnier, 1990), vol. 1, 267; Murray, *Voltaire's "Candide,"* 150.

ings. One might read Voltaire's poem on the Lisbon earthquake as claiming that it would be impossible to be happy if one realized that one lived in a universe of suffering. But Voltaire can scarcely have thought this, for he constantly declares both that he is happy and that others suffer. Rather, it seems, he objects to those whose optimism leads them to belittle or dismiss the sufferings of others. But if the world outside one's sweet retreat contains so much unhappiness, is one not under an obligation to do something about it? Here Voltaire and Candide part company, for Voltaire was not content (despite his frequent protestations to the contrary) simply to cultivate his land. In trying to do anything, though, about injustice and suffering, Voltaire faced a central problem: criticism of the authorities was not permitted.

FORBIDDEN BOOKS

It is very easy to forget that Voltaire knew from the very first moment he conceived *Candide* that it would be a forbidden book.[26] Of necessity it had to be published anonymously and sold under the counter. Certain that attempts would be made to suppress it, he took elaborate precautions to ensure its survival. The first edition, of two thousand copies, was printed by the brothers Cramer in Geneva (although of course the publishers were as careful as the author to conceal their identity), and was ready by 15 January, but no copies were released in Geneva until the greater part of the printing was safely out of the country. Voltaire seems also to have sent at least one copy of the manuscript abroad (the one we know of went to a printer in London), presumably to ensure that were the Cramer edition to be suppressed an edition would still appear elsewhere. By 22 February an edition had already been published in Lyon. On that day the Parisian authorities began to move against *Candide,* and on the 25th they seized an edition of five hundred copies in the course of being printed—apparently the sixth Paris edition in the space of a few days. The phrase "Let's eat a Jesuit" was already being echoed on all sides. At the end of the month Voltaire was estimating that six thousand copies had been sold in Paris, of which a thousand had been supplied by the Cramers. On the 23rd the authorities in Geneva also knew of the book's existence, and began to search bookshops for it, but they were unable to find a single copy (which is perhaps only to say that no bookseller was so foolish as to sell it openly). Once the book's existence was no longer a secret Voltaire could write letters to the Cramers designed to make it seem that neither he nor they

---

26. On forbidden books, see Robert Darnton, *The Forbidden Best-Sellers of Pre-Revolutionary France* (New York: W. W. Norton, 1995). On the publication of *Candide*: *Candide,* ed. Pomeau, 86–110.

had had anything to do with its publication. "What is this booklet called *Candide*?" he asked, adding later, "I have just finished reading, at last, this *Candide*. . . . I advise you not to sell copies . . ." He did not admit that he was the author of *Candide* until 1768.

The attempts to suppress *Candide* were futile. There were at least sixteen editions in French in the course of 1759, and while two of these French editions were printed in England there were also six editions in the British Isles of three different translations, and one edition in Italian. We may guess that all told there were some twenty thousand copies in French, six thousand in English, and five hundred in Italian within twelve months. (For all but the first two thousand of these Voltaire would have received no payment.) The numbers seem modest to us, but were enormous by the standards of the eighteenth century: no newly written work in French had ever sold in such numbers before. There were to be more than fifty editions in Voltaire's lifetime.

In Paris and Geneva the authorities (in the one case Catholic, in the other Calvinist) had no doubt that *Candide* was contrary to religion and morality. "Impiety" and "indecency" are words that recur in the official documents (and, indeed, it is a remarkable fact that the first unexpurgated edition for use in French schools did not appear until 1969). Voltaire's friend La Vallière claimed there was general agreement that the chapter on Paris (which Voltaire had already recast once) was the least successful, and Thiriot thought it was a mistake to mention (in the same chapter) Damiens's attempt to assassinate the king. Voltaire obviously agreed, for he added substantially to this problematic chapter for the 1761 edition, shifting its focus from religion and politics to literature.

Voltaire was acutely aware of the sensitivities of the French authorities as he prepared *Candide* for the press, for they had just suppressed Helvétius's *De l'esprit*, despite the fact that it had originally been published with official permission.[27] A lazy censor had missed Helvétius's republicanism and egalitarianism, which were obvious to all later readers. Diderot and D'Alembert's *Encyclopédie*, to which Voltaire had contributed articles, was also coming under sustained attack, and was to be definitively banned at the same time as *Candide*. Voltaire was also well aware that a book could be officially forbidden, but effectively allowed to circulate; or it could be systematically suppressed. That *Candide* would be a forbidden book, that it would be regarded as impious and indecent, he took for granted; but at the same time it was crucial that it circulate, that it merely irritate rather than infuriate the authorities. It was therefore essential that

27. Roland Desné, "Voltaire et Helvétius," in *Le Siècle de Voltaire*, ed. Christine Mervaud and Sylvain Menant (2 vols., Oxford: Voltaire Foundation, 1987), vol. 1, 403–16.

the chapter on Paris should strike no more than a glancing blow at the French authorities. Here, far more than anywhere else in the book, Voltaire had to practice self-censorship.

In the chapter on El Dorado Voltaire freely expressed his religious ideals: it is easy to find echoes of his long-standing admiration for the Quakers. But his account of El Dorado as a society in which there are neither law courts nor prisons provides no indication of his practical political commitments. Much more interesting is the account of the six deposed kings in chapter 26, for its central message seems to be that there is nothing stable about monarchy (a point that Pangloss reiterates in chapter 30), and that kings are no different from the rest of us. *"Je vous parle en républicain,"* "I speak to you as a republican," wrote Voltaire to d'Alembert in January 1758, as he was beginning work on *Candide*.[28] In *Candide* he dared not say as much; but in letter 8 of the *Letters Concerning the English Nation* he had praised the English for having resisted tyranny, executed a king, and fought a war against Louis XIV out of a disinterested love of liberty. There is no indication that he was shocked by the radical republicanism of Helvétius (as he was, for example, by Helvétius's claim that friendship was merely a form of enlightened self-interest).[29] In the last paragraph of *Candide,* the small holding that Candide has purchased becomes the common property of "the little society" who live on it. *"Il faut cultiver notre jardin,"* says Candide. If this little society is a model for others, then it would appear to have been silently transformed from a monarchy into a republic.

Where Cacambo had been doing all the agricultural work, Candide, Pangloss, and Martin, now (we are to understand) roll up their sleeves and grasp a spade. Given their social background, it would have been their first experience of manual labor. Like Candide, Voltaire worked his own land: he wore clogs like a peasant, and visitors would come across him laboriously sowing his own grain, planting his own cabbages. He criticized his niece Mme. de Fontaines for being too much of a lady to do likewise. In his letters he calls himself a gardener, a mason, a carpenter, a farmhand, a laborer.[30] In a society where the most important social division—more important even than that between commoners and aristocrats—was between those who worked with their hands and those who did not, between those whose hands were soft and those whose hands were hard, Voltaire deliberately got his hands dirty and callused. Implicit in the decision that

---

28. D7592.

29. On Helvétius, see David Wootton, "Helvétius: From Radical Enlightenment to Revolution," *Political Theory,* 28 (2000), 467–96.

30. Murray, *Voltaire's "Candide,"* chs. 1 and 5.

both Voltaire and Candide take to work the land is a radical egalitarianism. "Voltaire always remained a good bourgeois," writes Peter Gay, who correctly interprets the *Letters Concerning the English Nation* as a defense of commercial values.[31] But by the time he wrote *Candide,* Voltaire's sympathies were with the peasants rather than the merchants.

THE NEW POLITICS

By the time Voltaire finished writing *Candide* he was already planning to transform his life once again.[32] There were a number of factors influencing his decision. First, as the war went on his investments were increasingly at risk. Although he had hedged his bets by spreading his money around, trade was suffering increasingly severe disruption, and the whole of the six hundred thousand francs Voltaire had invested in Cadiz shipping was in danger of disappearing. There was a risk that the French government would cease to be able to pay his pension or the interest on his loans. Taxes were bound to rise and prices with them. In these circumstances he judged land to be the safest investment and self-sufficiency to be a key objective. For this he needed more land: Les Délices was an estate of sixty (rather unproductive) acres, about three times the size of the old man's small holding. He employed five men to work the land—just as there were five men on Candide's farm. Like Candide, he produced fruit and vegetables, plus a little wine, but not enough to feed his large household and his innumerable guests; above all he needed to buy wheat. Moreover he only had a life interest in Les Délices. He wanted to leave Mme. Denis a home that she could inherit. And his situation on Genevan territory was becoming slightly precarious: who knew whether the storm over the article on Geneva in the *Encyclopédie* would be followed by an even greater storm over *Candide*?

So Voltaire, as he finished writing *Candide,* was also negotiating to buy two large estates, Ferney and Tournay, just over the border in France. He now owned, not a few acres, but land that stretched for six miles. With these estates came privileges which meant that he was immune from taxation. He was judge in his own courts. He could even claim the title of count. Moreover because he now held land from two governments, and was on the borders of a third (Savoy), he was in effect answerable to no one. To an English correspondent he wrote, "I have willfully sought a free and pleasant retreat, where I enjoy peace and plenty, free from all ties, lord

---

31. Peter Gay, *Voltaire's Politics. The Poet as Realist* (2nd ed., New Haven: Yale University Press, 1988), 53.

32. Murray, *Voltaire's "Candide,"* ch. 6.

of my lands and of myself. I would settle at Borneo if liberty was but there."[33]

Above all a much larger community had now been added to the little community of Les Délices. Several entire villages, dilapidated, run down, and depopulated, now depended on him. Indeed the belief that he might be able to do these impoverished peasants some good was one of Voltaire's motives in purchasing the property. On 18 November 1758, around the time he finished *Candide,* he wrote: "Half of the inhabitants are dying of misery, and the other half are rotting in dungeons. One's heart breaks when one witnesses so much suffering. I am only buying the estate of Ferney in order to do a little bit of good there."[34] Over the remaining years of his life Voltaire was remarkably successful in building up the local economy, and with it the size and prosperity of the community over which he ruled. Ferney, we might say, became Voltaire's private El Dorado.

Shortly afterward, Voltaire found a new way of mediating the relationship between his sweet retreat and the horrors of the outside world. Candide, when he forms his little community, leaves the world behind. Voltaire, by contrast, had written *Candide* in order to bring about some change in the world around him. By publishing an attack on religious bigotry he was coming to the aid of Helvétius, Diderot, and d'Alembert, who were engaged in a decisive battle: "We are on the point of a great revolution in human thinking," Voltaire wrote to Diderot as he began work on *Candide.*[35] At such a time a major transformation of values could be achieved by the publications of a few determined philosophers if they would hold together and overcome the threat of censorship. But the critique of authority in *Candide* was displaced. Voltaire might dare attack the Jesuits (who were widely unpopular) and the Portuguese Inquisition, but he dared not directly attack the French government. With his newfound freedom this was to change.

Before *Candide* Voltaire had tried to intervene to prevent the execution of Admiral Byng, accused by the English government of cowardice for having failed to engage the French with sufficient determination. But Byng was an important personage, and in seeking to rescue him Voltaire was engaged in the politics of the establishment as it argued over the fate of one of its own. The case of Jean Calas, a Protestant businessman from Toulouse, marks the beginning of Voltaire's new politics. Calas's son had hanged himself, but in order to obtain for him a Christian burial (a motive that would immediately have won Voltaire's sympathy, for his fear that he himself would be denied a proper burial was acute) Calas had pretended

33. 29 Sept. 1759 (D8500).

34. D7946.

35. D7570.

he had been murdered. This relatively innocent deception backfired: Calas was accused of having murdered his son to prevent him from converting to Catholicism. Calas was brutally executed (by breaking on the wheel) in March 1762. Voltaire gave shelter to his widow and children, and, after three years of campaigning, succeeded in having his conviction overturned.

The case of Calas was followed by others: those of Pierre Sirven (condemned to death for supposedly murdering his daughter in 1764, he escaped to Switzerland and was rehabilitated in 1771) and that of the chevalier La Barre (executed for blasphemy in 1766). Voltaire had become a campaigner for religious toleration (*Treatise on Tolerance*, 1763) and law reform (*Commentary* on Beccaria's *Crimes and Punishments*, 1766). This new politics, which relied on the mobilization of a still-embryonic public opinion, depended on Voltaire's ability to tell true stories of personal disaster, which inspired sympathy and indignation.[36] Calas, we might say, was Candide made flesh.

We can see these developments foreshadowed in *Candide* if we choose.[37] Candide's little community prefigures the larger community of Ferney; Candide's bitter experiences with the law prefigure Voltaire's later campaigns for justice. But if we do so we must also acknowledge that the success of *Candide* itself must have helped to change Voltaire's relationship to the outside world. The surface message of *Candide* is that one should stop talking and work the land; but the impact of *Candide* surely encouraged Voltaire to keep talking about injustice, for if a fictional story could win such an enormous audience, might not as many people be persuaded to listen to true stories of disaster?

---

36. Despite his close involvement in such tragic cases, Voltaire continued to delight in his happiness. Thus the historian Edward Gibbon wrote to Mrs. Gibbon, 6 Aug. 1763: "After a life passed in courts and Capitals, the Great Voltaire is now a mere country Gentleman, and even (for the honor of the profession) sometimes of a farmer. He says he never enjoyed so much true happiness." *Letters of Edward Gibbon*, ed. J. E. Norton (3 vols., London: Cassell, 1956), vol. 1, 154–5.

37. I am not convinced by David Langdon, "On the Meanings of the Conclusion of *Candide*," *SV* 238 (1985), 397–432, which denies that the ending of *Candide* implies a rejection of politics. At this point it seems to me essential to distinguish the lesson Candide has drawn from his experiences from the lesson Voltaire intends his reader to draw. Nor do I accept that the *topos* of noninvolvement in politics is always disingenuous when it appears in Voltaire's letters: see for example D7848, 5 Sept. 1758, to countess Bentinck: "It is princes who are responsible for the miseries of the human race. Happy is the person who places themselves at a distance so that they are independent of them." Noninvolvement seems like a real option to Voltaire in 1758; though not the only option, nor the option he takes.

Here again, we must acknowledge that Voltaire brought something of himself to this task. By talking of others' sufferings he was compensating for his inability to talk about his own childhood distress. In 1767 Voltaire published another story, *L'ingénu*, about an honest man on whom terrible sufferings (including incarceration in the Bastille) are inflicted. For *L'ingénu*, as for Candide, all turns out well. But in *L'ingénu*'s case telling stories is not just part of the process of traveling toward a sweet retreat, for even when he has reached safety Voltaire can say of him (in what are very nearly the last words of the novel): "He never spoke of this adventure without shuddering, and yet he comforted himself by speaking of it." It is the old woman's storytelling, not Candide's silence, which Voltaire chose to imitate.

22 Nov. 1694: François-Marie Arouet baptized. (Voltaire was later to claim that his true father was not François Arouet, a lawyer, but M. de Rochebrune, a retired officer and poet.)

1697: Bayle's *Historical and Critical Dictionary,* the origin of the debate on optimism, published.

1704–11: Arouet a student at the elite Jesuit college of Louis-le-Grand.

1710: Leibniz's *Essais de Théodicée,* a reply to Bayle, published.

1711: Shaftesbury's *Characteristics* published.

May 1717–April 1718: Arouet in the Bastille for writing satirical poetry.

Nov. 1718: Voltaire (as he now calls himself) has his first literary success with the play *Oedipe.*

May 1726–Nov. 1728: Voltaire in exile in England. He publishes there his epic poem, *La Henriade.*

1731: Voltaire establishes himself as a historian with *The History of Charles XII.*

1733: Beginning of his affair with Mme. du Châtelet.

1733: *Letters Concerning the English Nation* published (in English)

1733–4: Pope's *Essay on Man* published.

1734: The *Lettres philosophiques* (the French translation, with an additional letter on Pascal, of the *Letters Concerning the English Nation*) published; the resulting controversy drives Voltaire into exile at Mme. du Châtelet's château, Cirey.

1736: Correspondence with Frederick, heir to the throne of Prussia, begins.

1737: Voltaire publishes *Elements of the Philosophy of Newton.*

1740: First meeting with Frederick.

1743–7: In favor with the French court: appointed royal historiographer (1745); elected to the Académie Française (1746).

1745: Voltaire's affair with Mme. Denis, his niece, begins.

1747: Voltaire publishes his first philosophical novella, *Memnon, histoire orientale,* revised under the title *Zadig* (1748).

1749: Death of Mme. du Châtelet.

1750–3: Voltaire lives in Berlin, at the court of Frederick II.

1751: Voltaire publishes *The Age of Louis XIV.*

1753–5: Voltaire in exile and homeless until he finds Les Délices.

1 Nov. 1755: The Lisbon earthquake.

1756: Voltaire's poem on the Lisbon earthquake published; also the first edition of his universal history, *Essai sur les moeurs* (but he continued to work on an expanded edition, which appeared in 1761).

1756–63: The Seven Years War, started by Frederick II.

1758: Voltaire writes *Candide* and buys the estate of Ferney.

Jan. 1759: Publication of *Candide*.

1762: Voltaire's campaign for the rehabilitation of Calas, executed for murdering his son.

1763: Voltaire's *Treatise on Toleration* published.

1764: The *Portable Philosophical Dictionary* published.

1766: Voltaire's campaign of protest over the execution of the chevalier de la Barre, executed for blasphemy. Publication of his commentary on Beccaria's *On Crimes and Punishments*.

1778: Voltaire returns triumphantly to Paris, and dies there.

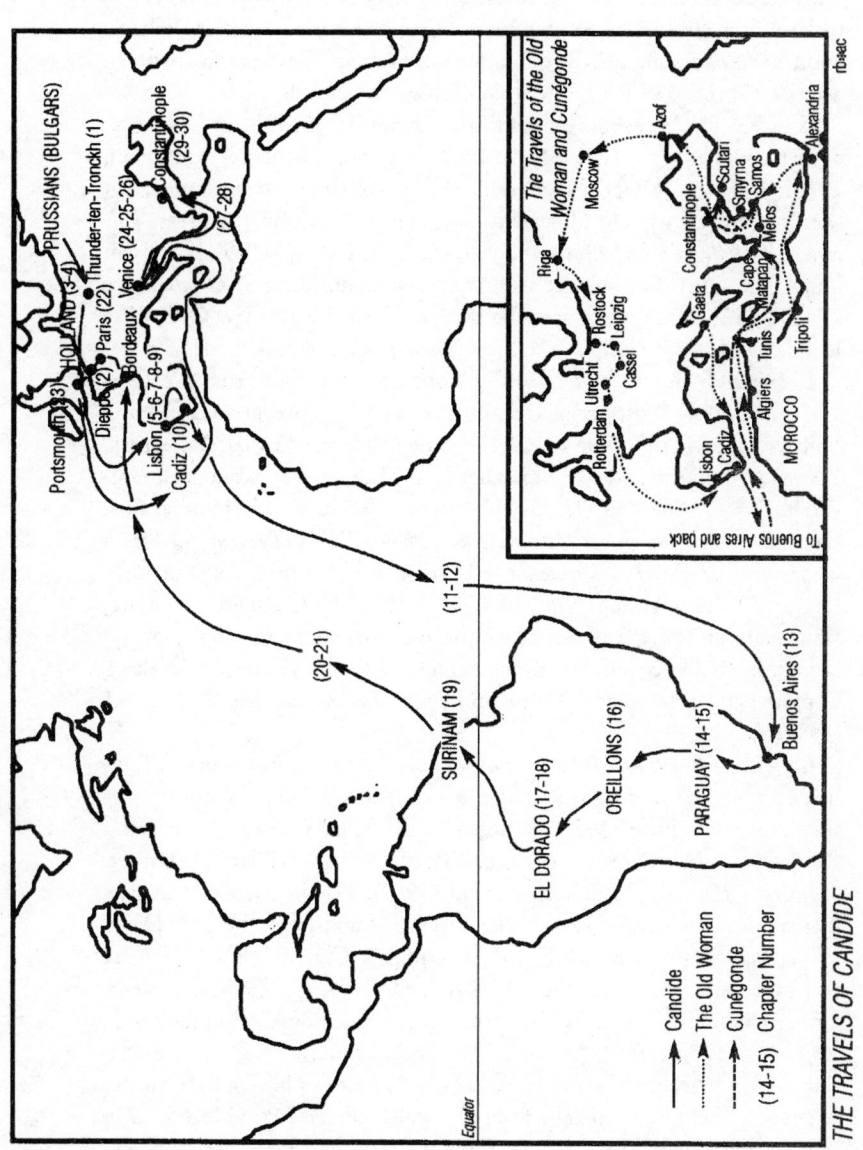

THE TRAVELS OF CANDIDE

This guide to further reading is restricted to books in English in order to make it manageable; but it should be noted that most works on Voltaire and *Candide* contain lengthy quotations in French. I have marked with an asterisk (*) those which are written entirely in English.

Voltaire: The best short biography is Haydn Mason, *Voltaire: A Biography* (London: Granada, 1981).* Much longer is Theodore Besterman, *Voltaire* (3rd ed., Oxford: Blackwell, 1976). Voltaire's correspondence at the time he was writing *Candide* is the subject of Geoffrey Murray, *Voltaire's "Candide": The Protean Gardener, 1755–1762* (*SV* 69 [1970]): an important study. On Voltaire's life, and the significance of *Candide*, see also David Wootton, "Unhappy Voltaire, or 'I Shall Never Get Over It As Long As I Live'," *History Workshop Journal* No. 50 (2000), 141–59.

Lisbon and "Scarmentado": On Lisbon: R. A. Leigh, "From the *Inégalité* to *Candide:* Notes on a Desultory Dialogue between Rousseau and Voltaire (1755–1759)," in *The Age of Enlightenment: Studies Presented to Theodore Besterman,* ed. W. H. Barber et al. (Edinburgh: Edinburgh University Press, 1967), 66–92; Haydn Mason, "Voltaire's 'Sermon' against Optimism: The *Poème sur le désastre de Lisbonne*," in *Enlightenment Essays in Memory of Robert Shackleton,* ed. Giles Barber and C. P. Courtney (Oxford: Voltaire Foundation, 1988), 189–203; Rita Goldberg, "Voltaire, Rousseau, and the Lisbon Earthquake," *Eighteenth-Century Life* 13 (1989), 1–20.* Excellent on "Scarmentado" is Roy S. Wolper, "The Black Captain and Scarmentado. Tyrant and Fool," *Eighteenth-Century Fiction* 1 (1988/9), 119–31.

Candide—Books and Bibliography: There have been five books in English on *Candide:* Ira O. Wade, *Voltaire and "Candide"* (Princeton: Princeton University Press, 1959); William F. Bottiglia, *Voltaire's "Candide": Analysis of a Classic* (1959; rev. ed., *SV* 7A [1964]); William H. Barber, *Voltaire: "Candide"* (London: Arnold, 1960); Haydn Mason, *Candide: Optimism Demolished* (New York: Twayne Publishers, 1992);* David Williams, *Voltaire: Candide* (London: Grant & Cutler, 1997). There are two collections of essays: Milton P. Foster, ed., *Voltaire's "Candide" and the Critics* (Belmont, Calif.: Wadsworth, 1962)* and Renée Waldinger, ed., *Approaches to Teaching "Candide"* (New York: Modern Language Association, 1987).* And two recent books look at Voltaire's philosophical stories in general, including *Candide:* Robin Howells, *Disabled Powers: A Reading of Voltaire's 'Contes'* (Amsterdam: Rodopi, 1993), and Roger Pearson, *The Fables of Reason: A Study of Voltaire's 'Contes Philosophiques'* (Oxford: Clarendon Press, 1993). The most recent bibliographical survey is Robin

Howells, "Voltaire's *Contes:* A Review of Studies, 1969–1993," *SV* 320 (1994), 229–81.

Essays on "Candide": There are several valuable essays on *Candide* in Jean Starobinski, *Blessings in Disguise: The Morality of Evil* (Cambridge, Mass.: Harvard University Press, 1993).* For two stimulating debates see Roland Barthes, "The Last Happy Writer" in *A Barthes Reader,* ed. Susan Sontag (New York: Hill and Wang, 1982),* 150–8, and the reply by Patrick Henry, "Contre Barthes," *SV* 249 (1987), 19–36; and Roy S. Wolper, "Candide, Gull in the Garden," *Eighteenth-Century Studies* 3 (1969), 265–77, and the replies by Theodore E. D. Braun, "Voltaire and His *Contes:* A Review Essay on Interpretations Offered by Roy S. Wolper," *SV* 212 (1982), 312–7, and Vivienne Mylne, "Wolper's View of Voltaire's Tales," *SV* 212 (1982), 318–27. There is much to learn from C. J. Betts, "Exploring Narrative Structures in *Candide,*" *SV* 314 (1993), 1– 131. On particular themes in *Candide* see Patrick Henry, "Sacred and Profane Gardens in *Candide,*" *SV* 176 (1979), 133–52 and David Langdon, "On the Meanings of the Conclusion of *Candide,*" *SV* 238 (1985), 397–432.

Voltaire and Feminism: The literature is thin. Worth reading are Arthur Scherr, "Candide's Garden Revisited: Gender Equality in a Commoner's Paradise," *Eighteenth-Century Life* 17 (1993), 40–59, and Gloria M. Russo, "Voltaire and Women," in *French Women and the Age of Enlightenment,* ed. Samia I. Spencer (Bloomington: Indiana University, 1984), 285– 95; but neither mentions "Wives Obey Your Husbands."

Other Voltaire Texts in English: For a useful collection of nonfiction texts see *Political Writings,* ed. David Williams (Cambridge: Cambridge University Press, 1994). For a translation of the *Dictionnaire philosophique,* see *Philosophical Dictionary,* trans. Theodore Besterman (Harmondsworth: Penguin Books, 1971). Nicholas Cronk's edition of *Letters Concerning the English Nation* (Oxford: Oxford University Press, 1994) is important for respecting Voltaire's original English text. For other stories by Voltaire (including *Zadig,* but not *Jenni*), see Roger Pearson's translation of *Candide and Other Stories* (Oxford: Oxford University Press, 1990).

The Debate on Theodicy—Sources: A valuable selection from Bayle (including "Manicheans," "Paulicians," and the "Second Clarification," but not "Xenophanes") is to be found in Pierre Bayle, *Historical and Critical Dictionary,* ed. R. H. Popkin (Indianapolis: Hackett, 1991). For Leibniz see G. W. Leibniz, *Theodicy* (La Salle, Ill.: Open Court, 1985). Among recent editions of Shaftesbury see Anthony Ashley Cooper, Third Earl of Shaftesbury, *Characteristics of Men, Manners, Opinions, Times,* ed. Lawrence E. Klein (Cambridge: Cambridge University Press, 1999). The standard edition of Alexander Pope's "essay" is *An Essay on Man,* ed. Maynard Mack (London: Methuen, 1950). It is interesting to compare the

Voltaire texts translated here with two nearly contemporary works by
Samuel Johnson: his 1757 review of Soames Jenyns's *A Free Inquiry into
the Nature and Origin of Evil* (a substantial excerpt is reprinted in Simon
Eliot and Beverley Stern, ed., *The Age of Enlightenment* [2 vols., E.
Grinstead: Ward Lock, 1979], vol. 1, 108–20), and his novel *Rasselas,
Prince of Abyssinia* (1759) (which has been frequently reprinted). There
are no modern editions of Wolff or Bolingbroke.

Theodicy—Intellectual History: For a brief discussion of Enlightenment
providentialist philosophy see Charles Taylor, *Sources of the Self: The
Making of the Modern Identity* (Cambridge: Cambridge University Press,
1989), ch. 16. The best introduction to Pope is A. D. Nuttall, *Pope's
"Essay on Man"* (London: Allen and Unwin, 1984). Relevant are W. H.
Barber, *Leibniz in France, from Arnauld to Voltaire* (Oxford: Clarendon
Press, 1955); Richard A. Brooks, *Voltaire and Leibniz* (Geneva: Droz,
1964); Haydn Mason, *Pierre Bayle and Voltaire* (Oxford: Oxford University Press, 1963); particularly helpful is Mason, "Voltaire and Manichean
Dualism," *SV* 26 (1963), 1143–60. On the interpretation of Bayle see
David Wootton, "Pierre Bayle, Libertine?" in *Oxford Studies in the History
of Philosophy*, vol. II, ed. M. A. Stewart (Oxford: Oxford University Press,
1997), 197–226.

A Note on the Texts

The translation of *Candide* is based on the standard edition, edited by René Pomeau, *The Complete Works of Voltaire*, vol. 48 (Oxford: The Voltaire Foundation, 1980). "Scarmentado," and "The Comforter Comforted" are translated from Voltaire, *Romans et contes*, ed. Frédéric Deloffre and Jacques van den Heuvel (Paris: Gallimard, 1979); Preface and Notes to "Poem on the Lisbon Disaster" from Voltaire, *Oeuvres*, ed. Louis Moland (52 vols., Paris: Garnier Frères, 1877–85), vol. 9, 465–79; "Wives Obey Your Husbands" from Voltaire, *Mélanges*, ed. Emmanuel Berl and Jacques van den Heuvel (Paris: Gallimard, 1961); "Well (All is)" from *Dictionnaire philosophique*, ed. Alain Pons (Paris: Gallimard, 1994); Voltaire's letters, and Rousseau's "Letter on Optimism" from Voltaire, *Correspondence*, ed. Theodore Besterman, *Complete Works*, vols. 85–135 (Oxford: The Voltaire Foundation, 1968–77); Leibniz's "Metaphysics Summarized" from *Opuscules et fragments inédits*, ed. Louis Couturat (Paris: F. Alcan, 1903).

NOTES ON THE TRANSLATION

GENDERED LANGUAGE

Voltaire, like every other eighteenth-century author, often uses "man" and similar masculine terms when he intends "person." In my translation I have used gender-neutral expressions when I think Voltaire had both men and women in mind. Although Voltaire could never have considered the adoption of such a practice, certain features of his thought make it less anachronistic than it would be in the case of most of his contemporaries. For Voltaire was not only a feminist (see "Wives Obey Your Husbands"), he was also acutely conscious of the gendered nature of language. When his long-time lover, intimate friend, and companion Mme. du Châtelet died in 1749 he wrote a whole series of letters (D4015, D4025, D4035, D4037, D4039) in which he described her as a great man ("*un grand homme*"), meaning someone who had excelled in traditionally masculine activities such as science and philosophy, and we find him addressing his intimate friend Charlotte-Sophie, countess of Bentinck, a woman of striking independence with an interest in military affairs, as *Monsieur* (D4692, D4694, D4752: all from January 1753). Similar gender-bending occurs in his account of Jeanne, the hero(ine) of his poem *La Pucelle,* and it may of course be linked to Voltaire's own bisexuality.

RACIAL STEREOTYPES

Voltaire, like most eighteenth-century thinkers, believed in the siginificance of racial differences; moreover, unlike many eighteenth-century thinkers, he did not believe that racial differences were the result of differences of climate; and, unlike most eighteenth-century thinkers, he rejected the Christian view that all humans are descended from the same common ancestor. In other words he was a "polygenist," not a "monogenist." He thus came very close to regarding racial differences as comparable to differences between species. (For his views in 1756 see *Essai sur les moeurs,* ed. Pomeau, vol. 1, pp. 6–9.)[1] Nevertheless, his attack on slavery in *Candide* is unequivocal. On the other hand, he loved sugar, and his taste for it was not diminished by his knowledge that it was the product of slave labor (e.g. D8126, 17 February 1759).

Voltaire was also hostile to Jews. One can note that on several occasions he had lost significant sums of money as a result of Jewish financiers going bankrupt; and that many of his attacks on Judaism are meant to be under-

---

1. I am grateful to Silvia Sebastiani for bringing this to my attention.

stood as attacks on Christianity. But this takes one only so far, and is no justification. The subject of Voltaire's anti-Semitism has been much discussed: e.g., Peter Gay, *Voltaire's Politics. The Poet as Realist* (2nd ed., New Haven: Yale University Press, 1988), appendix 3 (351–4); Arthur Hertzberg, *The French Enlightenment and the Jews: The Origins of Modern Anti-Semitism* (New York: Columbia University Press, 1968, repr. 1990), 280–313. Bertram E. Schwarzbach, "Voltaire et les juifs: bilan et plaidoyer," *SV* 358 (1997), 27–91, surveys the literature on this question and seeks to put Voltaire in the best possible light.

Problems of Translation

Let two stand for many. The last words of *Candide* are "*Il faut cultiver notre jardin.*" Word for word this is "It is necessary to cultivate our garden." The Everyman edition (1937, but a revision of an eighteenth-century translation) has "Let us take care of our garden." John Butt (Penguin, 1947) has "We must go and work in the garden." Robert M. Adams (Norton, 1991) and Daniel Gordon (Bedford/St. Martin's, 1999) both have "We must cultivate our garden." But what Candide is talking about is not a garden in the normal modern sense of the word. It is a small farm, a small holding, a market garden. In the eighteenth century, both French *jardin* and English "garden" mean (in the definition of the *Shorter Oxford English Dictionary*, 1933) "an enclosed piece of ground devoted to the cultivation of flowers, fruit, or vegetables," which excludes pastures, arable fields, and woods, but includes orchards, vegetable gardens, and kitchen gardens. Translators thus have a choice. They can use the word "garden," in which case they should add a note saying the word is not used in its normal modern sense; or they can do what a translator should always seek to do—convey the author's meaning in modern English. Hence the translation here: "We must work our land." This corresponds to a phrase Voltaire uses both in his correspondence and in the manuscript of *Candide*, "*cultiver la terre*," and is closely paralleled by another of his phrases, "*cultiver ses champs*" ("cultivate his fields"). For confirmation that this is Voltaire's meaning, see below, page 135. However, one must note that Voltaire was probably drawn to the word *jardin* because it would remind readers of both the Garden of Eden and the garden of the ancient philosopher Epicurus. Thus it is important to bear in mind the ideas that an eighteenth-century reader would have associated with the word "garden," even though Voltaire is not talking about a garden in the sense in which we would normally understand the term.

Secondly, Voltaire regularly uses "*raisonner*" (to reason, to argue) and "*philosopher*" (to philosophize) with the implication that these are activities to avoid. In conventional English, the verb "rationalize" and the adjective "logical" are often used with negative connotations, but it is very hard to use the verb "to reason" negatively; and "to argue," unless followed by "that," implies passion. I have therefore translated *"raisonner"* as either synonymous with *"philosopher"* ("to philosophize"), or with a phrase including the noun "logic."

CANDIDE,

OR

OPTIMISM[1]

TRANSLATED FROM THE GERMAN OF
DR. RALPH
WITH THE ADDITIONS[2] THAT WERE
FOUND IN THE DOCTOR'S POCKET WHEN
HE DIED AT MINDEN,[3] IN THE YEAR OF
OUR LORD 1759

CHAPTER ONE: *How Candide was brought up in a beautiful castle,
and how he came to be driven out of it*

In Westphalia, in the castle of His Excellency the Baron of Thunder-ten-tronckh, there was once a young man on whom nature had bestowed the sweetest of dispositions. You could read his soul by watching the expressions on his face. He was not without intelligence, but he was incapable of being devious; I presume this was why he was called Candide.[4] The older household servants suspected that he was the son of His Excellency the Baron's sister, and that his father was a good and honest gentleman who lived in the neighborhood. The baron's sister had never been willing to marry this man because he could only demonstrate that seventy-one of his

---

1. The word *optimisme* is rare in French in 1758: the first recorded usage is 1737, and it appears in the *Dictionnaire de Trévoux* in 1752: "It is the name that is given to the system of those who claim that all is for the best, that the world is the best that God could create; that the best possible is to be found in all that which is and which happens. Even crimes exist to further the beauty and the perfection of the moral order, for they give rise to good. The crime of Tarquin, who raped Lucretia, produced the liberty of Rome, and consequently all the virtues of the Roman republic. See the *Théodicée* of M. Leibniz." It is used once in the text of *Candide* (below, p. 43) in a passage that is a late addition to the text. It would therefore seem that Voltaire hesitated to use a word that might prove ephemeral. It first appears in English in one of the 1759 translations of *Candide*; but of the six editions, five translate *optimisme* as "all for the best." The publication of *Candide* was followed promptly by the invention of the word *pessimisme* (1759).

2. Chapter 22 was substantially revised in the edition of 1761.

3. The French army suffered a severe defeat at Minden on 1 August 1759, after the first publication of *Candide*.

4. In Latin the word *candidus* means "white," "unspotted," and by extension "honest" and "fair-minded."

ancestors were nobles; the others may also have been, but it had proved impossible to trace his genealogy far enough back in time.

His Excellency the Baron was one of the most powerful noblemen in Westphalia, for his castle had a door and it had windows. His great hall was even decorated with a tapestry. When required, all the dogs in the farm yards would be assembled to form a pack; his stable boys were transformed into huntsmen; the priest in the local village became his chaplain. They all addressed him as "Your Excellency," and laughed at the stories he told.

The baron's wife, who weighed around three hundred and fifty pounds, was regarded as a person of substance, and welcomed guests with a self-possession that made her all the more distinguished. Her daughter Cunégonde[5] was seventeen, with pink cheeks and a fresh complexion; she was plump and delectable. The baron's son appeared to be in every respect worthy of his father. Nobody disagreed with anything that their tutor, who was called Pangloss,[6] said, and as little Candide listened to his teaching he was as tractable as one might expect a student of his age and his character to be.

Pangloss taught metaphysico-theologico-cosmolonigology.[7] He demonstrated beautifully that there is no effect without a cause, and that, in this the best of all possible worlds, the castle of His Excellency the Baron was the most beautiful of all castles, and his wife was the best of all possible baronesses.[8]

"It can be demonstrated," he would say, "that things could not be other than they are: for everything has been made to serve a purpose, and so nothing is susceptible to improvement. Just see how noses are designed to support spectacles, and indeed we have spectacles. It's obvious that legs were constructed to fit trousers, and we have trousers to fit them. Rock was made to be quarried, cut, and turned into castles, and thus his excellency has a very beautiful castle; naturally the most important baron in the province ought to be the best housed. Pigs were made to be eaten, and we eat pork throughout the year. So I conclude that those who have argued that all is well can't be taken seriously; they should have said that nothing could be better."

---

5. There was an eleventh-century German queen called Kunigunde; but Voltaire surely expects the reader to find in the name two Latin words: *cunnus* (vagina) and *gonades* (ovaries).

6. From the Greek for "all-tongue."

7. Metaphysics and theology were long-established disciplines, but "cosmology" was invented by Leibniz. Wolff had written a book on it, which Voltaire said he had had the misfortune to read.

8. Leibniz had argued that this is best of all possible worlds and that there is no effect without a cause.

Candide listened carefully and believed without hesitation; for he was of the view that Miss Cunégonde was extremely beautiful, though he never summoned up the courage to tell her so. He concluded that after the happiness of being born Baron of Thunder-ten-tronckh, the second degree of happiness was to be Miss Cunégonde, the third to see her every day, and the fourth to listen to Dr. Pangloss, the finest philosopher in the province, and consequently the most important in the whole world.

One day Cunégonde was out for a stroll near the castle, in the little wood that was called "the park." Through the bushes she caught sight of Dr. Pangloss, who was giving a lesson in experimental physics to her mother's serving girl, a little brunette who was very pretty and very pliable. As Miss Cunégonde had a genuine interest in the sciences, she watched (without so much as breathing) the series of experiments of which she was the witness; she could plainly see the doctor's sufficient reason,[9] the effects and the causes. She set out for home exceedingly agitated, very thoughtful, entirely suffused with the desire for knowledge, thinking to herself that she could well be the sufficient reason of young Candide, while he could be hers.

She bumped into Candide when she got back to the castle, and blushed; Candide blushed too. She said "good day" to him with a catch in her breath. Candide replied to her without knowing what he was saying. Next day, after dinner, when everyone was getting down from table, Cunégonde and Candide found themselves hidden behind a screen. Cunégonde let her handkerchief drop; Candide picked it up. Innocently she took his hand in hers; innocently the young man kissed the hand of the young lady, doing so with a liveliness, a sensitivity, a gracefulness that was all his own. Their lips met; their eyes shone; their knees trembled; their hands strayed. His Excellency the Baron of Thunder-ten-tronckh passed near the screen and saw this cause and this effect. He chased Candide out of the castle with a series of hefty kicks on his backside. Cunégonde fainted. She was whipped by Her Excellency the Baroness as soon as she regained consciousness. And in the most beautiful and the most delightful of possible castles everything was upside down and back to front.

CHAPTER TWO: *What became of Candide among the Bulgars*[10]

Candide, driven out of the Garden of Eden, walked and walked without knowing where he was going. He cried; he lifted his eyes to the heavens; he

---

9. A technical term from Wolff.

10. Voltaire intends the reader to recognize that the Bulgars represent the Prussians. He was aware that the word "Bulgar" has the same etymological root as the word "bugger."

looked back frequently in the direction of the most beautiful of all castles, in which was to be found the most beautiful of all noble youngsters. He fell asleep without having had anything to eat; he lay in the open fields between two furrows. The snow was falling in large flakes. Next day, frozen to the core, Candide dragged himself toward the nearest town, which was called Valdberghoff-trarbk-dikdorff. He had no money and was dying of hunger and exhaustion. He came to a halt at the entrance to a bar. Two men dressed in blue watched him.[11] "Comrade," said one, "there is a young man who is well built and who meets the height requirements." They came up to Candide and very politely they invited him to eat with them. "Gentlemen," replied Candide, with a charming modesty, "your invitation is an honor, but I don't have any money with which to pay my share of the bill." "But sir!" said one of the men in blue to him, "people of your build and of your distinction never have to pay for themselves! Aren't you nearly six feet tall?"[12] "Yes, gentlemen, that's my height," he said bowing. "Oh sir! Come and sit down. Not only will we pay your share, but we would never permit a chap like you to go short of money. We were put on earth to give each other a helping hand." "You're quite right," said Candide, "that's what Mr. Pangloss always told me, and I can certainly see that everything is as good as could be." They urged him to accept a small amount of money; he accepted and made to pay for his meal; they objected and everyone sat down to eat. "Aren't you terribly fond . . . ?" "Oh yes!" he replied, "I'm terribly fond of Miss Cunégonde." "No," said one of the gentlemen, "we were asking you if you aren't terribly fond of the king of the Bulgars?"[13] "By no means," he said, "for I've never seen him." "What! He's the most delightful of kings, and we must drink his health." "Oh! I'd be happy to do so, gentlemen," and he drank. "That's enough," they said to him. "Now you are the support, the prop, the defender, the hero of the Bulgars; your fortune is made and your glory is assured."[14] Straightaway they put shackles on his legs and took him off to the regiment. They made him turn left and turn right; raise his ramrod; lower his ramrod; lie on his face; fire; march at the double; and they gave him thirty strokes of the cane. Next day he did the exercise a little less badly and he was given only

---

11. Blue was the color of the uniform of the Prussian army.

12. "Five feet five inches"; but the "foot" in pre-Revolutionary France was longer than in Britain and America (see Voltaire, *Candide*, ed. and trans. Daniel Gordon [Boston: Bedford/St. Martin's, 1999], 44). To allow for this I have increased all such measurements by about ten percent.

13. I.e., Frederick II.

14. Candide, by accepting the king's money and toasting the king's health is regarded as having signed up for military service.

twenty strokes. The day after he was given only ten, and he was regarded by his comrades as a prodigy.

Candide, stunned by the course of events, could not quite work out in what sense he was supposed to be a hero. One fine spring day he took it into his head to go for a walk, putting one foot in front of the other, believing it to be a privilege of the human species, as of the various animal species, to make use of one's legs as one pleases. He had not gone five miles when there were four other six-foot-six-tall heroes who were catching up on him, who tied him up, who led him away to a cell. He was asked by an official of the court which he would prefer: to be beaten thirty-six times by the whole regiment, or to have twelve little lead balls enter his skull simultaneously. It was all very well for him to say that human beings have freedom of the will,[15] and that he wanted neither option; he had no choice but to make a choice. He decided, making full use of the divine gift that is called freedom, to run the gauntlet thirty-six times.[16] He survived two circuits. The regiment was composed of two thousand men; which meant that two circuits meant that he received four thousand blows of the cane, and these stripped the skin off his muscles and his nerves from the nape of his neck to his ass. When the third circuit was about to begin Candide begged for the only clemency he could hope for, that they would be so good as to smash his skull. They were kind enough to agree; his eyes were blindfolded and he was placed in a kneeling position. As it happened, the king of the Bulgars passed by at this moment, and he inquired as to why Candide was being punished. As the king was a man of genius, he grasped from the account he was given that Candide was a young metaphysician who knew very little about the ways of the world,[17] and he remitted his punishment with a clemency that will be praised in every newspaper and will be remembered through the centuries. A fine surgeon cured Candide in three weeks using unguents concocted according to the recipes of Dioscorides.[18] He already had a little bit of skin, and could walk, when the king of the Bulgars declared war on the king of the Abars.[19]

---

15. In *Eléments de la philosophie de Newton* (1738), Voltaire had defended the doctrine of freedom of the will; but Frederick II had converted him to determinism or fatalism by 1740, when he wrote his *Métaphysique de Newton*.

16. Voltaire reports in his *Mémoires* that this punishment was inflicted on deserters from the Prussian army while he was in Berlin—indeed Frederick II took pleasure in watching.

17. Frederick's father had expelled Wolff from Prussia because a number of soldiers had used his argument against freedom of the will to justify desertion.

18. A Greek doctor of the first century C.E.

19. The Abars, like the Bulgars, are a Scythian nation, but Voltaire expects us to identify them with the French.

CHAPTER THREE: *How Candide escaped from the midst of the*
Bulgars, and what became of him

Nothing could be more beautiful, more fine, more glittering, more orderly than the two armies. Trumpets, fifes, oboes, drums, and artillery made a beautiful music such as they never have the chance to hear in hell. First of all the artillery knocked over about six thousand men on each side; then the muskets removed from the best of all worlds about nine or ten thousand bastards who infested its surface. The bayonet, in addition, was the sufficient reason for the death of some thousands of men. All added together there may well have been thirty thousand corpses. Candide, who trembled like a philosopher, hid himself as best he could during this heroic butchery.

Finally, while the two kings each had a *Te Deum* sung in his camp,[20] he took the decision to go and philosophize about effects and causes somewhere else. He climbed over piles of the dead and dying, and came first of all to a neighboring village. It was reduced to ashes: it was an Abar village that the Bulgars had burned in conformity with international law. Here old men, crippled by the blows they had received, watched their wives, their throats cut, die while holding their babies to their bleeding breasts. There girls, disemboweled after having satisfied the natural instincts of some hero, breathed their last. Others, half burned, screamed for someone to come and finish them off. Brains were scattered on the ground, alongside arms and legs that had been cut off.

Candide ran off as fast as he could until he reached another village. It belonged to some Bulgars, and Abar heroes had given it the same treatment. Candide, still walking though his legs trembled and he had to stumble over ruins, finally found himself outside the war zone, carrying a few bits and pieces to eat in his backpack, and never forgetting Miss Cunégonde. His supplies ran out when he reached Holland: but having heard that everybody living in that country was rich, and that they were all Christians, he had no doubt that he would be treated there just as well as he had been in the château of His Honor the Baron—before he was driven out of it on account of Miss Cunégonde's beautiful eyes.

He begged several respectable people to give him some spare change; they all replied that if he carried on begging he would be locked up in a house of correction in order to teach him how to live.[21]

Next he accosted a man who had just been speaking to a large gathering on the subject of charity for a whole hour, uninterrupted and on his own. This fine speaker looked askance at him and asked, "What are you doing

---

20. A religious ceremony traditionally employed to give thanks for victory.
21. Begging was illegal in Holland.

here? Are you here to give your support to the cause of right?" "There is no effect without a cause," Candide modestly replied; "everything is linked together by necessary connections, and arranged for the best. It was inevitable that I would be driven away from Miss Cunégonde's side, that I should have to run the gauntlet, and it is necessary that I beg for food until I can earn my own keep. All this could not be otherwise." "My friend," said the distinguished speaker to him, "do you believe that the pope is antichrist?"[22] "I've never been told that before," replied Candide, "but whether he is or is not, I'm in need of food." "You don't deserve to eat," replied the other; "go away you wretch; go away you miserable creature; never come near me again as long as you live." The speaker's wife had just put her head out of the window, and, seeing somebody who was not convinced that the pope is antichrist, she emptied over his head a full . . . Oh heavens! Women are capable of dreadful excesses when motivated by religious zeal!

A person who had never been baptized, an authentic Anabaptist,[23] called Jacques, saw the cruel and shameful way in which one of his fellow human beings was being treated, a creature like him with two legs and no feathers, one with a soul.[24] He took him back to his house, cleaned him up, gave him some bread and some beer, presented him with two florins, and even wanted to teach him to earn a living working in one of his workshops manufacturing the "oriental" cloth that is made in Holland. Candide almost threw himself at his feet, and cried out, "Dr. Pangloss was quite right to tell me that all is as good as could be in this world; for I am infinitely more moved by your extraordinary generosity than by the inhumanity of that gentleman in a black coat and the good lady his wife."

Next day, while out for a walk, he came across a cripple all covered in pustules, his eyes infected, the end of his nose eaten away, his mouth crooked, his teeth black, his voice hoarse. He was tormented by a dreadful cough, and spat out a tooth with every spasm.

CHAPTER FOUR: *How Candide met Dr. Pangloss, who used to teach him philosophy, and what became of it*

Candide, more touched with compassion than horrified, gave this repulsive cripple the two florins that he had been given by his honest Anabaptist, Jacques. The ghost stared at him, burst into tears, and threw his arms

---

22. This was the view held by orthodox Calvinists.

23. Anabaptists believed that only adults could choose to become Christians and therefore rejected infant (but not adult) baptism.

24. This definition of a human being comes from Plato.

around him. Candide was terrified, and stepped back. "Alas," said one poor wretch to the other, "do you no longer recognize your beloved Pangloss?" "What are you saying? Is it you, my dearest teacher? You, in this awful state! What dreadful thing has happened to you? Why are you no longer in the most beautiful of all castles? What has become of Miss Cunégonde, who is so much more beautiful than other girls, and is nature's masterpiece?" "I can't bear any more," said Pangloss. At once Candide took him to the Anabaptist's stable, where he gave him a bit of bread to eat. And when Pangloss had recovered his strength, "Well," he asked, "what about Cunégonde?" "She is dead," Pangloss replied. Candide fainted at the word "dead"; his friend brought him to his senses with some foul vinegar, a bottle of which happened to be in the stable. Candide opened his eyes. "Cunégonde dead! Oh, best of worlds, where are you! But of what illness did she die? Did she die of grief on seeing me literally kicked out of the beautiful castle that belongs to her noble father?" "No," said Pangloss, "she was disemboweled by some Bulgar soldiers, after being raped until she could be raped no more. They smashed in the head of the noble baron, who tried to defend her, and they chopped her ladyship into little pieces. My poor pupil, her brother, was treated exactly as his sister was. And as for the castle, there's not a single stone standing on another; there's not a barn, not a sheep, not a duck, not a tree left. But we've been properly revenged, for the Abars have done the same to a neighboring castle that belonged to a Bulgar nobleman."

At this speech Candide fainted again, but, having regained consciousness, and having said all that needed to be said, he inquired after the cause, the effect, and the sufficient reason that had reduced Pangloss to such a pitiable condition. "Alas!" said Pangloss, "It's love; love, the consolation of the human species; love, without which life would disappear from the face of the earth; love, which inspires all creatures capable of sensation; sweet love." "Alas!" said Candide, "I've had some experience of this love, this love that rules our hearts, which is the soul of our souls; all it got me was a kiss and twenty kicks in the ass. How could so beautiful a cause have produced in you such an abominable effect?"

Pangloss replied as follows: "O my dear Candide! You knew Paquette, that pretty serving girl who worked for her distinguished ladyship. In her arms I tasted the delights of Paradise, and it is they that have produced these hellish torments that you now see eating me alive. She was infected; she may now be dead. Paquette received this present from a learned friar who had traced it back to its origins. For he had had it from an old countess, who had been given it by a captain of artillery, who got it from a marquise, who had it from a young boy, who was given it by a Jesuit, who, when he was a novice, received it without any intermediaries from someone who had voyaged with Christopher Columbus.[25] As for me, I won't give it to anyone, for I am dying."

"O Pangloss!" Candide exclaimed, "what a strange genealogy that is! Surely the devil must have been the source of this disease?" "Not at all," replied this great thinker; "it was essential it should be present in the best of all possible worlds, it was a necessary ingredient. For if Columbus had not caught, on an island off the Americas, this disease that poisons the genital organs, and that often even makes people sterile, this disease that is obviously the antithesis of the primary purpose of all nature, we would have had neither chocolate not cochineal;[26] moreover one should note that so far this disease is peculiar to us Europeans, just like theological debate. The Turks, the Indians, the Persians, the Chinese, the Siamese, the Japanese—none of them have it yet. But there is a sufficient reason to ensure that they will catch it in their turn before too many centuries go by. Meanwhile it has made quite extraordinary progress among us, and especially in these great armies that decide the destiny of states, and that are made up of honest, well brought-up employees. One can be confident that when thirty thousand men advance into battle against an army of the same size drawn up in front of them, then there are around twenty thousand syphilitics on each side."

"Well, that's a remarkable fact," said Candide, "but we must get you cured." "And how can I get treatment?" said Pangloss. "For I don't have the money, my friend, and no matter where one goes on this planet one cannot get oneself bled nor obtain an enema without paying, or without having someone to pay for you."

This last remark made up Candide's mind; he went and threw himself at the feet of his charitable Anabaptist, Jacques, and portrayed to him in such moving terms the state to which his friend was reduced that the good chap did not hesitate to take up Dr. Pangloss; he had him treated at his own expense. In the process of being cured Pangloss lost only one eye and one ear. He wrote legibly and had a perfect command of arithmetic. Jacques the Anabaptist put him in charge of his accounts. At the end of two months, being obliged to go to Lisbon on business, he took his two philosophers with him in his ship. Pangloss explained to him how everything was so good it could not be better. Jacques didn't agree. "It must be the case," he said, "that human beings have corrupted the natural order of things somewhat; for they are not born wolves, and they have become

---

25. That syphilis had been brought to the Old World from the New was a well-established fact in Voltaire's day.

26. An insect from which a scarlet dye is produced.

wolves.[27] God did not give them twenty-four pounder guns or bayonets; and they have made themselves bayonets and cannons to destroy each other. Bankruptcy is something else that surely wouldn't be found in the best of worlds, nor the bankruptcy courts that seize the goods of the bankrupts in order to prevent their creditors from getting what they are owed." "That's how things have to be," replied the one-eyed doctor, "and the misfortunes of individuals go to make up the welfare of the whole, in such a way that the more personal misfortunes there are, the more everything is for the best." While he was arguing, the sky darkened, the winds blew from the four corners of the world, and the ship was struck by the most dreadful storm when it was within sight of the port of Lisbon.

CHAPTER FIVE: *The storm, the shipwreck, the earthquake, and what became of Dr. Pangloss, of Candide, and of Jacques the Anabaptist*

Half of those on board, struck down, dying of those inconceivable agonies that the rolling of a vessel conveys to the nerves and to all the fluids of a body when it is shaken in opposing directions, didn't even have the strength to worry about the danger they faced. The other half cried out and prayed aloud; the sails were torn, the masts broken, the vessel took on water. Those who could work did what they could; but they were all at cross purposes, and no one took command. The Anabaptist lent a hand; he was on the prow; a furious sailor hit him hard and laid him out on the deck; but the blow he gave him was so hard that he lost his balance and fell overboard head first. He was hanging upside down, caught up in a section of the broken mast. The good Jacques ran to his assistance, helped get him back on board, but in his struggles he slipped into the sea himself, in full view of the sailor, who left him to drown without even bothering to watch him go down. Candide ran to the side, and caught sight of his benefactor, who came to the surface for a moment before being swallowed forever. He wanted to throw himself into the sea after him, but the philosopher Pangloss prevented him, proving to him that the Bay of Lisbon had been especially made so that the Anabaptist could drown in it. While he was proving this by logical deduction, the vessel foundered and everyone died, with the exception of Pangloss, of Candide, and of the brutal sailor who had drowned the virtuous Anabaptist; the wretch swam successfully to the

---

27. There was a well-known adage "Man is a wolf to man," which is discussed, for example, by Erasmus in his *Adages* (1508).

shore, while Pangloss and Candide were carried ashore clinging to a plank.[28]

When they had recovered a little they set out on foot for Lisbon; they had some money in their pockets with which they hoped to save themselves from starvation now that they had escaped drowning.

No sooner had they passed through the gates of the town, weeping over the death of their benefactor, than they felt the earth tremble under their feet; the sea in the port began to boil, and the ships at anchor were smashed to pieces.[29] Gusts of wind showered sparks and glowing cinders over the streets and the squares of the city; the houses collapsed, their roofs leveled with their foundations, and their foundations shattered; thirty thousand inhabitants, randomly selected without regard to age or sex, were crushed in the ruins. The sailor said to himself, with a whistle and a swear word, "There'll be good pickings here!" "What can be the sufficient reason of this phenomenon?" asked Pangloss. "This is the end of the world," cried Candide. The sailor at once ran into the middle of the ruins, risked death looking for money, found some, took it, got drunk, and, having slept it off, bought the favors of the first willing woman that he met among the ruins of the shattered houses, surrounded by the dying and the dead. Pangloss, however, caught hold of his sleeve: "My friend," he said to him, "that's no good, you're falling short of the standard set by universal reason, you're not spending your time as you should." "Christ!" said the sailor. "I'm a sailor and I was born in the colonies. I've made four voyages to Japan, and four times I've walked on the crucifix.[30] I'm just the man to talk to about universal reason!"

Some falling rocks had wounded Candide, who was stretched out in the street and covered in debris. He said to Pangloss, "Alas! Get me a little wine and some oil; I'm dying." "This earthquake isn't something new," replied Pangloss. "The city of Lima in South America felt the same shocks

---

28. Voltaire had lost significant sums of money as a result of ships going down, and we find him writing on 4 or 5 Feb. 1757, "I must get used to shipwrecks" (D7142). But the theme of shipwreck also imposed itself because Petronius had described the world as one great shipwreck, a phrase Voltaire echoes repeatedly (e.g., D7263, 20 May 1757: "This world is a great shipwreck; let those who can save themselves is what I often say.") Storms, shipwrecks, planks, and "each man for himself" recur frequently as a linked set of images in the correspondence: D7096, D7097, D7839, D7848, D7862. See Murray, *Voltaire's "Candide,"* 315–9.

29. The Lisbon earthquake occurred on 1 Nov. 1755; contemporaries estimated that 30,000 were killed by it.

30. This symbolic repudiation of Christianity was a requirement for entry into Japan, at least in the early eighteenth century.

last year. The same causes, the same effects. There must be a fissure of sulfur underground that stretches from Lima to Lisbon."[31] "There is no better explanation," said Candide. "But for God's sake, get me a little oil and some wine." "What do you mean, there *is* no better explanation!" replied the philosopher. "I maintain that my answer is proven and there *could* be no better explanation." Candide fainted and Pangloss brought him a little water from a nearby fountain.

Next day, having found some bits and pieces to eat while picking their way between the ruins, they recovered some of their strength. Then they worked alongside everyone else to give what help they could to their companions who had escaped death. A few residents, whom they had helped, gave them as good a lunch as one could hope for after such a disaster. It is true that the meal was mournful; the guests mingled tears with their food, but Pangloss consoled them, assuring them that things could not be otherwise. "For," said he, "all this is the best there could be; for if there is a volcano under Lisbon, then it couldn't be anywhere else. For it is impossible that things could be placed anywhere except where they are. For all is well."

A little dark man, an agent of the Inquisition, who was sitting beside him, politely joined in the conversation, and said: "I gather, sir, that you do not believe in original sin; for if all is as good as could be, then there has not been a fall, nor are we punished for it."[32]

"I very humbly beg pardon of Your Excellency," replied Pangloss even more politely, "for the fall of mankind and their punishment were necessary events in the best of all possible worlds." "Good sir, then you don't believe in free will?" asked the agent.[33] "Your Excellency will excuse me," said Pangloss, "but free will is compatible with inflexible necessity; for it was necessary that we should be free; since after all the will is determined . . ." Pangloss was in the middle of his phrase when the agent gave a nod of his head to his guard, who poured him a glass of Port to drink.

CHAPTER SIX: *How they held a fine auto-da-fé to prevent further earthquakes, and how Candide was whipped*

After the earthquake, which had wrecked three quarters of Lisbon, the wise men of Portugal had identified no more effective method to prevent the rest being destroyed than to hold a fine auto-da-fé to educate the

---

31. "The fissure of sulfur" theory was expounded in Elie Bertrand, *Mémoire sur les tremblements de terre* (Berne, 1756).

32. Evidently he suspects Pangloss of being a Socinian (see below, p. 82).

33. Pangloss has presented Leibniz's view, but orthodox Catholics were required to believe in free will (while orthodox Calvinists were determinists).

people.[34] It was decided by the University of Coïmbra that the spectacle of a few people being burned over a slow fire, accompanied by the most elaborate rituals, was an infallible, if little known, method for preventing earthquakes.

In view of this decision they had arrested someone from Biscay who was convicted of having married his godmother, and two Portuguese who, when eating a chicken, had thrown away the fatty bacon in which it had been wrapped.[35] After the dinner they came and seized Dr. Pangloss and his disciple Candide, the first for having spoken, and the second for having listened with an air of approval. Both of them were taken separately to accommodation that was extremely cool, where one was never troubled by the sun. Eight days later they were both dressed in a *san-benito*,[36] and their heads were decorated with miters of paper.[37] Candide's miter and *san-benito* were decorated with upside down flames, and with devils who had neither tails nor claws; but the devils Pangloss wore had claws and tails, and his flames were right way up. They walked in procession, dressed up like this, and listened to a very moving sermon, followed by delightful music consisting of one chord played on the organ. Candide was whipped in time while the congregation sang; the chap from Biscay and the two men who had not wanted to eat fatty bacon were burned; and Pangloss was hanged, although this was a break with tradition. The same day the earth trembled once again, making a blood-curdling noise.

Candide, shocked, bewildered, taken aback, covered in blood, shaking all over, said to himself, "If this is the best of all possible worlds, what on earth are the others like? I wouldn't mind just being beaten, after all I was beaten by the Bulgars. But my dearest Pangloss! The greatest of philosophers! Did I have to see you hanged without knowing why? O my dear Anabaptist, the best of men, was it necessary that you should be drowned in the harbor? O Miss Cunégonde, the most beautiful of girls, was it inevitable that you should be disemboweled?"

He turned away, hardly able to stand up, having been preached at, whipped, absolved, and blessed, when an old woman accosted him and said: "Young man, take heart, and follow me."

---

34. Voltaire's understanding was that such an auto-da-fé had occurred on 20 June 1756.

35. According to Church law the Biscayan was guilty of incest. Many Jews had been forcibly converted to Christianity, and a refusal to eat pork was taken as evidence of apostasy.

36. A tunic made of sackcloth.

37. Voltaire's account of what happened at an auto-da-fé is drawn from C. Dellon, *Relation de l'Inquisition de Goa* (1688).

CHAPTER SEVEN: *How an old woman took care of Candide, and how
he rediscovered his true love*

Candide did not take heart, but he followed the old woman into a hovel.
She gave him a bottle of ointment to rub on himself, left him food and
drink, and showed him a little bed that was fairly clean. Next to the bed
there was a complete set of clothes. "Eat, drink, sleep," she said to him,
"and may Our Lady of Atocha, St. Anthony of Padua, and St. James of
Compostella take care of you! I will return tomorrow." Candide, still
shocked by all he had seen, by all he had suffered, and most of all by the
kind deeds of the old woman, wanted to kiss her hand. "It's not *my* hand
you should kiss," said the old woman. "I will return tomorrow. Rub
yourself with ointment, eat, and sleep."

Despite all that he had suffered, Candide ate and slept. The next day
the old woman brought him breakfast, had a look at his back, and rubbed a
different ointment into it herself; later she brought him his lunch; in the
evening she came back with his dinner. On the next day her hospitality was
the same as the day before. "Who are you?" Candide asked her over and
over again; "Who has persuaded you to treat me so well? What can I do for
you in return?" The good woman never replied; she came back in the
evening, but she had no dinner with her. "Come with me," she said, "and
don't say a word." She took him by the arm and walked about a quarter of
a mile with him through open countryside. They arrived at an isolated
house, surrounded by gardens and ornamental ponds. The old woman
knocked at a little door. It opened; she took Candide up a concealed
staircase into a study decorated in gold leaf, sat him on a brocade sofa,
closed the door, and went away. Candide thought he was dreaming; indeed
he thought all his life hitherto had been a nightmare, but that right now he
was having a pleasant dream.

Soon the old woman reappeared; she supported, not without some
difficulty, a woman who was trembling: a woman of noble stature, shining
with jewels, and hidden behind a veil. "Remove the veil," said the old
woman to Candide. The young man approached; he lifted the veil with a
timid hand. What an experience! What a surprise! He thought he saw Miss
Cunégonde, he really did see her, it actually was her. His strength deserted
him; he could not say a word; he fell at her feet. Cunégonde fell on the
sofa. The old woman soaked them in smelling salts; they came back to
their senses; they talked to each other: at first they cut across each other's
words, their questions and their replies became entangled with each other
and with sighs, tears, cries. The old woman advised them to make less
noise, and left them to themselves. "What! It's you," Candide said to her.
"You're alive. I've rediscovered you in Portugal! Were you not raped? Did
they not cut your belly open, as Pangloss the philosopher assured me they

had?" "Yes they did," said the beautiful Cunégonde, "but one doesn't always die from those two mishaps." "But your father and mother, were they killed?" "I wish they had not been," said Cunégonde, weeping. "And your brother?" "My brother was killed as well." "And why are you in Portugal? And how did you know I was here? And by what peculiar chance were you able to bring me to this house?" "I will answer all your questions," replied the lady, "but first I require you to tell me everything that has happened to you since the innocent kiss you gave me, and the kicks you were given."

Candide obeyed her implicitly and unquestioningly; and although he was taken aback, although his voice was feeble and trembling, although his spine still hurt a bit, he told her in the simplest way everything that had happened to him since the moment of their separation. Cunégonde lifted her eyes to the heavens. She wept when the good Anabaptist died, and wept again when Pangloss was killed; after which she spoke as follows to Candide, who listened attentively to every word, and devoured her with his eyes.

CHAPTER EIGHT: *Cunégonde's story*

"I was sound asleep in my bed when the fates chose to send the Bulgars to our beautiful castle of Thunder-ten-tronckh. They cut the throats of my father and brother, and chopped my mother up into pieces. A large Bulgar, six-foot-six tall, seeing that I had fainted at the sight, set about raping me; this brought me back to consciousness; I recovered my senses; I cried; I fought; I bit; I scratched; I wanted to poke out the eyes of this enormous Bulgar, not realizing that everything that was happening in my father's castle was customary on such occasions. The brute gave me a blow with a knife in my left side—I carry the scar to this day." "Alas! I hope I'll see it," said Candide ingenuously. "You'll see it," said Cunégonde. "But let me continue." "Continue," said Candide.

So she picked up her story where she had left off. "A Bulgar captain came in; he saw me covered in blood, and the soldier didn't bother to get off me. The captain fell into a rage at the lack of respect that this brute had shown him, and killed him while he was on top of me. Then he had me treated, and took me to his camp as a prisoner of war. I washed the few shirts he had; I cooked for him; he found me very pretty, I must confess; and I won't deny that he was a fine figure of a man, nor that he had skin that was white and soft; but he had little intelligence, and almost no philosophy; it wasn't difficult to tell that he hadn't been educated by Dr. Pangloss. At the end of three months, having lost all his money, and having lost his taste for me, he sold me to a Jew named Issachar, who engaged in business in Holland and Portugal, and who had a passionate love of

women. This Jew took a great liking to me, but he could not have his way
with me; I put up a better resistance to him than I had to the Bulgar
soldier. A person of honor can be raped once, but their virtue is strength-
ened by it. The Jew, in order to tame me, brought me to this country house
that you are now in. I had believed, until I came here, that there was
nothing on earth more beautiful than the castle of Thunder-ten-tronckh; I
was mistaken.

"The Grand Inquisitor saw me one day when I was at Mass; he kept
making eyes at me, and sent a message to me that he had to speak to me
about a secret matter. I was taken to his palace; I told him who my parents
were; he pointed out to me how unsuitable it was for someone of my rank
to belong to a Jew. He arranged for the proposal to be put to Don Issachar
that he should give me to him. Don Issachar, who is the court's banker,
and a man of wealth, wanted nothing to do with it. The Inquisitor threatened him with an auto-da-fé. Finally my Jew, intimidated, reached an
agreement whereby the house and I would belong to both of them in
common, the Jew having Mondays, Wednesdays, and the Sabbath for
himself, and the Inquisitor having the other days of the week. This agreement has been in operation for six months. Though there have been
quarrels; often they have been unable to agree as to whether the night
between Saturday and Sunday belongs to the old law or the new.[38] As for
me, so far I have resisted both of them, and I believe this is the reason why
they both love me still.

"Finally, in order to ward off the scourge of earthquakes, and in order to
intimidate Don Issachar, his Lordship the Inquisitor was pleased to cele-
brate an auto-da-fé. He did me the honor of inviting me. I was seated
where I would have an excellent view; the ladies were served with refreshments between the Mass and the executions. Truth to tell I was overcome
with horror to watch those two Jews burn and that decent chap from
Biscay who had married his godmother. But that was nothing to my
surprise, my shock, my dismay when I saw, in a *san-benito*, half-hidden by a
miter, a face which looked like that of Pangloss! I rubbed my eyes, I
watched carefully, I saw him hanged; I fell into a swoon. I had barely
regained consciousness when I saw you stripped naked; this was the ultimate of horrors, of dismay, of pain, of despair. I will tell you, speaking
truthfully, that your skin is even whiter, and tinged with an even more
perfect pink, than that of my Bulgar captain. The sight of it redoubled all
the feelings that were overwhelming me, that were devouring me. I cried

38. The Old Law is the law of Moses, the New Law the law of Christ. As the
Jewish Sabbath runs from sunset on Friday to sunset on Saturday, there could be
uncertainty as to whether the night between Saturday and Sunday belonged to
Saturday or Sunday.

out. I wanted to say: 'Stop, you barbarians!' But my voice failed me, and my cries would have done no good. When you had been well whipped, 'How can it be,' I said to myself, 'that the lovable Candide and the wise Pangloss are here in Lisbon, the first to receive one hundred lashes, and the second to be hanged on the orders of His Lordship the Inquisitor, whose beloved I am? Pangloss certainly cruelly deceived me when he said that all goes as well as could be.'

"Upset, bewildered, sometimes taking leave of my senses, and sometimes on the point of dying of weakness, I had my head full of the massacres of my father, of my mother, of my brother, of the insolence of my foul Bulgar soldier, of the stabbing he had given me, of my enslavement, of my occupation as a cook, of my Bulgar captain, of my wretched Don Issachar, of my abominable Inquisitor, of the hanging of Dr. Pangloss, of this great *miserere*[39] accompanied by a droning organ while they whipped you, and above all of the kiss I had given you behind a screen, the day when I had seen you for the last time. I praised God who had brought you back to me through so many trials. I told my old woman to take care of you, and to bring you here as soon as she could. She has carried out my instructions faithfully; I have tasted the inexpressible pleasure of seeing you again, of listening to you, of speaking to you. You must be starving; I'm very hungry; let's begin by eating dinner."

So they both sat down to eat, and after dinner they sat down again on the fine sofa I have already mentioned; they were there when the honorable Don Issachar, one of the owners of the house, arrived. It was the Sabbath day. He had come to enjoy his rights, and to put his feelings of tender love into words.

CHAPTER NINE: *What became of Cunégonde, of Candide, of the Grand Inquisitor, and of a Jew*

This Issachar was the most hot-tempered Jew that had been seen in Israel since the captivity in Babylon. "What!" he said, "Christian bitch! Isn't it enough that I have to put up with His Lordship the Inquisitor? Must this bastard also have a share of you?" While saying this, he drew a long dagger that he always carried on him; and, believing his adversary to be unarmed, he threw himself on Candide. But our good Westphalian had received a fine sword from the old woman along with his complete outfit of clothes. He drew his sword, and, although he was a perfectly good-natured chap, he laid the Jew out stone dead on the tiles, right at the feet of the beautiful Cunégonde.

---

39. Psalm 50, often sung to express penitence.

"Mary Mother of God!" she cried, "What's going to become of us? A man killed in my house! If the police come we are done for!" "If Pangloss hadn't been hanged," says Candide, "he would have given us good advice in this crisis, for he was a great philosopher. Since he's not here, let's ask the old woman what to do." She had excellent judgment and was beginning to give her opinion when another little door opened. It was one minute after midnight, Sunday was just beginning. This day belonged to His Excellency the Inquisitor. He came in and saw the beaten Candide with a sword in his hand, a corpse spread out on the ground, Cunégonde looking scared, and the old woman giving her advice.

These are the thoughts that, at that precise instant, occurred to Candide, and this is the logic he followed: "If this holy man calls for help, he will unquestionably have me burned; he may also have Cunégonde burned; he had me whipped without mercy; he is my rival; I am in the middle of killing; there's no alternative." This logic was clear-cut and rapid; and without giving time to the Inquisitor to recover from his surprise, he ran him through, and tossed his body beside that of the Jew. "And now there's another one," said Cunégonde; "we won't be pardoned now; we are excommunicated; our last hour has come! How could you do it, you who were born so good-natured, how could you kill in the space of two minutes both a Jew and a clergyman?" "My dear miss," replied Candide, "when one is in love, jealous, and has been whipped by the Inquisition, one becomes a stranger to oneself."

The old woman then broke in, and said: "There are three Andalusian horses in the stables with their saddles and bridles. Let our brave Candide go and get them ready. My lady has some gold coins and some diamonds. Let us quickly mount our horses—though I have only one buttock on which to sit—and make for Cadiz. The weather is perfect, and there's nothing nicer than traveling in the cool of the night."

At once Candide saddled the three horses. Cunégonde, the old woman, and he traveled thirty miles without stopping. While they were making their escape, the police arrived at the house; the Inquisitor was buried in a beautiful church; and Issachar was thrown on the garbage dump.[40]

Candide, Cunégonde, and the old woman were already in the little town of Avacena, in the middle of the mountains of the Sierra Morena, and this is the conversation that was taking place between them in an inn.

---

40. The theme of what happened to those denied Christian burial preoccupied Voltaire, and recurs in chapter 21.

CHAPTER TEN: *The distress in which Candide, Cunégonde, and the old woman arrived in Cadiz; they board ship*

"Who could have stolen my doubloons and my diamonds?" asked Cunégonde, weeping. "What will we live on? How will we get by? Where will I find an Inquisitor or a Jew who will give me more?" "Alas," said the old woman, "I strongly suspect a priest, a Franciscan friar, who slept last night in the same hotel as us in Badajoz. God prevent me from jumping to the wrong conclusion, but he came twice into our room, and he left long before us."[41] "Oh dear!" said Candide. "Good Pangloss often demonstrated to me that the goods of this world are owned in common by all human beings, that each person has an equal right to them.[42] If one accepts Pangloss's argument, this friar should certainly have left us enough to enable us to pay for the rest of our journey. Have you got nothing left at all, then, my beautiful Cunégonde?" "Not even small change," she replied.

In the same inn there was a Benedictine prior. He bought one of the horses at a bargain price. Candide, Cunégonde, and the old woman traveled by Lucena, by Chillas, by Lebrixa, and finally reached Cadiz. There a fleet was being prepared to sail, and troops were being collected to teach a lesson to the Jesuit priests in Paraguay, who were accused of having encouraged one of their tribes to revolt against the kings of Spain and Portugal, attacking the town of Sacramento.[43] Candide, having been enrolled in the Bulgar army, performed the Bulgar drill in front of the general and his tiny army with such grace, such speed, such skill, such pride, and such dexterity that he was given a company of infantry to command. So now he was a captain. He embarked with Miss Cunégonde, the old woman, two servants, and the two remaining Andalusian horses that had belonged to His Excellency the Chief Inquisitor of Portugal.

Throughout the crossing they discussed at length the philosophy of

---

41. The modern reader finds the notion of the friar coming into their room (not once but twice) deeply puzzling. But eighteenth-century buildings normally required one to pass through one room to get to another—the corridor was a comparatively recent invention. The friar may therefore have simply been on his way to and from bed. Expectations regarding privacy were quite different then— the nearest contemporary example would be an overnight flight.

42. Pangloss' arguments are normally a satirical version of those of Leibniz and Wolff; but not here (or below on p. 31). It is possible that Rousseau's *Discourse on Inequality* is Voltaire's target.

43. In fact some money Voltaire had invested in Cadiz helped fund this expedition (D6676, D7433). Spain had agreed to transfer part of Paraguay to Portugal, but the local inhabitants and the Jesuits were resisting this.

poor Pangloss. "We are going to another world,"[44] said Candide. "I'm sure in that world we'll find that all is well. For one has to admit that what happens in our world, both in terms of physical and moral events, is enough to make one shudder a bit." "I love you with all my heart," said Cunégonde, "but my spirit is still completely shocked by what I have seen, by what I have experienced." "All will be well," replied Candide; "the sea of this New World is already superior to the seas of our Europe. It's calmer, the winds are less changeable. It's obvious that the New World is the best of all possible worlds." "I pray that it may be so," said Cunégonde; "but I have been so dreadfully unhappy in my world that my heart is almost sealed against any hope." "You two complain about what's happened to you," said the old woman; "Alas! You have no experience of misfortunes such as the ones I have suffered." Cunégonde almost broke out laughing; and thought it very amusing that this good woman would claim to be more unhappy than her. "Alas! My good woman," she said to her, "unless you have been raped by two Bulgars; unless you have been stabbed twice in the belly; unless two of your castles have been destroyed; unless you have had to watch while two mothers and two fathers have had their throats cut; and unless you have seen two of your lovers whipped in an auto-da-fé, I don't see how you can claim to have outdone me. Let me add that I was born a baroness with seventy-two quarterings to my coat of arms, and that I have had to work as a cook." "Miss," replied the old woman, "you don't know what the status of my parents was; and if I showed you my behind you wouldn't talk as you do, and you would suspend your judgment." This speech engendered a burning curiosity in Cunégonde and in Candide. The old woman spoke to them as follows.

CHAPTER ELEVEN: *The old woman's story*

"I didn't always have sore eyes, rimmed with raw flesh; my nose did not always touch my chin; and I haven't always been a servant. I am the daughter of Pope Urban X and the Princess of Palestrina.[45] Until I was fourteen years old I was brought up in a palace, one so grand that none of

44. Literally, "We are going to another universe." Leibniz had claimed to show that this is the best of all possible *universes;* no individual world within it is necessarily the best of all possible worlds, any more than any particular country is necessarily the best of all possible countries, which means the question of where things are best is a perfectly sensible one, even for a follower of Leibniz. See below, p. 134.

45. There never has been a Pope Urban X. In the manuscript of *Candide* the pope is Clement X (1730–40). Papal "nephews" and "nieces," as the children of popes were politely termed, were not uncommon.

the castles of your German barons would be fit to serve as its stable; and one of my dresses was worth more than all the splendors of Westphalia. I grew up beautiful, graceful, talented, surrounded by delight, by deference, by hope. I already inspired men to fall in love with me. My chest was forming, and what a chest! White, firm, shaped like that of the Medici Venus![46] And what eyes! What eyelashes! What black eyebrows! What flames burned in my two pupils, and dimmed the twinkling of the stars, as the local poets said to me. The women who dressed me and undressed me fell into ecstasies when they looked at me from in front and from behind, and all the men would have wished to be in their place.

"I was engaged to the sovereign ruler of Massa-Carrara. What a prince! As beautiful as me, consisting entirely of sweetness and charming gestures, with a gleaming wit and a burning love. I loved him as one does when one loves for the first time; I idolized him; I was swept away. Preparations were made for the wedding. It was extravagant beyond precedent, magnificent beyond belief; there were feasts, tournaments, and comic operas one after another, and all Italy wrote sonnets about me, not a single one of which was any good. I was about to experience the ultimate happiness when an old marquise, who had been my prince's mistress, invited him to have a cup of chocolate at her place. He died in less than two hours in horrendous convulsions. But this is nothing, a trifle. My mother, in despair, although much less distressed than I was, wanted to get away for a while from such a dreadful event. She had a very beautiful estate near Gaeta. We boarded a local galley, covered in gold like the altar of St. Peter's in Rome. Suddenly a pirate ship from Salé[47] swooped on us and boarded us. Our soldiers defended us with all the courage you would expect of soldiers in the pope's service: they threw themselves on their knees, threw their weapons aside, and begged the pirates to absolve them of their sins as they were on the point of death.

"Immediately they were stripped as naked as monkeys; and my mother too; and our ladies-in-waiting; and myself. It was quite astonishing to see the speed with which these gentlemen got us all out of our clothes. But what surprised me even more is that each one of us had one of their fingers put in a place where we women, for our part, normally allow only an enema to be placed. This ritual seemed very peculiar to me; but everything seems peculiar if you have no experience of travel. I soon learned that it was in order to check that we hadn't hidden any diamonds there. It is a custom established since time immemorial among the civilized nations who hunt on the open sea. I learned that the knights of Malta, members of

---

46. A famous statue from ancient Greece, owned by the Medici family of Florence.

47. In Morocco, a safe haven for pirates preying on Christian ships.

a religious order, never fail to perform this ritual when they seize Turks, whether male or female. It is required by an article of international law, one that has never been broken.

"I will not try to tell you how painful it is for a young princess to be taken off to Morocco as a slave, accompanied by her mother. You will be able to imagine everything we had to suffer on the pirate ship. My mother was still very beautiful; our ladies-in-waiting, even our mere servants, were more attractive than any woman in the whole of Africa. As for me, I was ravishing; I was the embodiment of beauty and of grace, and I was a virgin—though not for long. This flower that had been reserved for the handsome prince of Massa-Carrara was torn from me by the pirate captain. He was a loathsome Negro, who imagined he was doing me a great honor. Certainly my mother the Princess of Palestrina and I had to be strong indeed to live through everything we experienced during our journey to Morocco. But let's move on; these things are commonplace, and the time spent describing them is wasted.

"Morocco was bathed in blood when we arrived there. Fifty sons of the Emperor Muley Ismael each had a faction of his own, which resulted in effect in fifty civil wars: wars of blacks against blacks; of blacks against browns; of browns against browns; of half-castes against half-castes. The whole empire had been turned into one vast slaughterhouse.

"Scarcely had we put foot on dry land when the blacks of a faction opposed to that of my pirate arrived to take his booty from him. We were—second only to the diamonds and the gold—the most valuable part of his cargo. I was witness to a battle such as you would never see between people raised in your European climate—northerners don't have hot enough blood. They don't lust after women to the same degree as is commonplace in Africa. It seems as though you Europeans have milk in your veins; while it is sulfuric acid, it is liquid fire that flows in the veins of the people who live on Mount Atlas and in the surrounding countries. They fought with the fury of the lions, the tigers, and the snakes of that part of the world, in order to determine who should have us. A Moor seized my mother by the right arm; my captain's second-in-command had her by the left; a Moorish soldier grabbed her by one leg, and one of our pirates had her by the other. Almost all our servants found themselves at that same moment being pulled between four soldiers. My captain kept me hidden behind himself. He had his scimitar in his fist, and, in a blind rage, killed anyone who got in his way. Finally I saw all our Italian girls and my mother torn apart, cut up, massacred by the monsters who were fighting over them. My companions and fellow captives, those who had captured them, soldiers, sailors, blacks, browns, whites, half-castes, and finally my captain were all killed, and I remained, dying on top of a pile of dead bodies. Comparable events took place, as is well known, across a vast area more than seven hundred and fifty miles across, while everyone continued faithfully to pray five times a day as required by Mohammed.

"I struggled to untangle myself from the heap of so many bloody bodies piled on top of each other, and dragged myself into the shade of a large orange tree that stood beside a nearby stream. There I fell to the ground, overwhelmed by fear, exhaustion, horror, despair, and hunger. Before long I slipped into a sleep that was more a loss of consciousness than a rest. I was in this state of feebleness and insensibility, hanging between life and death, when I felt myself being pressed down by something that was rubbing against my body. I opened my eyes; I saw a white man, rather good-looking, who moaned and grimaced, muttering, '*O che sciagura d'essere senza c. . . .!*48' "

CHAPTER TWELVE: *Continuation of the dreadful experiences of the old woman*

"Astonished and delighted to hear the language of my homeland, and equally surprised by the words this man was uttering, I replied to him that there were worse things that could happen to one than the loss of which he was complaining. I explained to him in a few words just what horrors I had endured, and I slumped back exhausted. He carried me into a neighboring house, had me placed on a bed, gave me food to drink, looked after me, comforted me, humored me, told me that he had never seen anyone as beautiful as me, and that never before had he so much regretted the loss of that which had been his and which nobody could return to him. 'I was born in Naples,' he told me; 'there two or three thousand boys are castrated each year; some die as a result; some acquire a voice more beautiful than a woman's; and some are sent to govern whole provinces. In my case the operation was extremely successful, and I became a musician in the chapel of Her Lady the Princess of Palestrina.' 'In my mother's chapel!' I cried out. 'In your mother's chapel!' he cried, bursting into tears. 'What, are you that little princess whom I brought up until she was six years old, and who already showed signs of becoming as beautiful as you indeed are?' 'Yes, it's me. My mother is four hundred yards from here, cut into quarters under a pile of corpses . . .'

"I told him everything that had happened to me; and he told me his own adventures, and explained to me how he had been sent to the king of Morocco by a Christian ruler in order to conclude a treaty with him, under the terms of which he would be supplied with powder, cannons, and ships to assist him to destroy the trade of the other Christian states. 'My mission

---

48. "Oh what a misfortune to have no balls!"

is complete,' said this honest eunuch; 'I am going to board ship at Ceuta, and I will take you back to Italy. *Ma che sciagura d'essere senza c. . . .!*'

"I thanked him with tears of affection, and instead of taking me to Italy, he took me to Algiers and sold me to the governor of that province. I had scarcely been sold when the plague, which has made the circuit of Africa, Asia, and Europe, broke out in Algeria in a dreadful epidemic. You have seen earthquakes, but, miss, have you ever been infected with plague?" "Never," replied the baroness.

"If you had been," continued the old woman, "you would have to admit that it is far worse than an earthquake. It is very common in Africa; I fell victim to it. Imagine my situation, the daughter of a pope, fifteen years of age, who in the space of three months had experienced poverty and slavery, had been raped almost every day, had seen her mother cut into four, had survived hunger and battle, and was dying of plague in Algeria. However I didn't die. But my eunuch, and the governor, and almost the whole harem of Algiers did die.

"When the death toll caused by this awful plague began to diminish, they sold the slaves who had belonged to the governor. A merchant bought me, and took me to Tunis. He sold me to another merchant, who sold me again at Tripoli; from Tripoli I was taken to Alexandria for resale; from Alexandria to Smyrna; from Smyrna to Constantinople. In the end I was the property of a general of the Janizaries,[49] who was soon commanded to go to the defense of Azof against the Russians who were besieging it.

"The general, who was a very gallant man, took his whole harem with him, and we stayed in a small fort overlooking the Sea of Azof. We were guarded by two black eunuchs and twenty soldiers. Enormous numbers of Russians were being killed, but they were killing just as many of our men. Azof was sacked,[50] and no distinction was made between men and women, old and young: all were killed. Only our little fort still held out. The enemy wanted to take us by starving us out. The twenty Janizaries had sworn never to give themselves up. The extreme hunger to which they were reduced forced them to eat our two eunuchs, for fear that otherwise they would break their oaths. After twenty days they resolved to eat the women.

"We had an imam[51] who was very pious and very tenderhearted. He made a fine speech to them trying to persuade them not to kill us outright. 'Cut,' said he, 'just one buttock off each of these women, and you will eat well. If you have to come back to them you will be able to obtain as much

---

49. Elite troops in the sultan's army.

50. Azof fell in 1696, which implies the old woman was born around 1681 and is about seventy-five when she tells her story.

51. The equivalent of a chaplain.

again in a few days time. God will smile on you for so charitable an action, and you will have the sustenance you need.'

"He was eloquent indeed and he persuaded them. The dreadful operation he had proposed was carried out on us. The imam applied to our wounds the same ointment that they put on boys who have just been circumcised. We were all near death.

"Scarcely had the Janizaries eaten the meal that we had provided for them when the Russians arrived on flat-bottomed boats. Not a single Janizary escaped. The Russians were not at all interested in the condition in which we found ourselves. Wherever you go there are French surgeons; one of them who was fortunately very skillful took care of us; he cured us; and as long as I live I will not forget that when my wounds had properly healed, he propositioned me. However he told us all to console ourselves; he assured us that similar things had happened at other sieges, and that it was in accordance with the law of war.

"As soon as my companions could walk they were made to travel to Moscow. We were shared out amongst our captors, and I became the property of a boyar[52] who decided I should be his gardener and struck me twenty times a day with his whip. But two years later this lord was broken on the wheel with around thirty other noblemen because of some disagreement at court.[53] I seized my chance and ran away. I crossed the whole of Russia. For a long time I was a waitress in an inn in Riga; then in Rostock, in Vismar, in Leipzig, in Cassel, in Utrecht, in Leyden, in The Hague, in Rotterdam. I grew old in misery and disgrace, having only half of a backside, but I always remembered that I was the daughter of a pope. A hundred times I wanted to kill myself; but I was still in love with life. This ridiculous weakness is perhaps one of our most disastrous attachments; for is there anything more stupid than to choose to carry continuously a burden that at the same time one constantly wants to let drop to the ground? To hate one's existence, and to cling to it? To stroke the serpent that bites us, until it has eaten our heart out?

"In the countries that, carried along by chance, I traveled through, and in the inns in which I waited on table, I saw a vast number of people who loathed their lives; but I only saw twelve who put an end to their misery of their own free choice—three Negroes, four Englishmen, four Genevans, and a German professor named Robek.[54] I finished up as a servant in the household of Don Issachar the Jew; he sent me to work for you, my beautiful miss; I have attached myself to your destiny, and I have been

---

52. A minor nobleman.

53. The revolt of the strelitz, 1698.

54. Johann Robeck (1672–1739) advocated suicide and drowned himself. Voltaire had read about him in S. Formey, *Mélanges philosophiques* (1754).

more occupied with your adventures than with my own. I would never even have spoken about my own terrible experiences, if you hadn't prodded me a bit to make me do it, and if it wasn't customary while on a voyage to tell stories in order to pass the time. Finally, miss, I am a person of experience, I know the world. Give yourself some fun; require each passenger to tell you their life story; and if you find a single one who has not repeatedly cursed their life, who has not said to themselves over and over again that they are the most unhappy person in the world, throw me in the sea head first."

CHAPTER THIRTEEN: *How Candide was obliged to separate from lovely Cunégonde and from the old woman*

Lovely Cunégonde, having heard the old woman's story, treated her with all the politeness that one should show to a person of her rank and her condition. She accepted her proposal; she persuaded all the passengers, one after the other, to tell her their adventures. She and Candide had to admit that the old woman was right. "It's a great pity," said Candide, "that our wise Pangloss was hanged—contrary to established custom—during an auto-da-fé; he would tell us remarkable things about physical evil and moral evil, which between them cover both land and sea, and I would feel confident enough to dare formulate some objections, although I would of course express them with due respect."

As each person told their story the ship came closer to its destination. They made landfall at Buenos Aires. Cunégonde, Captain Candide, and the old woman went to see the Governor, Don Fernando d'Ibaraa y Figueora y Mascarenes y Lampourdos y Souza. This nobleman was as proud as someone with so many names ought to be. He spoke to people with an aristocratic disdain, his nose in the air, his voice painfully loud, his tone one that would permit no discussion, his manner so haughty that all who met him were tempted to hit him. He adored women beyond all reason. Cunégonde seemed to him the most beautiful thing he had ever seen. The first thing he did was to ask whether she was indeed the captain's wife. The manner in which he asked this question alarmed Candide. He did not dare say that she was his wife, for in truth she wasn't; he did not dare say she was his sister, because she wasn't that either; and although this white lie was long ago very fashionable, as history records, and although it could still be useful today, he was too decent a fellow to tell a lie.[55] "Miss Cunégonde," he said, "has promised to do me the honor of

---

55. Unlike Abraham, who twice described his wife as his sister (Genesis 12, 20): a famous article of Bayle's *Dictionary* ("Sara") is devoted to a discussion of the morality of such behavior.

marrying me, and we beg Your Excellency to be so gracious as to perform the ceremony."

Don Fernando d'Ibaraa y Figueora y Mascarenes y Lampourdos y Souza stroked his mustache and gave a wry smile. He ordered Captain Candide to go and inspect his company. Candide obeyed; the governor remained in the company of Miss Cunégonde. He declared his passion to her; assured her that tomorrow he would marry her in a Church ceremony, or not, for he would do whatever she preferred, for he could never say no to someone so charming. Cunégonde asked him for a quarter of an hour to collect her wits, to consult the old woman, and to reach a decision.

The old woman said to Cunégonde: "Miss, you have seventy-two quarterings on your coat of arms, and not a penny to your name. You have the opportunity to become the wife of the most powerful man in South America, a man with a very fine mustache. Do you really think you should take pride in resisting any and every temptation? You have been violated by the Bulgars; you have given yourself to a Jew and an inquisitor.[56] Your sufferings give you rights. I admit that if I was in your place I would have no scruples about marrying His Excellency the Governor, nor about making Captain Candide a rich man." While the old woman was talking, expressing herself with all the wisdom that age and experience give, a small ship was seen to enter the harbor; it carried an officer of the Inquisition and some guards, and this is what had happened.

The old woman had been quite right in her guess that, when they were in the town of Badajoz and she and Candide were fleeing from the law, Cunégonde's money and jewels had been stolen by a Franciscan friar. This friar wanted to sell some of the gems to a jeweler. The shopkeeper recognized them as belonging to the Grand Inquisitor. The Franciscan, before he was hanged, admitted that he had stolen them. He described the people from whom he had taken them, and the direction in which they were traveling. The flight of Candide and Cunégonde had already been discovered. They were followed to Cadiz. Without wasting time, a ship was sent off in pursuit of them. This ship had now arrived in the port of Buenos Aires. The news spread that an officer of the Inquisition was about to come ashore, and that he was pursuing the murderers of the Grand Inquisitor. The wise old woman immediately saw everything that had to be done. "You cannot fly," she said to Cunégonde, "and you have nothing to fear. It wasn't you who killed His Excellency; and in any case the Governor, who loves you, will not allow you to come to harm; stay here." She ran at once to Candide: "Flee," she said, "or within an hour they will burn

---

56. It would seem that Cunégonde lied to Candide in chapter 8, when she claimed to have resisted the Jew and the Inquisitor.

you. There is not a moment to lose." But how could he tear himself from Cunégonde? And where could he find safety?

CHAPTER FOURTEEN: *How Candide and Cacambo were received by the Jesuits of Paraguay*

Candide had brought with him from Cadiz a valet, a man of a sort that is common on the coasts of Spain and in the colonies. He was a quarter Spanish; his father was a half-caste in the province of Tucuman; he had been a choirboy, a sacristan, a sailor, a monk, a trader in the colonies, a soldier, a servant. He was called Cacambo, and was very attached to his master because his master was a very decent fellow. He saddled the two Andalusian horses without wasting a moment. "Let's go, master; let's do as the old woman advises; let's leave and gallop away without looking behind us." Candide broke into tears. "Oh my dear Cunégonde! Must I abandon you just when His Excellency the Governor was about to marry us! Cunégonde, brought here from so far away, what will become of you?" "She'll make the best of her situation," said Cacambo; "women are never at a loss when it comes to knowing what to do; God will look after her; let's be going!" "Where are you taking me? Where are we going? What will we do without Cunégonde?" was all Candide could say. "By St. Jerome of Compostella," said Cacambo, "you were going to fight against the Jesuits; now let's go and fight for them. I know the road well enough. I will take you to their kingdom.[57] They will be delighted to have a captain who knows how to do drill in the Bulgar fashion. You'll make yourself an enormous fortune. When one doesn't get what one wants in one world, one can find it in another. There's a great deal of pleasure in seeing and doing new things."

"So you've already been to Paraguay?"[58] Candide asked. "Oh yes, indeed I have," said Cacambo; "I was a kitchen hand in the college in Asunción,[59] and I am as familiar with the way in which Los Padres[60] run things as I am with the streets of Cadiz. Their rule is certainly remarkable. Their kingdom is already more than seven hundred and fifty miles across; it is divided into thirty provinces. Los Padres own everything in it, and the inhabitants own nothing. It's a masterpiece of logic and justice. In my view

---

57. There were reports that a Jesuit had been elected king of Paraguay.

58. Voltaire had written a chapter on Paraguay for his *Essai sur les moeurs* in Jan. 1758; it appeared in the edition of 1761. Among his sources is the *Histoire du Paraguay* (1756) by Charlevoix, a Jesuit.

59. The capital of Paraguay—the towns of Paraguay (Sacramento, Asunción) are named after doctrines of the Catholic Church.

60. I.e., the Jesuit Fathers.

there's nobody cleverer than Los Padres, for here they are at war with the king of Spain and with the king of Portugal, while in Europe it is Jesuits who are confessors to these kings; here they kill Spaniards, and in Madrid they unlock the gates of heaven for them. I think it's wonderful! Let's keep moving. You are going to be the happiest man in the world. Think how pleased Los Padres will be when they learn that a captain who knows the Bulgar drill has come to join them!"

When they came to the first checkpoint, Candide said to the lookout that a captain wanted to talk to His Reverence the commanding officer. Word was sent back to headquarters. A Paraguayan officer ran to the commanding officer, bowed low before him, and told him the news. Candide and Cacambo were first disarmed; then their two Andalusian horses were taken from them. The two foreigners were brought forward between two ranks of soldiers. The commanding officer was at the end, with his three-cornered cap on his head, his cassock tied up, his sword at his side, his lance in his hand.[61] He made a sign; at once twenty-four soldiers surrounded the two newcomers. A sergeant explained to them that they would have to wait; that the commanding officer could not talk to them; that the Reverend Father Provincial[62] did not allow any Spaniard to speak unless he was present, or to remain in the country for more than three days.[63] "And where is the Reverend Father Provincial?" asked Cacambo. "He is inspecting the troops after having said Mass," replied the sergeant, "and you will have to wait three hours before you can kiss his spurs." "But," said Cacambo, "my captain, who is starving to death, just as I am, is not a Spaniard; he's a German. So can't we eat while we wait for His Reverence to come?"

The sergeant went off at once to report what Cacambo had said to the commanding officer. "God be thanked," said this gentleman. "Since he is a German I can speak to him; take him to my arbor." Straightaway Candide was taken to an open-air room with living walls, ornamented with a very pretty colonnade of green marble and of gold, and with trelliswork that enclosed parrots, different sorts of hummingbirds, guinea fowls, and all sorts of rare birds. A fine meal was laid out ready in dishes of gold; and while the Paraguayans ate corn out of wooden bowls in the open fields under the burning sun, the reverend father the commanding officer entered his shady arbor.

---

61. It was contrary to Church law for a priest to wear a sword or engage in warfare.

62. The Jesuit with authority over all Jesuits in the province of Paraguay.

63. The text says "three hours"; but Voltaire says in the *Essai sur les moeurs* that Spaniards were never allowed to spend more than three days in Paraguay; "three hours" seems to be a corruption from the sentence after next; and if they could only stay three hours they couldn't be expected to wait three hours.

He was a very beautiful young man. His face was plump, white rather than brown, somewhat florid, with arched eyebrows, bright eyes, red ears, crimson lips, an air of pride, but his pride was not that of a Spaniard, nor a Jesuit. Candide and Cacambo were given back the weapons that had been taken from them, along with the two Andalusian horses; Cacambo fed them hay near the arbor, keeping his eye on them, in case they needed to escape.

First Candide kissed the hem of the cassock worn by the commanding officer, and then they sat down to table. "So you are German," the Jesuit said to him in that language. "Yes, my reverend father," said Candide. While these words were exchanged they both stared at each other in extreme surprise, feeling an emotion that they could not control. "And from what part of Germany do you come?" asked the Jesuit. "From the wretched province of Westphalia," said Candide; "I was born in the castle of Thunder-ten-tronckh." "Oh heavens! Is it possible?" cried the commanding officer. "What a miracle!" cried Candide. Both fell backward; they embraced each other; they wept rivers of tears. "What! Is it you, my Reverend Father? Are you the brother of the beautiful Cunégonde? You, who were killed by the Bulgars! You, the son of my lord the baron! And now you're a Jesuit in Paraguay! One has to admit that this world is a strange place. Oh Pangloss! Pangloss! How happy you would be, had you not been hanged!"

The commanding officer ordered the Negro slaves to withdraw, and, along with them, the Paraguayans who were serving them drinks in goblets of rock crystal. He thanked God and St. Ignatius a thousand times; he grasped Candide in his arms; their faces were bathed in tears. "You would be even more astonished, more moved, more unable to control yourself," said Candide, "if I were to tell you that Miss Cunégonde, your sister, whom you believed disemboweled, is in perfect health." "Where?" "Quite nearby, for she is staying with His Excellency the Governor of Buenos Aires; and I came here to go to war against you." Every word they spoke during this long conversation gave new cause for astonishment, such prodigies they recounted. Their whole beings were speaking through their tongues, listening through their ears, sparkling through their eyes. As they were Germans they stayed at table for ages, while waiting for the Reverend Father Provincial; and the commanding officer spoke as follows to his beloved Candide.

CHAPTER FIFTEEN: *How Candide killed the brother of his beloved Cunégonde*

"As long as I live I will never cease to remember the dreadful day when I saw my mother and my father killed and my sister violated. When the

Bulgar troops withdrew, my adorable sister could no longer be found; and my mother, my father, myself, two maids and three little boys who had had their throats cut were loaded onto a cart to be taken for burial at a Jesuit chapel five miles from the castle of my ancestors. A Jesuit sprinkled us with holy water which was dreadfully salty; a few drops got into my eyes; the priest saw that my eyelash had made a tiny movement; he placed his hand on my heart and felt it beating; I was rescued, and after three weeks I had fully recovered. You know, my dear Candide, that I was very pretty, and I became prettier still. As a result the Reverend Father Croust,[64] who was in charge of the community, developed a passionate attachment to me; he gave me a novice's uniform to wear; soon after I was sent to Rome. The General of the Order needed to send additional numbers of young German Jesuits into the field. The rulers of Paraguay try and keep to the minimum the number of Spanish Jesuits sent to them; they prefer foreigners whom they believe will be easier to form. I was judged suitable by the Reverend Father General to go and labor in this vineyard. We set out: a Pole, someone from the Tyrol, and I. When I arrived I was promoted to subdeacon and lieutenant. I now hold the ranks of colonel and priest. We're putting up a stiff resistance against the forces of the king of Spain; I can assure you that they will be excommunicated and beaten. Providence has sent you here to assist us. But is it really true that my dear sister Cunégonde is nearby, staying with the Governor of Buenos Aires?" Candide assured him with a solemn oath that this was absolutely true. Their tears began to flow again.

The baron hugged Candide, and wanted never to let him go. He called him his brother, his savior. "Ah! Perhaps," he said to him, "we will be able, my dear Candide, to enter Buenos Aires together as conquerors, and be reunited with my sister Cunégonde." "There's nothing I want more," said Candide, "for I was planning to marry her, and I still hope to do so." "What insolence!" replied the baron. "Would you have the nerve to marry my sister, whose coat of arms has seventy-two quarterings! I think you're absolutely shameless to dare talk to me of such an outrageous plan!" Candide, terrified by this outbreak, replied "My Reverend Father, all the quarterings in the world have nothing to do with it; I rescued your sister from the arms of a Jew and of an Inquisitor; she is deeply in my debt; she wants to marry me. Dr. Pangloss always told me that all human beings are equal, and I will certainly marry her." "We'll see about that, you bastard!" said the Jesuit baron of Thunder-ten-tronckh, and at the same moment he gave him an enormous blow on his face with the flat of his sword. Immediately Candide drew his sword, and stuck it into the stomach of the Jesuit baron right up to the hilt; but when he pulled it out, steaming with blood,

---

64. Rector of the Jesuit college at Colmar, and an enemy of Voltaire's.

he began to cry. "Alas, oh God!" he said, "I have killed the man who used to be my master, who is my friend, who would have been my brother-in-law; I am the finest fellow in the world, and look, I've already killed three men; and of these three, two have been priests."

Cacambo, who was keeping a lookout at the door of the arbor, ran up. "We have no choice but to sell our lives dearly," his employer said to him. "Someone is bound to come into the arbor soon; we must die with our weapons in our hands." Cacambo, who had been in tight spots before, did not lose his wits. He took the Jesuit cassock that the baron was wearing, and dressed Candide in it. He put the dead man's three-cornered hat on Candide's head, and shoved him onto a horse. This happened in the blink of an eye. "Let us gallop, master. Everyone will think you are a Jesuit rejoining his troops, and we will have crossed the frontier before they set out after us." He was already galloping as he spoke, and he began to shout aloud in Spanish: "Make way, make way for the Reverend Father Colonel."

CHAPTER SIXTEEN: *What happened to the two travelers when they met two girls, two apes, and the savages who are called Oreillons*

Candide and his manservant were past the guards, and no one in the garrison had yet realized that the German Jesuit was dead. Cacambo, always thinking ahead, had filled his pack with bread, chocolate, ham, fruit, and some bottles of wine. Mounted on their Andalusian horses, they were riding into an unknown land, one in which they could not identify any road. After a long journey, a beautiful meadow, with little streams cutting across it, lay in front of them. Our two travelers allowed their horses to graze. Cacambo urged his master to eat, and set him a good example. "How," said Candide, "can you expect me to eat ham when I have killed the son of His Excellency the Baron, and when it seems I am fated never to see my beautiful Cunégonde again as long as I live? What's the point of my surviving in misery for a few extra days, if I have to drag out my life far from her, eaten up by remorse and drowning in despair? And what do you think the *Journal de Trévoux* will say?"[65]

All the time he was speaking he was eating. The sun went down. The two lost travelers heard some faint cries that appeared to have been uttered by women. They could not tell if they were cries of pain or of delight; but they leaped to their feet. They were in an unknown land, and it didn't take much to make them anxious and alarmed. These shouts were coming from two completely naked girls who were running athletically along the edge of

---

65. An intellectual journal edited by the Jesuits.

the meadow while two apes bounded after them biting at their buttocks. Candide took pity on their plight. He had learned to shoot while in the Bulgar army, and he could have hit a nut in a bush without disturbing the surrounding leaves. He grabbed his double-barreled Spanish gun, fired, and killed the apes. "God be praised, my dear Cacambo. I have rescued those two poor creatures from a terrible danger; if I committed a sin when I killed an Inquisitor and a Jesuit, I have certainly made up for it now by saving the lives of two girls. Perhaps they are two young women of noble rank, and this adventure may ensure us a warm welcome in this country."

He was about to say more, but his tongue seized up when he saw these two girls tenderly embrace the two apes, melt into tears as they held their bodies, and heard them fill the air with the most heart-rending cries. "I didn't expect them to be so tenderhearted," he said eventually to Cacambo, who replied: "Well, that was really clever, master! You have killed the two young women's lovers." "Their lovers! Is it possible? You're making fun of me, Cacambo! Why would I believe you?" "Dear master," replied Cacambo, "you're taken by surprise at every turn of events; why do you find it so incredible that in some countries there are apes who win the hearts of young women? They are a quarter human, just as I am a quarter Spanish." "Alas!" Candide cried. "Now I remember hearing Dr. Pangloss say that such things had happened in the past, and that these unions had produced pans, fauns, and satyrs;[66] he said that several important people in the ancient world had seen them; but I thought these were only myths." "Well perhaps now you will admit that this is fact not fiction," said Cacambo, "and you can see how people behave when they haven't been brought up to think as we do. My only fear is that these ladies may get us into trouble."

These sensible remarks convinced Candide that they must leave the meadow and disappear into the woods. There he dined with Cacambo; and there they both, having cursed the Portuguese Inquisitor, the Governor of Buenos Aires, and the baron, fell asleep on a bank of moss. On waking they felt they could no longer move their limbs; the explanation for this

---

66. Antoine Banier, *La Mythologie et les fables* (1740) argued that pans, fauns, and satyrs were in reality apes, misdescribed in antiquity. But this was not Voltaire's view, for he believed such creatures were the result of intercourse between humans and other species. His notebooks contain the following: "The apes called Jockos, orang-outangs, baboons mate with women, and it is not impossible that they produce offspring." (*Complete Works,* vol. 81 [Geneva: Institut et Musée Voltaire, 1968], 179.) In *Essai sur les moeurs* (1756), he suggests that such offspring would have been infertile (ed. Pomeau, vol. 1, p. 8). The view that apes were biologically extremely close to humans (perhaps even were humans) was commonplace, and is supported by Rousseau in his *Discourse on the Origins of Inequality* (1755), which Voltaire had read.

was that the two women had reported them to the Oreillons,[67] who live in that part of the continent, and during the night they had come and tied them up with ropes made from the bark of trees. They were surrounded by about fifty Oreillons, completely naked, armed with bows and arrows, clubs, and hatchets made of stone. Some of them were boiling water in a large cooking pot; others were preparing skewers, and they were all chanting: "We've got a Jesuit; we've got a Jesuit; we'll revenge ourselves and we'll eat well; let's eat a Jesuit! Let's eat a Jesuit!"

"I told you so, dear master," Cacambo cried out in dismay. "Those two girls have paid us back." Candide, catching sight of the cooking pot and skewers, cried out, "It's clear that we are going to be either roasted or boiled![68] Ah! What would Dr. Pangloss say, if he saw what mankind is like in its natural state.[69] All is well; perhaps it is, but I confess it is very cruel that I should lose Miss Cunégonde, and be skewered by the Oreillons." Cacambo never lost his composure. "Don't despair," he said to Candide, who was devastated. "I know a bit of the lingo these people speak. I'll have a word with them." "Don't forget," said Candide, "to explain to them how frightful and inhuman it is to cook human beings, and to point out to them how contrary to Christian principles this is."

"Good sirs," said Cacambo. "I gather you're planning on eating a Jesuit today. It's an excellent plan. Eating one's enemies is a fair and admirable practice. Indeed, the law of nature teaches us to kill our neighbor, and this is how people behave throughout the world. If we Europeans don't exercise our right to eat our enemies, it's because we're not short of good food to eat; but you aren't as prosperous as we are; and it certainly makes more sense to eat one's enemies than to leave the fruit of one's victory to the crows and ravens. But gentlemen, you wouldn't want to eat one of your friends! You think you are about to have a kebab of Jesuit, but it's your defender, the enemy of your enemies, whom you are about to grill. As for me, I was born in your country; the gentleman you see is my employer, and, far from being a Jesuit, he has just killed a Jesuit, and is wearing the clothes he took off his back. That's why there's been a misunderstanding. In order to verify what I am saying, take off his cassock, take it to the nearest guard-post of the kingdom of Los Padres; and find out if my employer has not killed a Jesuit officer. It won't take you long; you can still

---

67. Garcilaso de La Vega, *L'Histoire des Incas* (1744) describes the *Orejones* or Indians with large ears, who live north of Paraguay. An *oreillon* is an earflap attached to a cap.

68. Voltaire discusses cannibalism at length in chapter 146 of the *Essai sur les moeurs* (written Jan. 1758) and in an article of the *Dictionnaire philosophique* ("Anthropophages").

69. Again, a dig at Rousseau may be intended.

eat us later, if you discover that I have lied to you. But if I have told you the truth, then, since you are perfectly familiar with the principles of international law, with custom and due process, you will of course let us go."

The Oreillons agreed that what Cacambo said was perfectly reasonable. They selected two senior members of the tribe to go as fast as they could and find out the truth; the two representatives carried out their responsibilities with good sense, and soon came back carrying the good news. The Oreillons untied the two prisoners, treated them with great respect, offered young women to them, gave them refreshments, and accompanied them to the limits of their territory, chanting happily, "He's no Jesuit! He's no Jesuit!"

Candide couldn't stop talking about the reasons for his release. "What a people!" he said. "What men! What customs! If I hadn't had the good fortune to stick a sword right through the body of the brother of Miss Cunégonde I would have been eaten, and no plea of mitigation would have been accepted. But after all, mankind in its natural state is good, for these people, instead of eating me, have treated me terribly well since they discovered that I am not a Jesuit."

CHAPTER SEVENTEEN: *The arrival of Candide and his manservant in the country of El Dorado,*[70] *and what they saw there*

When they had reached the limits of the Oreillons' territory Cacambo turned to Candide and said: "Now you can see that this hemisphere is no better than the other one; take my advice; let us go back to Europe by the shortest route we can find." "How can we get back there?" asked Candide. "And where would we go if we did? If I go to my own country, then the Bulgars and the Abars are murdering everyone there. If I go back to Portugal, I'll be burned. And if we stay here we might at any moment be turned into a kebab. But how can I agree to leave the part of the world that is inhabited by Miss Cunégonde?"

"Let's go to Cayenne," said Cacambo; "there we will find some of the French people who wander all over the world; they will be able to help us. Perhaps God will have pity on us."

It was not easy to go to Cayenne. They had a good idea as to which direction they ought to walk in; but mountains, rivers, cliffs, highwaymen, and savages were dreadful obstacles that had to be overcome again and again. Their horses died of exhaustion. Their supplies ran out. For a

---

70. Voltaire was familiar with Sir Walter Raleigh's account of El Dorado, which he placed near Guyana, and he summarizes accounts of El Dorado in chapter 151 of the *Essai sur les moeurs* (written Jan. 1758).

whole month they lived on wild fruits, and eventually they found themselves on the banks of a little river, alongside which coconut trees grew.
The coconuts gave them new strength and new hope.

Cacambo, who always gave advice as good as that given by the old
woman, said to Candide: "We can't go on. We've walked enough. I see an
empty canoe on the river bank; let us fill it with coconuts, climb into this
little boat, and allow ourselves to float with the current. A river must lead
in the end to some habitation. If we don't end up somewhere we like, we
will at least end up somewhere we haven't been before." "Let's go," said
Candide. "Let's put our trust in Providence."

They sailed for some miles between river banks that were sometimes
covered in flowers, sometimes bare; sometimes flat and sometimes sheer.
The river got bigger with every mile; finally it disappeared under an arch
of terrifying rocks that rose upward until they seemed to touch the sky.
The two travelers were so bold as to allow the current to carry them into
the darkness. The river, squeezed between the rocky walls, carried them
along at great speed with a terrifying roar. After twenty-four hours they
saw daylight again; but their canoe smashed against an underwater rock.
They had to clamber from rock to rock for two whole miles: finally they
emerged on a vast plain surrounded by unclimbable mountains. The land
was cultivated to provide beautiful vistas as well as food. Everywhere what
was useful was also delightful. The roads were crowded, or rather decorated with carriages of a design and material that was absolutely splendid,
carrying men and women who were exceptionally beautiful, drawn rapidly
along by large red sheep[71] who were faster than the handsomest horses in
Andalusia, Tetouan, or Meknes.[72]

"Well," said Candide, "this country is certainly better than Westphalia." He descended with Cacambo at the first village they reached.[73]
Some local children, dressed in golden brocades that were torn and
ragged, were playing at quoits at the entrance to the small town. Our two
men from another world amused themselves by watching them. Their
quoits were fairly large, round platters, colored yellow, red, and green,
which glinted strangely. The travelers soon wanted to pick up one or two
of them; they were made of gold, of emeralds, of rubies. The smallest one
would have been the finest ornament on the throne of the Mogul Emperor.
"Doubtless," said Cacambo, "these children playing at quoits are the sons
of the king of this country." The village schoolmaster appeared at that
moment to make them go back to school. "There," said Candide, "is the
tutor to the royal family."

---

71. These are llamas, though llamas do not in fact serve as draft animals.

72. Tetouan and Meknes are in North Africa.

73. Presumably they have mounted in one of the carriages.

The little scamps immediately abandoned their game, leaving their quoits on the ground, and all the rest of the apparatus that they had employed in their game. Candide picked them up, ran to the teacher, and handed them to him respectfully, gesturing to convey to him that their royal highnesses had forgotten their gold and their precious stones. The local schoolmaster, smiling, threw them back on the ground, looked Candide in the face for a moment with considerable puzzlement, and continued on his way.[74]

Our travelers did not fail to pick up the gold, the rubies, and the emeralds. "Where are we?" cried Candide. "It would seem that in this country the king's children are very well brought up, for they are taught to despise gold and jewels." Cacambo was every bit as surprised as Candide. Finally they approached the first house on the edge of the village. It was built like a palace in Europe. A crowd of people pressed against the door, and even more were crammed in doors. There was beautiful music being played, and a delightful smell of cooking reached them. Cacambo came closer to the door, and discovered they were speaking Peruvian.[75] This was his mother tongue, for you all know that Cacambo was born in Tucuman, in a village where that was the only language spoken. "I will be your interpreter," he said to Candide. "Let's go in, for this is a hotel."

At once two boys and two girls who worked there, and were dressed in cloth of gold, with their hair tied up with ribbons, invited them to sit at the top table. Four soups were being served, each garnished with two parrots; a boiled condor that weighed two hundred pounds; two apes, roasted, which tasted delicious; three hundred hummingbirds in one dish; and six hundred hummingbirds of a different species in another; some exquisite stews and delicious pastries; and everything was served on plates made from some type of rock crystal. The waiters and waitresses served several drinks made from cane sugar.

Their companions were for the most part businessmen and carters, all of them extremely polite, who asked Cacambo some questions, but with the utmost discretion, and who replied to his inquiries in a straightforward manner.

When the meal was finished, Cacambo believed—and Candide did too—that they would more than pay their bill by tossing onto the table two of the large pieces of gold they had picked up; the landlord and landlady burst out laughing, and for a long time they could barely stand. Finally they recovered. "Gentlemen," said the landlord, "we can certainly

74. Gold was supposed to be so common in El Dorado as to be worthless; but Voltaire is perhaps also thinking of More's *Utopia*, where contempt for gold and jewels is carefully inculcated.

75. Voltaire must intend to refer to the language of the Incas.

see that you are foreigners, although we very rarely see foreigners here. Forgive us if we burst into laughter when you tried to pay with pebbles picked up from our high street. You probably don't have any of our local money, but you don't need any to eat here. All the hotels established to further trade are funded by the government.[76] You have had a rather second-rate meal here, as this is a poor village, but everywhere else you will be received as you deserve to be." Cacambo explained to Candide everything that the landlord had said, and Candide listened to his words with the same astonishment and bewilderment as his friend Cacambo felt in speaking them. "What country is this?" they asked each other, "which is unknown to the rest of the world, and where the whole order of nature is quite different from ours?" "This is probably the country in which all goes well; for it is absolutely necessary that there should be one place that can be so described. And, whatever Dr. Pangloss said, I often noticed that in Westphalia everything went badly."

CHAPTER EIGHTEEN: *What they saw in the land of El Dorado*

Cacambo explained to the landlord just how eager he was for information. The landlord said to him, "I'm terribly ignorant, which suits me fine. But we have an old chap here who has retired from life at court. He is the most knowledgeable person in the kingdom, and the most voluble." At once he took Cacambo to meet the old man. Candide was now reduced to a supporting role, and accompanied his valet. They went into a very humble dwelling, for the door was only made of silver and the paneling of the rooms was only of gold, although worked in such good taste that it would have stood comparison with the most luxurious. The antechamber, one must admit, was only encrusted with rubies and emeralds, but the skill with which the overall effect was achieved certainly justified this extreme simplicity.

The old man received the two foreigners on a sofa upholstered in hummingbird feathers, and offered them drinks in glasses made of diamond; after which he satisfied their curiosity as follows:

"I am one hundred and seventy-two years old, and I learned from my late father, who was equerry to the king, the astonishing political revolutions that took place in Peru, of which he was an eyewitness. The kingdom we are in is the original homeland of the Incas, who very unwisely left it to conquer a vast empire, and who were eventually destroyed by the Spaniards.

"The princes of the royal household who remained in the country of their birth were wiser; they decreed, with the consent of the nation, that

---

76. Garcilaso de La Vega reports the Incas had state-funded hotels for travelers.

no inhabitant should ever leave our little kingdom; and this is what has preserved our innocence and our happiness. The Spaniards have had a rather hazy knowledge of the existence of this country; they have called it El Dorado, and an Englishman, named Sir Raleigh, even came close to here about a hundred years ago; but as we are surrounded by unclimbable mountains and by cliffs, we have always been, so far, sheltered from the rapacity of the European nations, who have an incredible mania for the pebbles and mud of our land, and who, in order to get their hands on them, would kill every one of us and leave not a single survivor."

Their conversation lasted a long time; they discussed the structure of the government, the customs of the people, the women, the public spectacles, and the arts. Finally Candide, who still had a taste for metaphysics, had Cacambo ask whether the inhabitants had a religion.

The old man blushed a little. "How on earth," he asked, "could you doubt it? Do you imagine we are without gratitude?" Cacambo asked respectfully what the religion of El Dorado was. The old man blushed again. "Do you mean that there can be more than one religion?" he asked. "We have, I believe, the same religion as everyone else; we worship God during every free moment." "Do you only worship one god?" asked Cacambo, who continued to serve as an interpreter for Candide's queries. "It would seem obvious," said the old man, "that there aren't two, or three, or four gods. I must confess that the people from your world ask some rather strange questions!" Candide was not tired of having questions put to this good old man on his behalf. He wanted to know how one prayed to God in El Dorado. "We don't pray to him," said the good and respectable man of wisdom; "we don't have anything to ask of him; he has given us everything we need, and we thank him continuously." Candide was curious to see some priests; he asked where they could be found. The good old man smiled. "My friends," he said, "we are all priests; every morning the king and all the heads of families solemnly sing hymns of thanksgiving, and five or six thousand musicians accompany them." "What, you don't have monks who teach, who argue, who rule, who conspire, and who burn people who don't agree with them?" "We'd have to be mad," said the old man. "Here we all agree with each other, and we don't understand what you're trying to say with your talk about monks." Candide was thrilled by every word he heard, and said to himself "This is quite different from Westphalia and from life in the castle of my lord the baron; if our friend Pangloss had seen El Dorado he would not have said that the castle of Thunder-ten-tronckh was the best place on earth; it's evident that one should travel."

After this long conversation, the good old man had six sheep harnessed to a carriage, and lent a dozen of his servants to the two travelers to take them to the court. "Forgive me," he said to them, "if my old age deprives me of the honor of accompanying you. The king will receive you in such a manner that you will have no complaints, and I trust you will excuse the local customs if any of them displease you."

Candide and Cacambo climbed into a carriage; the six sheep galloped; and in less than four hours they arrived at the palace of the king, which was situated at one end of the capital city. The entrance was an arch eighty yards high and thirty-five wide; it is impossible to describe the material of which it was made. But you can imagine the immense degree to which it must have been superior to the pebbles and sand that we call gold and precious stones.

Twenty beautiful women of the royal guard received Candide and Cacambo as they descended from the carriage and took them to the baths; there they were dressed in clothes made of a fabric consisting of the down of hummingbirds; after which great officers (both male and female) of the monarchy took them to the state rooms of His Majesty; they passed between two rows of musicians, a thousand in each row, as was the custom. When they approached the throne room, Cacambo asked a senior official how one ought to behave in order to greet His Majesty? Should one throw oneself on one's knees, or prostrate oneself on the ground? Should one place one's hands on one's head or one's behind? Should one lick the dust off the floor?[77] In a word, what was the appropriate ceremony to observe? "The custom," said the senior official, "is to hug the king and to kiss him on both cheeks."[78] Candide and Cacambo threw themselves into His Majesty's arms; he received them with perfect politeness, and graciously invited them to dine.

While they were waiting for it to be time for dinner they were shown around the town. The public buildings were tall enough to touch the clouds; the markets were ornamented with a thousand columns. There were fountains that ran with pure water, fountains that ran with rose water, fountains that ran with a drink made from cane sugar. They gushed continually in the main squares, which were paved with some sort of precious stone that gave off a scent that resembled that of cloves or cinnamon. Candide asked to see the courts of justice and the Supreme Court; he was told that there were no such buildings, as law cases were unknown. He asked if there were any prisons, and he was told there were none. What surprised him even more, and delighted him the most, was the palace of knowledge, in which he saw a gallery a mile long, full of mathematical and astronomical instruments.

After having spent the whole afternoon looking at just a thousandth part of the whole city, they were taken back to the royal palace. Candide sat

---

77. Swift's *Gulliver's Travels* describes such behavior at the court of Luggnag.
78. This is how Voltaire would have greeted his friends.

at table between His Majesty, his manservant Cacambo, and several ladies. Never has there been better food served, and never has anyone enjoyed good food and good company more than His Majesty. Cacambo explained the king's witty remarks to Candide, and even in translation they did not lose their wit. There was much to astonish Candide; but this was as astonishing as anything could be.

They spent a month as the king's guests. Candide kept saying to Cacambo: "It is true, my friend, I admit it once more, that the castle where I was born is insignificant compared to where we now find ourselves; but, when all's said, Miss Cunégonde isn't here; and I'm sure you have a mistress or two in Europe. If we stay here we will never be anybody special; while if we return to our world, even if we take only twelve sheep laden with pebbles from El Dorado, we will be richer than all the kings added together. We will no longer have to fear any inquisitors, and we will easily be able to get back Miss Cunégonde."

Cacambo liked these sentiments. Everyone likes to compete, to make themselves seem important to their friends and relations, to boast about what they have seen on their travels. Candide and Cacambo were happy, but they decided to stop being happy and to ask His Majesty for permission to leave.

"You're making a bad mistake," the king said to them. "I know my country is nothing special; but when you find yourself in reasonable circumstances, wherever you may be, you should settle down there. But I certainly don't have the right to hold strangers against their will; that would be tyrannical, and contrary to both our customs and our laws.[79] All men are free; leave when you choose, but it is very hard to get out. It is impossible to go against the current, to go back up the fast-flowing river that brought you here by a miracle, and emerge on the other side of the tunnel through the rocks. The mountains that surround my kingdom are ten thousand feet high, and rise straight upward like walls. Each one of them is twenty-five miles across; and the descent is a sheer drop. However, since you are absolutely determined to leave, I will give instructions to the people who specialize in mechanical matters to make you a machine that can transport you conveniently. When you have been taken to the far side of the mountains you will have to proceed on your own, for my subjects have taken a vow never to leave their enclosure, and they are too wise to break their word. Ask me, before you go, for anything you please." "We ask Your Majesty only for a few sheep laden with food, with pebbles, and with the local mud." The king laughed. "I don't understand," he said, "what it is that makes you people from Europe so interested in our yellow mud; but take as much of it as you like, and a lot of good may it do you."

---

79. Frederick the Great had tried to prevent Voltaire from leaving Prussia in 1753.

He immediately ordered his engineers to make a machine that would transport these two strange men out of the country. Three thousand first-rate scientists worked on the problem; the machine was ready after a fortnight, and cost no more than twenty million English pounds sterling, which is the local currency.[80] Candide and Cacambo were put onto the machine; along with them there were two large red sheep with saddles and bridles for them to ride when they arrived on the other side of the mountains; twenty pack-sheep laden with food; thirty carrying gifts consisting of rarities from the region; and fifty laden with gold, precious stones, and diamonds. The king tenderly embraced the two wanderers.

Their departure was a fine spectacle, as was the ingenious way in which they and their sheep were hoisted to the top of the mountains. The scientists said good-bye to them, having seen them safely over, and Candide had no desire and no ambition except to go and present his sheep to Miss Cunégonde. "We have," he said, "enough to pay the Governor of Buenos Aires, should he be willing to exchange Miss Cunégonde for money. Let us walk toward Cayenne, find a boat, and then we will see what kingdom we can buy for ourselves."

CHAPTER NINETEEN: *What happened to them in Surinam, and how Candide got to know Martin*

The first day's journey was quite pleasurable. Our two travelers took heart from the idea that they would be owners of more wealth than could be found if the treasure of Asia, Europe, and Africa were collected together. Candide, carried away, carved Cunégonde's name on the trees. On the second day two of their sheep became bogged down in a marsh, and were swallowed up along with the loads on their backs. Two other sheep died of exhaustion a few days later. Seven or eight then died of hunger in a desert. A few days later some more fell over a cliff. Finally, after a hundred days of traveling they only had two sheep left. Candide said to Cacambo: "My friend, you see how the riches of this world slip away. There is nothing that endures except virtue, and the happiness of seeing Miss Cunégonde again." "I agree," said Cacambo, "but we still have two sheep, with more treasure on their backs than the king of Spain will ever own; and I can see in the distance a city that I suspect is Surinam, which belongs to the Dutch. We are at the end of our sufferings; our happiness begins here."

As they approached the city they came across a Negro stretched out on

---

80. Voltaire surely does not mean, as some have thought, that the currency of El Dorado is the English pound; rather he must mean that El Dorado, like England, measures value in terms of relative weights of pure silver (not gold, which is too common to serve as a currency).

the ground. He had lost half his clothes; he was wearing what remained of a pair of shorts made of blue canvas. This poor man had lost his left leg and his right hand. "Ah! Good God!" said Candide to him in Dutch, "what are you doing there, my friend, in this terrible state in which I find you?" "I am waiting for my master, Mr. Vanderdendur, the famous merchant," replied the Negro. "Was it Mr. Vanderdendur," asked Candide, "who treated you like this?" "Yes, sir," said the Negro. "It's customary. They give us a pair of canvas shorts twice a year, and these are the only clothes we have. When we work in the sugar refineries, and we get one of our fingers caught in the mechanism, they cut the hand off. When we try and escape, they cut a leg off. Both have happened to me. This is the price that has to be paid so that you can eat sugar in Europe.[81] But when my mother sold me on the coast of Guinea for ten Patagonian dollars she said to me: 'My dear child, bless your fetishes,[82] worship them as long as you live, and they will ensure that you live happily; you have the honor to be a slave to our lords the whites, and thereby you have made your father and your mother wealthy.' Alas! I don't know if I made them wealthy, but they certainly didn't make me happy. Dogs, apes, and parrots are a thousand times less miserable than we are: the Dutch witch doctors who have converted me say every Sunday that we are all the children of Adam, whites and blacks. I am no genealogist, but if these preachers tell the truth, then we are all second cousins. But you'll have to admit that one couldn't treat one's relatives in a more dreadful fashion."

"Oh Pangloss!" cried Candide, "you never imagined such an abomination could exist. That's it; in the end I have no choice but to give up your optimism."[83] "What's optimism?" asked Cacambo. "Alas!" said Candide, "it's the madness that leads one to maintain that all is well when one's own life is dreadful." And he wept at the sight of his Negro, and he was still weeping as he entered Surinam.

The first thing they did was inquire as to whether there was a boat in harbor that one could send to Buenos Aires. The person whom they asked was actually a Spanish ship owner, who said he could offer them a deal on favorable terms. He arranged to meet them in a bar. Candide and the faithful Cacambo went there to wait for him with their two sheep.

---

81. Voltaire received a copy of Helvétius's *De l'esprit* on 18 Oct. 1758, and draws on it for his attack on slavery, which is a late addition, for it is missing from the manuscript; he had already covered similar ground in chapter 152 of the *Essai sur les moeurs*, written in Jan. 1758. Voltaire's account of the customary treatment of slaves in Surinam is, unfortunately, accurate.

82. I.e., your gods.

83. This is the only time the word "optimism" appears in the text of *Candide*, and this section is a late addition.

Candide, who was incapable of deception, told the Spaniard all of their adventures, and admitted to him that he wanted to make off with Miss Cunégonde. "I'll take care not to take you to Buenos Aires," said the ship owner; "I would be hanged, and so would you. The beautiful Cunégonde is the favorite mistress of His Excellency." This was a wretched shock for Candide. He cried and cried. Finally he took Cacambo to one side: "Look, my dear friend," he said to him, "this is what you must do. We each of us have in our pockets five or six million in diamonds; you are better at getting things done than I am; go and get hold of Miss Cunégonde in Buenos Aires. If the governor tries to cause trouble, give him a million; if he doesn't become amenable, give him two. You haven't killed an inquisitor, they won't be suspicious of you. I will provision another ship, I will go to Venice and meet you there. It's a free country where one doesn't need to fear Bulgars and Abars, nor Jews and inquisitors." Cacambo applauded this sound proposal. He was in despair at the prospect of separating from such a good master, who had become his close friend, but the pleasure of being useful to him overcame his grief at leaving him. They embraced each other with tears rolling down their cheeks. Candide urged him not to forget the good old woman. Cacambo left that very day. What a fine chap this Cacambo was.

Candide remained for a while in Surinam, and waited for another ship owner who would be willing to take him to Italy, along with the two surviving sheep. He hired some servants, and bought everything that would be necessary for a long voyage; finally Mr. Vanderdendur, captain of a large ship, came and introduced himself. "How much do you want," Candide asked this fellow, "to take me straight to Venice, that is myself, my servants, my baggage, and the two sheep you see over there?" The ship owner agreed to charge ten thousand piastres. Candide didn't hesitate.

"Ah! Ha!" said Vanderdendur, who knew about business, "this foreigner pays ten thousand piastres without a moment's anxiety. He must be rich indeed." So he came back a moment later, and explained that he could not sail for less than twenty thousand. "Very well," said Candide, "I'll pay."

"Ohhh!" the merchant said under his breath, "this chap pays twenty thousand piastres as easily as ten thousand." He turned round again, and said that he could not take him to Venice for less than thirty thousand piastres. "Then I will pay you thirty thousand," replied Candide.

"Ah! Ha!" the Dutch merchant said to himself again, "thirty thousand piastres seems like nothing to this chap here. Presumably the two sheep are carrying immense wealth. Let's not ask for more. Let's first get him to pay the thirty thousand and then we'll see." Candide sold two little diamonds, the smallest of which was worth more than the whole sum requested by the ship owner. He paid him in advance. The two sheep were put on board. Candide followed in a little boat to join the vessel that was moored in the channel; the ship owner saw his opportunity, raised the sails, cast off; the wind was behind him. Candide, shocked and amazed, soon lost sight of him. "Alas!" he cried. "That was a trick worthy of the Old World." He returned to the shore sunk in depression; for after all he had lost a treasure that would have transformed the finances of twenty kings had it been shared among them.

He went to see the Dutch judge; and as he was a little distressed, he banged hard on his door. He went in, described what had happened to him, and shouted a bit louder than was appropriate. The judge began by fining him ten thousand piastres for the noise he had made. Then he listened patiently to him, promised him that he would look into the matter as soon as the merchant had returned, and charged another ten thousand piastres in fees for attending to the matter.

This hearing finally drove Candide to despair. In truth he had survived blows that were a thousand times more painful; but the heartlessness of the judge, along with that of the ship owner who had robbed him, made him bilious, and plunged him into a black despair. The wickedness of men was now apparent to him in all its ugliness; his mind was full of dark and dismal thoughts. Finally he discovered that a French ship was on the point of leaving for Bordeaux. As he no longer had any sheep laden with diamonds to ship, he rented a cabin at a fair price, and let it be known around town that he would pay the passage and board, and would give two thousand piastres to an honest man who would travel with him, on condition that this man should be the most disgusted with his situation and the most unhappy in the province.

A crowd of applicants, so numerous a whole fleet would not have had room for them all, came to his door. Candide, wanting to make a short-list of those who appeared the most suitable, picked out twenty people who seemed to him to be reasonably sociable, and all of whom claimed to be more deserving than the rest. He gathered them together in his inn and gave them dinner on condition that each one took an oath to give an accurate account of the story of his life, promising that he would choose the person who seemed to him to be the most pitiable, and to have the best reasons for being the most discontented with his situation, and would give each of the rest a small gift.

The session lasted until four in the morning. Candide, listening to all their stories, remembered what the old woman had said to him on the way to Buenos Aires, and the wager she had made, that there was no one on the boat who had not experienced terrible ill fortune. He thought of Pangloss as he listened to each story. "That Pangloss," he said, "would find it very difficult to demonstrate the truth of his system. I wish he were here. Certainly if everything is well then it is so in El Dorado, and not elsewhere on the earth." Finally he decided to select a poor scholar who had spent ten years working for publishers in Amsterdam. He decided that there was no occupation in the world with which one was entitled to be more disgusted.

This scholar, who was, moreover, a good chap, had been robbed by his wife, beaten up by his son, and abandoned by his daughter, who had eloped with a Portuguese. He had just lost a poorly paid job on which he had relied to keep body and soul together, and the preachers of Surinam were persecuting him because they thought he was a Socinian.[84] One must admit that the other applicants were at least as miserable as he was; but Candide hoped that the scholar would entertain him during the voyage. All those in competition with him were of the view that Candide had done them a terrible injustice, but he pacified them by giving each of them one hundred piastres.

CHAPTER TWENTY: *What happened to Candide and Martin while they were at sea*

Thus the old scholar, who was called Martin, set sail for Bordeaux with Candide. Both had seen a great deal and suffered a great deal. Even if the ship had been supposed to sail from Surinam to Japan via the Cape of Good Hope they would have had enough to say to each other about moral evil and physical evil to occupy the whole voyage.

However Candide had a great advantage over Martin, for he still hoped to see Miss Cunégonde again, while Martin had nothing to hope for; moreover Candide had some gold and some diamonds, and, although he had lost one hundred large red sheep laden with the most valuable treasures in the world, though the thought of the way in which the Dutch ship owner had robbed him gnawed at him constantly, yet, when he thought of what he had left in his pockets, and when he spoke of Cunégonde, especially when he was finishing a meal, at such times he tended to favor the philosophy of Pangloss.

"But you, Mr. Martin," he said to the scholar, "what do you think of all that? What's your opinion with regard to moral evil and physical evil?" "Sir," replied Martin, "the local priests accused me of being a Socinian, but the truth is that I am a Manichean." "You're making fun of me," said Candide, "there are no Manicheans left in the world."[85] "There's me,"

---

84. Faustus and Laelius Socinus, sixteenth-century Italian founders of Socinianism, were unitarians who rejected the doctrine of original sin.

85. Mani was a Persian philosopher of the third century C.E. who taught that there were two gods, one good and one evil. St. Augustine was in his youth a Manichean, and the Manicheans influenced the Cathars who flourished in southern France in

said Martin. "I don't know what to do about it, but I can't think differently." "You must be possessed by the devil," said Candide. "He is so busy occupying himself with what happens in this world," said Martin, "that he could easily be possessing my body, just as he is present everywhere else; but I admit to you that if I look at this globe, or rather at this globule,[86] it seems to me that God has handed it over to some malevolent being—with the exception, of course, of El Dorado. I don't think I've seen a town that didn't want to see the town nearest to it destroyed, or a family that didn't want to see some other family wiped out. Everywhere the weak loathe the powerful, while cringing before them, and the powerful treat them like sheep whose wool and meat go to market. A thousand assassins organized in regiments run from one end of Europe to another, carrying out murder and robbery to feed themselves while never disobeying orders, for there is no more respectable occupation. And in those towns that seem to be enjoying peace, where commerce and the arts flourish, people are so eaten up with envy, anxiety, and disquiet that they would be less miserable in a city under siege. Their secret sufferings are even more painful than their public miseries. In a word, I have seen so much, and experienced so much, that I am a Manichean."

"But there is good in the world," replied Candide. "That may be," replied Martin, "but I have no experience of it."

In the middle of this discussion they became aware of the sound of artillery. With every passing moment the noise became twice as loud. Each picked up his telescope. They could see two ships about three miles away that were firing at each other. The wind brought them both so close to the French vessel that they had the pleasure of watching the battle in comfort. Finally one of the two ships let fire at the other a broadside so low and so accurate that it sank. Candide and Martin clearly saw a hundred or so men on the deck of the vessel that was going under; they all raised their hands to the heavens and let out terrible cries; in a moment they and their ship were swallowed up.

"Well," said Martin, "that is how people treat each other." "It is true," said Candide, "that there is something diabolical in such an event." While he was talking he caught sight of something—one couldn't tell quite what—colored bright red, which was swimming close to their ship. A boat was lowered to see what it might be; it was one of Candide's sheep. He was more delighted at recovering this sheep than he had been dismayed at

---

the twelfth century. Pierre Bayle, in his *Dictionary* (article "Manicheans"), had argued that dualists were in the best position to give an account of the world as we experience it.

86. Voltaire is the first to use the word "globule" in this way; in his correspondence it occurs on 26 June 1758 and 9 Dec. 1758.

losing a hundred of them, each laden with large diamonds from El
Dorado.

The French captain was soon able to tell that the captain of the ship
doing the sinking was Spanish, and the captain of the ship being sunk was
a Dutch pirate; it was the very person who had robbed Candide. The
immense wealth that this evil man had stolen was buried with him at sea,
and only one sheep was saved. "You see," said Candide to Martin, "that
crime is sometimes punished; this bastard Dutch ship owner has suffered
the fate he deserved." "Yes," said Martin, "but was it necessary that the
passengers who were on his ship should die as well? God may have
punished this wretch, but it was the devil who drowned the rest of them."

However the French and Spanish vessels continued on their journey,
and Candide continued his conversations with Martin. They argued for
fifteen days nonstop, and at the end of fifteen days they were no further
forward. But at least they talked to each other, they exchanged ideas, they
comforted each other. Candide stroked his sheep. "Since I've met up with
you again," he said, "there's no reason why I shouldn't meet up with
Cunégonde."

CHAPTER TWENTY-ONE: *Candide and Martin approach the coast of
France, philosophizing all the while*

Finally they could see the coast of France. "Have you ever been to France,
Mr. Martin?" asked Candide. "Yes," said Martin, "I have traveled through
several parts of the country. In some places half the inhabitants are crazy;
in some places people are too cunning; in others most people are rather
good-natured and rather stupid; in some places people cultivate their
intelligence; and wherever you go the people's first preoccupation is love;
their second is speaking ill of each other; and their third is talking nonsense." "But, Mr. Martin, have you been to Paris?" "Yes, I've been to
Paris; there's something of everything I've described to be found there; it's
a chaos, a crowd in which everybody is looking for pleasure, and where
almost no one finds it, at least as far as I could tell. I didn't stay there long;
no sooner had I arrived than I was robbed of everything I had by pick-
pockets at the St. Germain fair. Then I was accused of being a thief myself
and I spent eight days in prison; after which I did some proofreading in
order to earn enough money to be able to walk back to Holland. I knew
writers, religious revivalists, politicians—every one of them worthless.
They say there are some very civilized people in Paris; I suppose I'm
prepared to believe it."

"For my part, I have no interest in seeing France," said Candide; "you'll
have no difficulty in understanding that when one has spent a month in El
Dorado one loses all interest in seeing anything else on this earth, except

for Miss Cunégonde. I'm going to wait for her in Venice; I'm going to go across France to get to Italy; won't you come with me?" "I'd be happy to," said Martin. "They say that Venice is a decent place to be only if you're a Venetian noble, but they also say that foreigners are warmly welcomed there if they have plenty of money. I have none; you have lots; I'll stick close to you." "By the way," said Candide, "do you think the earth was originally covered by the sea, as is maintained in that fat book that belongs to the ship's captain?"[87] "I think that's nonsense," said Martin, "just like all these other fabrications that people keep coming up with these days." "Well then, for what purpose was the world originally constructed?" asked Candide. "In order to frustrate us at every turn," replied Martin. "Aren't you absolutely astonished," Candide continued, "by the love those two girls from the country of the Oreillons felt for those two apes—you remember I've told you the story?" "Not at all," said Martin, "I don't see anything odd about their passion at all; I have seen so many extraordinary things that nothing seems extraordinary to me any more." "Do you believe," asked Candide, "that men have always massacred each other, as they do today? That they have always been liars, cheats, and robbers; unreliable, ungrateful, weak, fickle, lazy, envious, greedy, drunken, avaricious, ambitious, violent, debauched, fanatical, hypocritical, stupid, and with nothing good to say for each other?" "Do you think," asked Martin, "that hawks have always eaten pigeons when they've had the chance?" "Why yes of course," said Candide. "Well," said Martin, "if hawks have always had the same nature, why do you want to imagine that the nature of man has changed?" "Oh!" said Candide, "there's an essential difference, for free will . . ." While philosophizing like this they arrived in Bordeaux.

CHAPTER TWENTY-TWO: *What happened to Candide and Martin*
while they were in France

Candide did not stay in Bordeaux any longer than was necessary to sell some pebbles from El Dorado and to get hold of a good two-seater, for he could no longer bear to be without his philosopher Martin. He was very distressed to have to part from his sheep, which he donated to the Scientific Academy of Bordeaux.[88] That year the question set in the Academy's annual essay competition was, "Why is the wool of this sheep red?"; the prize was awarded to a scholar from the North, who demonstrated by A

---

87. Probably not the Bible as is sometimes claimed (for the captain was presumably Catholic), but De Brosses, *Histoire des navigations aux terres australes* (1756), which Voltaire read in Sept. 1758.

88. Voltaire was an associate member of the Academy.

plus B, minus C, divided by Z, that the sheep was red of necessity, and bound to die of sheep pox.

However, all the travelers that Candide met in the inns along the road said to him, "We're going to Paris." This general eagerness finally gave him a desire to see the capital himself; it didn't involve much of a detour off the road to Venice.

He entered by the suburb of Saint Marceau, and for all he could tell he was in one of the most poverty-stricken villages in Westphalia.

Candide had scarcely reached his hotel when he was attacked by a mild illness caused by his exertions. Since he had on his finger an enormous diamond, and an astonishingly heavy money box had been noticed in his baggage, he quickly had two doctors he hadn't sent for at his side, some intimate friends who stayed by his side night and day, and two pious women who heated soup for him. Martin said: "I remember that I too fell ill during my first trip to Paris; I was very poor; and so I had neither friends, nor pious women, nor doctors; and I got better."

However, as a result of laxatives and blood-lettings, Candide's illness became serious. A curate from the parish came to him to ask gently if he had a passport to show at the frontier of the next world.[89] Candide wanted to do nothing about it; the pious women explained to him that it was a new fashion. Candide replied that he wasn't a man of fashion. Martin wanted to throw the curate out of the window. The clergyman swore that Candide would be refused burial. Martin swore that he would bury the clergyman if he continued to harass them. The quarrel became heated; Martin grabbed the clergyman by his shoulders and pushed him roughly out of the room; this caused a great scandal and was reported to the authorities.

Candide got better. And during his convalescence he had very good company dining with him. They played cards for high stakes. Candide was simply astonished that there was never an ace to be found in his hand; Martin wasn't at all surprised.

Among those who welcomed Candide to the city there was a little abbot from Périgord. He was one of those people who are always eager, always paying attention, always ready to please, who are impudent, flattering, adaptable. They lie in wait for passing strangers, tell them of all the

---

89. Jansenism (which denied freedom of the will and opposed frequent communion) had been condemned as a heresy by the pope in 1713. In order to receive extreme unction and to be buried in holy ground it was necessary to have a certificate of orthodoxy. This measure, which was primarily directed against Jansenism, was to oblige Voltaire (who was very concerned to have a decent burial) to go to considerable lengths to obtain a certificate when he was dying. See John McManners, *Reflections at the Death-Bed of Voltaire* (Oxford: Clarendon Press, 1975).

scandalous goings-on, and offer them a range of delights from the cheapest to the most expensive. This specimen of the type first took Candide and Martin to the theater. There a new tragedy was being performed. Candide found himself seated among some fashionable wits. That didn't prevent him from weeping at some scenes that were exquisitely performed. One of his sophisticated neighbors said to him during an intermission: "You're quite wrong to weep. This actress is dreadful. The actor who plays opposite her is even worse. The play is even worse than the performers. The author doesn't know a word of Arabic, yet his play is set in Arabia; moreover he's someone who doesn't believe in innate ideas.[90] Tomorrow I'll bring you twenty pamphlets written against him." "Sir, how many plays have been written in French?"[91] Candide asked the abbot, who replied, "Five or six thousand." "That's a lot," said Candide. "How many of them are any good?" "Fifteen or sixteen," was the reply. "That's a lot," said Martin.

Candide was rather taken with an actress who played Queen Elizabeth in a rather dull tragedy that is performed occasionally.[92] "This actress," he said to Martin, "pleases me a lot. There's something about her that reminds me of Miss Cunégonde; I would really very much like to meet her." The abbot from Périgord offered to take him to meet her. Candide, who had been brought up in Germany, asked how one was supposed to conduct oneself, and in particular how one should behave toward a Queen of England if one met her in France. "One must distinguish," said the abbot; "in the provinces one takes them to a bar; in Paris one treats them with respect while they are beautiful, and one throws them on the garbage dump when they are dead." "Queens thrown out with the garbage!" said Candide. "Yes, indeed," said Martin, "father abbot is right; I was in Paris when Miss Monime passed, as the saying is, from this world to the next; she was refused what those people call 'the honor of a Christian burial,' that's to say the chance to rot alongside all the beggars of the parish in a wretched cemetery. She was buried, alone rather than in the company of others of her own kind, at the corner of Burgundy Street.[93] This must have been dreadful for her, as she had a very high opinion of herself."

---

90. In the manuscript it is explicit, here implicit, that this is a play by Voltaire.

91. Here begins a section added in 1761.

92. Corneille's *Le Comte d'Essex*.

93. Adrienne Lecouvreur became famous playing the role of Monime. She was denied Christian burial because all actresses were, according to Church Law, excommunicated. Voltaire published a poem in protest, *La Mort de Mlle Lecouvreur* (1730). In 1761 Huerne de la Mothe published a pamphlet attacking the abuse of excommunication (for which he was punished by being deprived of the right to practice as a lawyer), and Voltaire came to his support.

"That's not very friendly," said Candide. "What do you expect?" said Martin. "That's how these people are. Think of all the contradictions and inconsistencies that are theoretically possible; you will find them all in the government, in the courts, in the churches, in the theaters of this peculiar country." "Is it true that everyone in Paris is always laughing?" asked Candide. "Yes," said the abbot, "but they laugh as they lose their tempers; for here everyone complains about everything while laughing loudly, and people even do the most wicked things while they are laughing."

"Who was," asked Candide, "that fat pig who was so critical of that play where I cried so much, and of the actors who gave me so much pleasure?" "He's a ne'er-do-well," replied the abbot, "who makes his living by speaking ill of all plays and all books. He hates anyone who is successful, just as eunuchs hate lovers. He is a snake in the world of letters, who lives by eating mud and poison. He's a scribbler." "What do you mean by a 'scribbler'?" asked Candide. "Someone," said the abbot, "who is always writing, someone like Fréron."[94]

This is how Candide, Martin, and the abbot from Périgord were chatting on the stairs, watching the audience come out at the end of the play. "Although I'm eager to see Miss Cunégonde again," said Candide, "I would still rather like to go to dinner with Miss Clairon,[95] for I thought she was wonderful."

The abbot was not someone who could go and speak to Miss Clairon, for she moved only in the best society. "She is tied up this evening," he said. "But let me have the honor of taking you to meet a lady of distinction; at her house you will get to know Paris as well as if you had been here for four years."

Candide, who was naturally curious, allowed himself to be taken to the lady, who lived at the end of the district of Saint Honoré. There they were playing a game of cards called faro. A dozen unhappy punters sat, each holding a hand of cards that were dog-eared as they were being used to record their losses. The game was played in complete silence; the punters were pale-faced; the banker looked anxious; the lady of the house sat next to this merciless banker, watching with the eyes of a lynx all the bets being placed and indicated by the dog-earing by each player of their cards; she made them straighten the dog-ears by keeping a strict eye on them, while remaining friendly, and certainly without expressing irritation, as she had

---

94. Fréron had written an amusing review of *Candide* in the *Année littéraire* (1759), claiming it could not possibly be by Voltaire because Voltaire was an optimist—a claim he convincingly supported by quotations from his previous works. He describes *Candide* as advocating *pessimism*.

95. A famous actress, who had starred in Voltaire's *Tancrède* (first performed 3 Sept. 1760).

no desire to lose her customers. This lady called herself the Marquise de Parolignac.[96] Her daughter, who was fifteen, was one of the punters, and alerted her mother with a movement of her eyebrow when one of her unlucky companions cheated in an attempt to win back something of what cruel chance had taken from them. The abbot from Périgord, Candide, and Martin entered. Nobody stood up; nobody greeted them; nobody looked at them. They all had their attention fixed on their cards. "Her Excellency the Baroness of Thunder-ten-tronckh was more polite," said Candide.

However, the abbot whispered into the ear of the marquise, who half stood up, directed a gracious smile toward Candide, and a haughty glance toward Martin. She gave instructions that a seat and a hand of cards should be given to Candide, who lost fifty thousand francs in the course of two games. After that they ate, and everyone was very cheerful. They were all surprised that Candide was not distressed by his losses; the servants said to each other, using the slang they use when talking to each other, "He must be some sort of English lord."

The dinner was like most dinners in Paris: first there was silence; then a babble of indistinguishable words; then some witticisms which were for the most part banal; then false reports about current events, bad arguments, a little politics, and lots of backbiting; there was even some discussion of recent books. "Have you seen," asked the abbot from Périgord, "the novel by father Gauchat, doctor of theology?"[97] "Yes," replied one of their companions, "but I couldn't finish it. We are swamped with worthless books; but if you added them all together they wouldn't be able to compete for worthlessness with the work of Gauchat, doctor of theology. I am so fed up with this endless flood of detestable books in which we are drowning that I have taken to gambling at faro." "And the *Essays* of Archdeacon T. . . . ,[98] what do you think of them?" asked the abbot. "Ah!" said Lady Parolignac, "what a boring man! What a fuss he makes of telling you things that everybody knows already! What heavy weather he makes of arguments so insignificant that they would not be worth mentioning in passing! How witless he is in repeating the witticisms of others! How he ruins what he steals! He disgusts me! But he won't disgust me in future; once you've read a few pages by the archdeacon there's no need to read more."

At the dinner table there was a learned man of good taste, and he agreed with what the marquise had said. Then they talked about tragedies. Her Ladyship wanted to know why there are some tragedies that are performed

---

96. A *paroli* is a type of bet at faro.
97. Gauchat had attacked Helvétius and Voltaire.
98. Trublet, another enemy of Voltaire's.

every now and again, but which are unreadable. The man of taste explained very clearly how a play might be fairly interesting, and be almost entirely worthless. He proved in the space of a few words that it wasn't enough to set up one or two of the situations that are to be found in every novel. One needed to be new without being eccentric; to be frequently sublime but always natural; to know the human heart and to give it a voice; to be a great poet without any of the characters in one's play appearing to be a poet; to know one's language perfectly and to speak a purified version of it, with every phrase sounding harmonious, and without the use of rhyming couplets ever interfering with what one has to say. "Whoever," he added, "fails to observe all these rules may succeed in writing one or two tragedies that are applauded on the stage, but he will never be considered a fine writer. There are very few good tragedies. Some are mere romances, though with dialogues that are well written and well rhymed; others are political diatribes that send you to sleep or go on so long they would put anyone off; yet others are the concoctions of barroom brawlers, written in a barbaric style, with characters interrupting each other and lengthy monologues addressed to the gods—because the author can't write a convincing dialogue—which are designed to illustrate false views of how the world works or to provide puffed up illustrations of trite and conventional views."

Candide listened to this speech with great attention and formed a very favorable opinion of the speaker. Since the marquise had taken care to place him at her side, he leaned over and whispered in her ear, taking advantage of his privileged position to ask her to tell him about this man who spoke so well. "He's a scholar," said the marquise, "who does not play cards, and whom the abbot sometimes brings to my house to dine. He is a great expert on plays and on books. He once wrote a play that was booed, and a book, of which only one copy has ever been seen, aside from the copies in his publisher's window, and that was a copy he presented to me." "What a great man," said Candide. "He deserves to be compared to Pangloss."

So, turning toward him, he said, "Sir, you think, I feel sure, that everything is as good as could be in the world, both the physical world and the moral world, and that nothing could be other than it is?" "Me, sir?" replied the scholar. "I don't agree with any of that. In my experience everything goes wrong in the world we inhabit. Nobody knows what their status is, nobody knows what their responsibilities are, nobody knows how to do what they are trying to do, nor do they know what they ought to be doing, and—with the exception of this dinner party, where the company is rather entertaining and where there seems to be little conflict—people pass the whole of their time in pointless squabbling: Jansenists against

Molinists,[99] supporters of the Supreme Court[100] against supporters of the Church, authors against other authors, courtiers against other courtiers, financiers against the nation, wives against husbands, relatives against relatives. It's a war that goes on forever."

Candide replied to him, "I've seen worse. But a wise man, now deceased, for he had the ill fortune to be hanged, taught me that all that is just perfect. These are like shadows that form part of a beautiful painting." "This chap who was hanged was pulling everyone's leg," said Martin. "What you call shadows are horrible smudges and stains." "It is human beings who make these stains," said Candide, "and they can't live without making them." "In that case they aren't to be blamed for them," said Martin. Most of the card players had no interest in this sort of conversation, but were happily drinking, while Martin argued with the scholar, and Candide told stories about his adventures to his hostess.

After dinner the marquise took Candide into a private room and sat him down on a couch. "Well," she said to him, "are you still hopelessly in love with Miss Cunégonde of Thunder-ten-tronckh?" "Yes, ma'am," replied Candide. The marquise smiled tenderly at him as she said, "Your answer is what I would expect from a young man from Westphalia. A Frenchman would have said to me: 'It is true that I have been in love with Miss Cunégonde, but now I have seen you, ma'am, I fear I can love her no more.'" "Oh dear! Ma'am," replied Candide, "I will say whatever you think I should say." "Your passion for her," said the marquise, "was awakened when you picked up her handkerchief; I want you to pick up my garter." "I'd be delighted," said Candide, and he picked it up. "But I want you to slip it back on," said the lady, and Candide slipped it back on. "Look," said the lady, "you're a foreigner. Sometimes I make my Parisian lovers pine for two weeks, but I'm going to give myself to you on the first night, as it's only right to welcome a young man from Westphalia to France."[101] This beautiful woman, having noticed two enormous dia-

---

99. Followers (including the Jesuits) of Luis Molina, who had defended the doctrine of the freedom of the will.

100. I have used this term to translate the French *parlement*. The *parlement* was a court, not a representative assembly. It was often in conflict with the Church, for it favored a weakening of the ties between French Catholicism and Rome, a view called "Gallicanism."

101. Candide had already been "welcomed" (the French phrase is *faire les honneurs*) by the Périgordian abbot. Daniel Gordon suggests we are supposed to understand he had a sexual relationship with both the abbot and the marquise (*Candide*, p. 32). This appears to be confirmed below, p. 59, when Candide refers to the marquise and the abbot as if they had both taken Cunégonde's place.

monds, one on this young foreigner's left hand, and one on his right, praised them so sincerely that they slipped from Candide's fingers to the fingers of the marquise.

Candide, on his way home in the company of the abbot from Périgord, felt some remorse for having been unfaithful to Miss Cunégonde; father abbot shared his distress, for he was getting only a small percentage of the fifty thousand francs that Candide had lost at cards, and of the value of the two diamonds that had been half given by Candide, half extorted from him. His plan was to make as much money as he could from the opportunities that his acquaintance with Candide might open up for him. He spoke at length to Candide about Cunégonde, and Candide told him that he would beg his beloved to pardon him for his infidelity when he saw her again in Venice.

The Périgordian became even more attentive and considerate, and showed a genuine interest in everything that Candide said, in everything he did, in everything he wanted to do.[102]

"So I gather, sir," he said to him, "that you have an arrangement to meet in Venice?" "Yes, sir," said Candide; "it's imperative that I go and meet Miss Cunégonde." So, caught up in the pleasure of talking about the person he loved, he told the story—as he now often did—of some of his adventures with this member of the Westphalian nobility.

"I imagine," said the abbot, "that Miss Cunégonde is very witty, and that she writes absolutely delightful letters." "I've never had a letter from her," said Candide; "for bear in mind that I was driven out of the castle because I loved her, and so I couldn't write to her; that soon afterward I learned that she was dead; that next I found her again and lost her again; and that I sent a messenger to her when I was seven thousand five hundred miles from here, and that I'm waiting for her reply."

The abbot listened carefully and seemed lost in thought. He soon took leave of the two foreigners, first hugging them warmly. The next day when he woke up Candide found waiting for him a letter written as follows:

Sir,
My dearest lover, I have been sick in bed here in Paris for eight days; now I learn that you are here too. I would run to your arms if I could move at all. I knew you had sailed to Bordeaux. I have left the faithful Cacambo and the old woman there; they should soon come to join me. The Governor of Buenos Aires took everything, but your heart is still mine. Come. Having you with me will bring me back to life, or else I will die of delight.

---

102. Here ends the section added in 1761.

This charming letter, this unhoped for letter filled Candide with an inexpressible joy; and at the same time the illness of his dearest Cunégonde overwhelmed him with pain. Torn between these two emotions, he took hold of his gold and his diamonds, and had himself and Martin driven to the house where Miss Cunégonde was staying. He entered, trembling with emotion. His heart was throbbing violently. He sobbed. He wanted to draw back the hangings surrounding the bed. He wanted lamps brought in. "You mustn't do that," said the maid, "light is dreadfully painful for her," and she quickly drew the hangings together. "My darling Cunégonde," said Candide weeping, "how is your health? If you can't see me, at least speak to me." "She can't speak," said the maid. The invalid then held out a plump hand, over which Candide wept tears for a long time. Then he filled the hand with diamonds, and left a bag full of gold on the armchair.

In the middle of his emotional turmoil a senior police officer arrived, followed by the abbot from Périgord and a squad of constables. "Are these they?" he asked. "Are these the two foreigners who are under suspicion?" He had them arrested at once, and ordered his underlings to drag them off to prison. "This isn't how they treat foreigners in El Dorado," said Candide. "I am more convinced than ever that the Manicheans are right," said Martin. "But, officer, where are you taking us?" asked Candide. "To a dungeon," said the officer.

Martin, having recovered his wits, concluded that the woman who was claiming to be Cunégonde was a cheat; that father abbot was a cheat who had seized the earliest opportunity to take advantage of Candide's unsuspecting nature; and that the police officer was another cheat of whom they could easily rid themselves.

Rather than face the criminal justice system, Candide, who had the benefit of Martin's advice, and who was still in a hurry to meet up with the real Cunégonde, offered the police officer three little diamonds worth three thousand pistoles each. "Ah, sir!," said this senior official to Candide, "even if you had committed every imaginable crime, you would be the most honest man in the world. Three diamonds! Each worth three thousand pistoles! Sir, far from throwing you in a dungeon, I would give my life for you. All foreigners are being rounded up, but I'll sort things out. I have a brother in Dieppe, in Normandy. I'll take you there. And if you have a diamond or two to give him he'll take every bit as good care of you as I would."

"And why are you arresting all foreigners?" asked Candide. The abbot from Périgord then spoke up and said: "It's because some wretch from the region of Arras overheard some people talking rubbish; that was enough to make him set out to kill a father figure. It wasn't like what happened in 1610, in the month of May, but like what happened in 1594, in the month of December; and like several other events that occurred in other years, and in different months, that were also carried out by other wretches who had overheard nonsense."[103]

The official then explained what had happened. "Oh! What monsters!" Candide exclaimed. "What! For such dreadful things to happen in a country where people dance and sing! I hope I can get out as quickly as possible from this country where monkeys provoke tigers. I saw bears in my own country; the only place I've seen human beings was in El Dorado. I beg you, good sir, take me to Venice where I am supposed to wait for Miss Cunégonde." "I can only take you to Lower Normandy," said the chief of police. Straightaway he had the handcuffs taken off him, told his subordinates that he had made a mistake, sent them away, took Candide and Martin to Dieppe, and left them with his brother. There was a little Dutch ship in the harbor. The Norman, encouraged by three more diamonds to become the most cooperative man in the world, had Candide and his people put on a ship that was going to sail to Portsmouth in England. This wasn't on the route to Venice, but Candide was happy to take any road that would enable him to escape from this country that seemed as dreadful as hell itself, and he intended to take the first opportunity to get back on the road to Venice.

CHAPTER TWENTY-THREE: *Candide and Martin reach the coast of England; and what they see there*

"Oh! Pangloss! Pangloss! Oh! Martin! Martin! Oh, my dear Cunégonde! What sort of world is this?" said Candide, on board the Dutch ship. "A quite mad world, and a quite dreadful one," replied Martin. "You know England; are they as mad there as in France?" "It's a different type of madness," said Martin. "You know that these two nations are at war over some acres of snow on the Canadian border; and that they are spending much more than the whole of Canada is worth on this fine war. To tell you precisely if there are more people who ought to be locked up in one country or in the other, that's something of which my limited intellect isn't capable. All I know is that the people we are going to see are very splenetic."

While talking like this they made landfall at Plymouth. A vast crowd covered the shore. All their eyes were fixed on a fairly fat man who was kneeling down, his eyes blindfolded, on the deck of one of the ships in the

---

103. Damiens, born near Arras, had tried to assassinate Louis XV on 5 Jan. 1757. May 1610: assassination of Henri IV, king of France. Dec. 1594: attempted assassination of Henri IV. All three (would-be) assassins had been influenced by the Jesuits.

fleet. Four soldiers, placed opposite this man, each fired three bullets into his skull as calmly as could be, and all those watching went home very well pleased. "What was happening there?" asked Candide, "and which devil is it who is the master of this whole world?" He asked who the fat man was who had just been killed so ceremoniously. "He was an admiral," they told him. "And why kill this admiral?" "It is," they said, "because he didn't have enough people killed; he began a battle with a French admiral, and it has been decided that he wasn't close enough to him." "But," said Candide, "the French admiral was as far from the English admiral as vice versa!" "There's no doubt about that," they replied, "but in this country it is thought a good idea to kill an admiral from time to time in order to encourage the others."[104]

Candide was so stunned and so shocked by what he had seen, and by what he had been told, that he didn't want to so much as put a foot on English soil, and so he made a deal with the Dutch ship owner (at the risk that he might rob him as his compatriot had done in Surinam) for him to take him straight to Venice.

The ship owner was ready to leave after two days. They followed the coast of France; they passed within sight of Lisbon, and Candide shuddered. They passed through the straits and into the Mediterranean; finally they reached Venice. "God be praised," said Candide, hugging Martin, "this is where I will see the beautiful Cunégonde again. I trust Cacambo as I would trust myself. All is well, all goes well, all goes as well as it possibly could."

CHAPTER TWENTY-FOUR: *About Paquette and brother Giroflée*

As soon as he arrived in Venice he began to search for Cacambo in all the bars, in all the cafés, in all the brothels; but he could not find him. He sent every day to inquire what ships and small boats had arrived in the harbor; he could obtain no news of Cacambo. "What!" he said to Martin, "I have had the time to sail from Surinam to Bordeaux, to travel from Bordeaux to Paris, from Paris to Dieppe, from Dieppe to Portsmouth, to sail along the coast of Portugal and Spain, to journey the length of the Mediterranean, to spend some months in Venice, and still the beautiful Cunégonde hasn't arrived! Instead of her the only people I have met up with have been a trollop and an abbot from Périgord! Doubtless Cunégonde is dead, and all that is left for me to do is die. Oh! It would have been better if I had stayed in the paradise of El Dorado rather than returning to this cursed conti-

---

104. Admiral Byng was executed on 14 March 1757. Voltaire had sought to organize a petition for clemency.

nent. How right you are, my dear Martin. There is nothing to life except illusion and calamity."

He fell into a black despair and did not go to the latest opera, nor to any of the other entertainments of the Carnival. Not a single woman tempted him in the slightest. Martin said to him, "You're really very naive, if truth be told, to imagine that a half-caste valet, who has five or six million in his pockets, is going to go to the end of the earth to look for your mistress and will then bring her to you in Venice. He'll take her for himself if he finds her. If he doesn't find her, he will replace her with someone else. I advise you to forget your valet Cacambo and your mistress Cunégonde." Martin's remarks were hardly cheering. Candide's despair deepened, and Martin kept on proving to him that there was very little virtue and very little happiness to be found on this earth, except perhaps in El Dorado, and nobody could go there.

While arguing about this important question, and waiting for Cunégonde, Candide noticed a young Theatine[105] in St. Mark's Square who had his arm around a girl. The Theatine looked fresh, chubby, vigorous; his eyes sparkled, his manner was proud, his expression superior, his stride confident. The girl was very pretty and was singing. She looked lovingly at her Theatine, and from time to time she pinched his fat cheeks. "At least you must acknowledge," said Candide to Martin, "that those people over there are happy. Wherever I have gone throughout the inhabited world—with the exception of El Dorado—I have so far found only the victims of ill fortune, but I'm prepared to wager that girl and that Theatine are both very happy." "And I'll bet they aren't," said Martin. "Well, we only have to invite them to have lunch with us," said Candide, "and you'll see if I'm mistaken."

They went up to them at once; Candide introduced himself, and invited them to come and eat some pasta, some Lombardy partridges, some caviar, and to drink some wine from Montepulciano, some from Vesuvius, some from Cyprus, and some from Samos. The young lady blushed; the Theatine accepted their invitation; and the girl followed him while looking at Candide with an expression of surprise and confusion, as tears began to fill her eyes. She had scarcely gone into Candide's hotel room when she said, "So! Mr. Candide doesn't recognize Paquette!" On hearing these words, Candide, who had not looked at her closely until then, for all his thoughts were of Cunégonde, said to her, "Alas! my poor child, so it was you who reduced Dr. Pangloss to the wretched state in which I saw him?" "Alas, sir, it was I," said Paquette; "I see you know all there is to know. I know about the dreadful sufferings undergone by the whole household of her ladyship and the beautiful Cunégonde. I promise you my own fate was scarcely less

---

105. A Catholic religious order founded in 1524.

awful. I was very innocent when you last saw me. A Franciscan who was my confessor seduced me without difficulty. The consequences were dire: I was forced to leave the castle some time after his lordship the baron sent you on your way with hefty kicks on your backside. If a distinguished doctor had not taken pity on me I would have died. For a while I expressed my gratitude to this doctor by being his mistress. His wife, who was mad with jealousy, beat me every day without mercy—she was a harpy. This doctor was the ugliest man alive, and I was the most miserable of creatures, being beaten all the time for sleeping with a man I did not love. You must know, sir, how dangerous it is for a cantankerous woman to be married to a doctor. This doctor, fed up with his wife's behavior, one day gave her, in order to cure her of a slight cold, a medicine so effective that she died two hours later while writhing in agony. Her relatives had him taken to court; he ran away, and I was thrown into prison. The fact that I was innocent would not have saved me, had I not also been good-looking. The judge released me on condition that he took over from the doctor. I was soon supplanted by a rival, driven out without any payment, and forced to continue this horrible profession, which you men think is good for a laugh, and which for us women is an ocean of misery. I went to Venice to practice my trade. Oh! Sir, if you could imagine what it is like to have to make love with the same enthusiasm to an elderly businessman, a lawyer, a monk, a gondolier, an abbot; to be the butt of every sort of insult and every sort of snub; to be reduced over and over again to borrowing a skirt so that one can go and have it lifted by some disgusting man; to have one man steal what you have earned from another man; to be blackmailed by the police; and to have no prospect but a horrific old age, a workhouse followed by a garbage dump.[106] If you could imagine all this you would conclude I am one of the unhappiest creatures in the whole world."

Thus Paquette opened her heart to honest Candide, in a private room, in the presence of Martin, who said to Candide, "You see that I have already won half the bet."

Brother Giroflée had stayed in the dining room and was having a drink while waiting for lunch. "But," said Candide to Paquette, "you looked so happy, so content, when I met you; you were singing; you fondled the Theatine with an affection that seemed entirely genuine; you seemed to me every bit as happy as you now claim to be miserable." "Ah sir!" replied Paquette, "that's another one of the miseries of my line of work. Yesterday I was robbed and beaten by a policeman, and today I have to seem cheerful in order to give pleasure to a monk."

Candide did not want to hear any more; he admitted that Martin was right. They sat down to eat with Paquette and the monk; they enjoyed

---

106. Prostitutes were, like actresses, denied Christian burial.

themselves during the meal; and as it was drawing to a close they were talking quite frankly to each other. "Father," said Candide to the monk, "it seems to me that your life is one that everybody else should envy. You're obviously in the peak of good health. It is clear from the expression on your face that you're happy; you have a very pretty girl to entertain you; and you seem very content with your life as a monk."

"Goodness, sir," said brother Giroflée, "I'd like to see every last Theatine drowned. On a hundred occasions I've been tempted to set fire to the monastery and to run off and convert to Islam. My parents forced me when I was fifteen to put on this hateful cassock, so that they would have more money to leave to my wretched elder brother, God damn him! Jealousy, conflict, and anger are at home in a monastery. It's true that I've preached some lousy sermons that have earned me a bit of money, though the prior has stolen half of that from me. What's left enables me to pay for female company; but, in the evening, when I go back to the monastery, I feel like banging my head against the walls of the dormitory; and all my fellow friars are in the same state."

Martin turned to Candide with his normal calm expression: "Well," he said to him, "don't you agree that I've won the whole bet?" Candide gave two thousand dollars to Paquette and a thousand dollars to brother Giroflée. "My reply is," he said, "that that will be enough to make them happy." "I don't believe it for a moment," said Martin; "it's quite possible that this money you've given them will make them even more miserable." "Well, what will happen will happen," said Candide; "but one thing consoles me; I've learned that one often meets up with people whom one never expected to see again; it could easily happen that, having met up with my red sheep and Paquette, I will also meet up with Cunégonde." "I hope," said Martin, "that one day she will make you happy; but I don't for a moment believe it will happen." "You've got a hard heart," said Candide. "That's because I've some experience of life," said Martin.

"But look at those gondoliers," said Candide, "don't they sing all the time?" "You don't see them at home, with their wives and their brats," replied Martin. "The doge[107] is familiar with sorrow and disappointment; and so are these gondoliers. It is true that, all in all, the life of a gondolier is preferable to that of a doge; but I believe the difference is so slight that it isn't worth the trouble of analyzing it."

"People talk," said Candide, "about a senator called Pococurante who lives in that beautiful palace on the river Brenta, and who is rather welcoming to foreigners. They claim he is someone who has never experienced sorrow or disappointment."[108] "I'd certainly like to examine such a

---

107. The constitutional head of the Venetian state.
108. The name means "few worries."

rare specimen," said Martin. At once Candide sent a messenger to His Lordship Pococurante asking if they might come and visit him tomorrow.

CHAPTER TWENTY-FIVE: *A visit to the home of His Lordship Pococurante, a Venetian nobleman*

Candide and Martin set out by gondola along the Brenta and came to the palace of Pococurante, a Venetian nobleman. The gardens were well laid out and ornamented with beautiful marble statues; the palace was beautifully designed. The master of the house, a man of about sixty and immensely wealthy, received our inquisitive duo very politely but with very little enthusiasm. Candide found this disconcerting, while Martin approved of it.

First two pretty girls, smartly dressed, served hot chocolate, which they had frothed to perfection. Candide could not prevent himself from praising them for their beauty, their charm, and their technique. "They are rather nice young women," said the senator; "I sometimes have them sleep with me, as I've had enough of the noblewomen of the town: enough of their flirtations, their jealousies, their quarrels, their moods, their self-obsession, their pride, their stupidity, and of the sonnets that one has to write—or have someone else write—in praise of them. But still, these two young women are really beginning to bore me."

Candide, after lunch, took a turn in a long gallery, and was astonished by the fine paintings. He asked which of the old masters had painted the first two. "They are by Raphael," said the senator; "I paid a lot for them a few years ago because I wanted to show off. People say they are the most beautiful paintings in Italy, but I don't like them at all. Their color has faded. The bodies seem flat and aren't three-dimensional. The fabrics don't seem real. In a word, no matter what people say, I don't think they are a successful imitation of nature herself. I will only love a painting when I find one that makes me think I am looking at real life; there are none that give this illusion. I have lots of paintings, but I no longer look at them."[109]

Pococurante, while waiting for dinner, had his orchestra perform a concerto. Candide found the music delightful. "This noise," said Pococurante, "can amuse one for half an hour; but if it lasts any longer than that it tires anybody listening to it, though nobody dares admit it.

---

109. Voltaire said he resembled Pococurante in a letter of 10 March 1759 (D8168), and Pococurante's views on Raphael (the great Renaissance painter), Homer and Virgil (the great epic poets of ancient Greece and Rome), and Milton (the great epic poet of seventeenth-century England) largely coincide with those expressed by Voltaire in the article "Goût" of *Questions de l'Encyclopédie* (1770–72) and in the *Essai sur la poésie épique* (1728). On the other hand Voltaire admired Cicero's skepticism (D9126, 9 Aug. 1760).

Music today is nothing but the technical skill of performing scores that are hard to play, and music whose only claim is that it is difficult to play cannot please its listeners for long.

"It's possible that I would prefer opera, if the secret had not been discovered of how to turn it into something monstrous that revolts me. Let anyone who wants to go to see dreadful tragedies set to music, where the story line has no purpose but to provide a poor excuse for two or three ridiculous songs, which serve to show off an actress's throat to good advantage. Let people swoon with pleasure if they want to, or if they can, while watching a castrato hum the role of Caesar or of Cato, and march up and down in a clumsy fashion upon the stage. As for me, I long ago gave up these miserable performances, in which Italy nowadays takes such pride, and which princes pay so dearly to see." Candide argued a bit, but cautiously. Martin agreed wholeheartedly with the senator.

They sat down to eat, and after an excellent dinner they went to the library. Candide, seeing a magnificently bound copy of Homer, praised the illustrious nobleman on his good taste. "That," he said, "is a book that used to delight that great man Pangloss, the finest philosopher in all Germany." "It doesn't delight me," said Pococurante. "It used to be possible to persuade me that I enjoyed reading it, but the continual repetition of battles, each indistinguishable from the others; the gods, who are constantly meddling but never do anything decisive; Helen, over whom the Greeks are fighting, but who scarcely appears in the story; Troy, which is under siege but does not fall; all that used to make me die of boredom. On several occasions I asked various scholars if they found reading Homer as boring as I did; all the honest ones admitted to me that they nodded off every time they tried to read him, but they said one must always have a copy in one's library, as a monument to a past age, just like those rusted old coins one collects but cannot use as money."

"Your Excellency wouldn't speak like this about Virgil?" asked Candide. "I admit," said Pococurante, "that the second, the fourth, and the sixth books of the *Aeneid* are excellent; but as for his description of pious Aeneas, and strong Cloanthes, and Aeneas' friend Achates, and little Ascanius, and the stupid king Latinus, and the respectable Amata, and the tedious Lavinia: I can't believe that anything more flat and disagreeable has ever been written. I prefer Tasso, and Ariosto's fantastical stories."[110]

"Might I be so bold as to ask you, sir," said Candide, "if you don't find reading Horace a true delight?"[111] "There are some maxims in Horace," said Pococurante, "that have something to teach a man of the world. And, since they are succinctly expressed in energetic verses, it is all the easier to

---

110. Tasso and Ariosto wrote romantic epics in sixteenth-century Italy.

111. A Roman poet of the first century C.E.

engrave them in one's memory. But I really don't care for his voyage to Brindisi, nor for his description of a bad dinner, nor for the quarrel between two porters, one called Pupilus, I think, whose words, he tells us, were 'full of pus,' and another whose words 'were like vinegar.' I felt absolute disgust while I was reading those coarse verses against old women and witches; and I can't see what makes it admirable for him to say to his friend Maecenas that if he includes him among the great lyric poets, then he will bump into the stars with his sublime forehead. Idiots admire everything written by a famous author. I only read to please myself, and I only like books I want to read." Candide, who had been brought up never to judge anything for himself, was very astonished by what he heard; and Martin found Pococurante's way of approaching these questions rather sensible.

"Ah! Here is a copy of Cicero," said Candide. "I take it you don't get bored reading such a great author as Cicero?" "I never read him," replied the Venetian. "What does it matter to me whether he represented Rabirius or Cluentius? I listen to enough speeches by lawyers in the trials where I serve as judge. I would have got on rather better with his philosophical works; but when I realized that he doubted everything and believed nothing, I concluded that I knew as much about these things as he did, and that I didn't need his help or anyone else's to be a know-nothing."

"Ah! Here are twenty-four volumes of papers published by one of the scientific institutions," cried Martin. "I imagine there's some good things in them." "There would be," said Pococurante, "if a single one of the authors of this pile of rubbish had invented something as useful as the technique for making pins; but in all these volumes there isn't a single useful thing, only pointless theories."

"What plays I see over there!" said Candide. "In Italian, in Spanish, in French." "Yes," said the senator, "there are three thousand of them, and not three dozen good ones. As for these collections of sermons, all of which together aren't worth a single page of Seneca,[112] and these fat volumes of theology, you can be sure that I never look inside them, not me, nor anybody else."

Martin saw that there were shelves of English books. "I imagine," he said, "that a republican must enjoy the majority of these works, which have been written without fear of censorship."[113] "Yes," replied Pococurante, "it's a fine thing to write what one thinks;[114] it's a privilege that every human being should have. No matter where you go in my Italy,

---

112. A Roman stoic philosopher of the first century B.C.E.

113. Venice was a republic, but it had (unlike England) an effective system of censorship.

114. This echoes a famous remark by the Roman historian Tacitus.

people only write what they don't think. The people who live in the land
of the Caesars and the Antonines don't dare have an idea that hasn't been
approved by a Dominican.[115] I would be delighted by the liberty that
inspires the brilliant writers of England, if partisan politics and doctrinaire
thinking did not corrupt everything that this precious liberty produces
which would otherwise be worth admiring."[116]

Candide, seeing a volume of Milton, asked him if he did not think that
Milton was a great man. "Who?" said Pococurante. "That barbarian who
wrote a long commentary on the first chapter of Genesis in ten books of
jangling verses?[117] That crude imitator of the Greeks, who misrepresents
the creation? Where Moses describes the eternal Being as producing the
world with his speech, Milton portrays the Messiah as taking a gigantic
compass out of a cupboard in heaven in order to measure out his project.
Do you imagine that I could admire the person who ruined the hell and
the devil described by Tasso; who turns Lucifer sometimes into a monster,
sometimes into a dwarf; who makes him deliver the same speeches a
hundred times; who has him enter into debates about theology, who,
imitating Ariosto's comic account of the invention of gunpowder, has
cannon being shot off in heaven by the devils, and expects us to take it
seriously? Neither I nor any other Italian could enjoy all these wretched
excesses. The marriage of sin and death, and the snakes to which sin gives
birth, are enough to make any man who has any delicacy of taste throw up,
and his long description of a hospital would only interest a gravedigger.
This poem, which is difficult to follow, bizarre, and disgusting, was
thought awful when it was first published; my attitude to it now is the
same as the attitude English contemporaries had to it when it first appeared. In any case, I say what I think, and I really don't care if other
people agree with me." Candide was distressed by this speech. He had a
high opinion of Homer; he liked Milton, even if he didn't love him.
"Alas!" he whispered to Martin, "I'm rather afraid this fellow will have a
lofty contempt for our German poets." "That wouldn't be such a serious
mistake," said Martin. "Oh what a high opinion he has of himself!"
Candide went on muttering to himself. "What a great genius this
Pococurante is! Nothing can please him."

Thus, having looked through all the books in his library, they went
down into the garden. Candide praised all its beauties. "I know nothing
that better illustrates bad taste," said its owner. "This is all just rubbish;

---

115. The Dominicans ran the Inquisition.

116. The notion that there was something inherently corrupt about partisan
politics was a commonplace. Few (apart from Machiavelli) were prepared to praise
political conflict.

117. I.e., *Paradise Lost*, which has twelve books.

but tomorrow I'm going to have another one constructed, following a much finer design."

When our two inquisitive travelers had said good-bye to His Excellency, Candide turned to Martin: "You'll have to admit that we've just seen the happiest man alive, for he is superior to everything he owns." "Don't you think," said Martin, "that he is disgusted by everything he owns? Plato said, long ago, that the best stomachs are not the ones that can't digest food of any sort." "But," said Candide, "isn't there a pleasure to be had in criticizing everything, in perceiving defects where everyone else believes they see beautiful works of art?" "You're saying," replied Martin, "that there's pleasure to be had out of not having pleasure?" "OK," said Candide, "in that case I'm the only happy person in the world, or will be when I meet up with Miss Cunégonde again." "It's always a good idea to keep hoping," said Martin.

However the days, the weeks, slipped away. Cacambo did not arrive, and Candide was so broken-down by his distress that he didn't even notice that Paquette and brother Giroflée had not taken the trouble to come and thank him.

CHAPTER TWENTY-SIX: *On a dinner that Candide and Martin ate with six strangers, and who they were*

One evening when Candide, followed by Martin, was going to sit down to dine with the other foreigners who were staying in the same hotel, a man with a face the color of soot came up to him from behind and, taking him by the arm, said to him: "Be ready to leave with us; don't be late." He turned around, and it was Cacambo. There was nothing, except for seeing Cunégonde, that could have astonished him more or given him more pleasure. He was on the point of going mad with happiness. He hugged his dear friend. "Cunégonde is here, I'm sure. Where is she? Take me to her so that I can die of joy in her arms." "Cunégonde isn't here," said Cacambo, "she's in Constantinople." "Oh Lord! In Constantinople! But even if she were in China, I'd run to her; let's go." "We'll go after we've had dinner," replied Cacambo; "I can't say any more. I am a slave; my master is waiting for me; I must go and wait on him at dinner; don't say a word; eat your dinner and be ready for the moment."

Candide was torn between joy and pain; delighted to have met up with his faithful servant; astonished to discover he was a slave; full of thoughts of rediscovering his mistress. With his heart agitated, his wits shaken, he sat down to eat with Martin, who watched all these remarkable events without losing his composure, and with six foreigners who had come to Venice to enjoy the Carnival.

Cacambo, who poured the drinks for one of these foreigners, lowered his head toward his master's ear as the dinner was ending, and said to him: "Sire, Your Majesty may leave when he wishes; the ship is ready." Having said these words he went out. The others around the table, astonished, looked at each other without saying a single word. Then another servant went up to his master and said, "Sire, Your Majesty's sedan chair is at Padua, and the boat is ready." His master gave a nod, and the servant left. All the fellow diners continued to look at each other, and their shared surprise was now twice as great. A third valet, coming up to a third foreigner, said, "Sire, believe me, Your Majesty should not stay here any longer; I will go and get everything ready." And at once he disappeared.

By this point Candide and Martin were sure that this was a performance put on for Carnival. A fourth servant said to the fourth master, "Your Majesty may leave when he wishes," and went out after the others. The fifth valet said the same to the fifth master. But the sixth valet spoke differently to the sixth master, who was sitting next to Candide. He said to him: "Believe me, Sire, no one's prepared any longer to accept your assurance of future payment, nor mine either; you and I could both end up in prison before the night is over; I'm going to look after myself; farewell."

All the servants had now disappeared, and the six foreigners, plus Candide and Martin, sat in a deep silence. Finally Candide broke it: "Gentlemen," he said, "this is a very strange joke. Why are you all pretending to be kings? For my part, I confess that neither I nor Martin are monarchs."

Cacambo's master then began to speak in solemn tones, saying, in Italian, "I am not joking. My name is Achmet III.[118] I was the grand sultan for several years; I overthrew my brother; and my nephew overthrew me. My viziers had their throats cut. I live out my life in the old seraglio. My nephew, the Grand Sultan Mahmoud, sometimes lets me travel for the sake of my health, and I have come to Venice to enjoy the Carnival."

A young man who was sitting next to Achmet spoke next, and said, "I am called Ivan;[119] I was emperor of all the Russias; I was overthrown while I was still an infant. My father and mother were locked up, and I was brought up in prison. Every now and again I am given permission to travel, accompanied by my guards, and I have come to Venice to enjoy the Carnival."

The third man said, "I am Charles Edward, king of England.[120] My father transferred to me his right to the throne. I have fought to uphold it.

118. 1673–1736; reigned 1703–1730.
119. Ivan VI, 1740–1764; reigned 1740–1756.
120. The Young Pretender, 1720–1788, grandson of the deposed James II.

Eight hundred of my supporters have had their hearts torn out, and their cheeks have been beaten with them.[121] I have been imprisoned. I am going to Rome to visit the king my father, who was denied his throne, as I have been, and as my grandfather was, and I have come to Venice to enjoy the Carnival."

The fourth spoke, "I am the king of the Poles; the fortunes of war have deprived me of my hereditary states; my father experienced the same fate.[122] I entrust myself to Providence, like the Sultan Achmet, Emperor Ivan, King Charles Edward, to whom God grant a long life. And I have come to Venice to enjoy the Carnival."

The fifth said, "I am also king of the Poles;[123] I have lost my kingdom twice, but Providence has given me another state, in which I have done more good than all the kings of Poland put together have been able to do on the banks of the Vistula. I too entrust myself to Providence, and I have come to Venice to enjoy the Carnival."

Only the sixth king had yet to speak. "Gentlemen," he said, "I am not so great a ruler as each of you; but in the end I too was as much a king as anyone else. My name is Theodore; I was elected king of Corsica;[124] people said, 'Your Majesty' to me, and nowadays people barely say 'sir' to me. I minted money, and now I've not even got change. I had two secretaries of state, and now I've scarcely got a valet. I have sat on a throne, and for a long time I was in prison in London, sleeping on straw. I am very much afraid I'll end up the same way here, although I came, like Your Majesties, to Venice to enjoy the Carnival."

The five other kings listened to this speech with regal compassion. Each of them gave twenty gold coins to King Theodore so that he could buy some suits and shirts. Candide gave him a present of a diamond and two hundred gold coins. "Who," said the five kings, "is this private person who is in a position to give a hundred times as much as each of us, and who gives indeed?"[125]

Just as they were getting up from the table, there arrived at their hotel four serene highnesses, who had likewise lost their states through the

---

121. Voltaire is accurately describing part of the process known as "hanging, drawing, and quartering."

122. Augustus III, 1696–1763, elector of Saxony; king of Poland, 1733–1763; expelled from Saxony in 1756.

123. Stanislas Leszczynski, 1677–1766; king of Poland, 1704–1709, and (disputing the claim of Augustus III) 1733–1736.

124. Theodore von Neuhof, 1690–1756; king of Corsica for eight months in 1736; he spent seven years in a London debtor's prison.

125. In 1758 Voltaire was lending money to the Duke of Wurtemburg, the Elector Palatine, and the Duke of Saxe-Gotha, each one virtually a king.

fortunes of war, and who had come to Venice to enjoy what remained of the Carnival. But Candide was not even aware of these new arrivals. He was entirely preoccupied with going to Constantinople to find his beloved Cunégonde.

CHAPTER TWENTY-SEVEN: *Candide's voyage to Constantinople*[126]

The faithful Cacambo had already obtained the agreement of the Turkish ship owner who was going to carry Sultan Achmet back to Constantinople that Candide and Martin could travel with him. Both set out for the ship after they had prostrated themselves before His miserable Highness. On the way Candide said to Martin: "There you have six kings who have been overthrown. We've had supper with them, and I've even given charity to one of these six monarchs. Perhaps there are many other rulers who are more unfortunate. As for me, I have only lost a hundred sheep, and I'm rushing toward the arms of Cunégonde. My dear Martin, once more I see that Pangloss was right, all is well." "I hope you are right," said Martin. "But," said Candide, "this adventure that we've had in Venice scarcely seems credible. No one had ever seen, or heard talk of six overthrown kings eating together at a hotel." "That's no more extraordinary," said Martin, "than the majority of the things that have happened to us. It's perfectly commonplace for kings to be dethroned;[127] and as for the honor we have experienced of dining with them, it's so insignificant that we should pay no attention to it."

Candide had scarcely boarded the boat when he grabbed hold of his former servant, his friend Cacambo. "Well," he said to him, "what's Cunégonde doing? Is she still prodigiously beautiful? Does she still love me? Is she in good health? I presume you've bought a palace for her in Constantinople?"

---

126. Why does Candide end in Constantinople? Voltaire loved to imagine (e.g., D7213) that the views of Lake Geneva from his home were similar to views of the Bosphorus from Constantinople (which he had never visited). His identification with the explorer Tavernier, who had traveled to Constantinople and died in Lausanne (D7215) is also significant. See Murray, *Voltaire's "Candide,"* ch. 6. Voltaire was perhaps struck by a comment in the *Correspondance littéraire* for 1 Jan. 1754, when he was effectively a refugee, expelled from Prussia and denied entry to France: "Those with an unpleasant sense of humor say that this author will go and have himself circumcised in Constantinople, *et que ce sera la fin de son roman* [and that will be the end of his story]."

127. The precarious position of contemporary rulers was a recurring subject in Voltaire's correspondence at this time, particularly as a result of the attempt to assassinate the king of Portugal (3 Sept. 1758): e.g., de Brosses' letter to Voltaire, c. 25 Oct. 1758 (D7918): "the job [of king] is no longer worth having."

"My dear Master," replied Cacambo, "Cunégonde washes dishes on the shores of the Sea of Marmara. She is a slave in the household of a prince who has very few dishes, a deposed ruler named Ragotski,[128] to whom the grand sultan pays a pension of three crowns a day while he is in exile. But what is much sadder is that she has lost her beauty, and she has become horribly ugly." "Ah! Beautiful or ugly," said Candide, "I am an honorable man, and my duty is to love her always. But how can she be reduced to so abject a condition when she has the five or six million that you took to her?" "Well," said Cacambo, "you must realize I had to pay two million to His Excellency Don Fernando d'Ibaraa y Figueora y Mascarenes y Lampourdos y Souza, governor of Buenos Aires, to obtain his permission for Miss Cunégonde to leave with me. And then you must realize that a bold pirate took all the rest away from us. This pirate, what did he do but take us to Cape Matapan, to Melos, to Nicaria, to Samos, to Petra, to the Dardanelles, to Marmara, to Scutari? Cunégonde and the old woman labor in the household of this prince I've told you about, and as for me, I'm the slave of the former sultan, now overthrown." "What dreadful calamities, each one the cause of the next!" said Candide. "But let's not forget, I've still got some diamonds; I'll easily obtain the release of Cunégonde. It's really a shame that she's become so ugly."

Then he turned to Martin: "What do you think?" he asked. "Who is most deserving of our pity—Emperor Achmet, Emperor Ivan, His Highness Charles Edward, or me?" "I haven't a clue," said Martin; "I'd have to be able to look into your hearts to know the answer." "Ah!" said Candide, "if Pangloss were here, he would know the answer, and he would teach it to us." "I don't know," said Martin, "what scales your Pangloss would have used to weigh the misfortunes of men, and to measure their sufferings. The only thing I presume to know is that there are millions of people on the earth who are a hundred times more deserving of our pity than His Highness Charles Edward, Emperor Ivan, and Sultan Achmet." "You may be right," said Candide.

In a few days they reached the channel that leads into the Black Sea. Candide began by paying a very high price for Cacambo; and without wasting time he leaped into a galley, followed by his companions, so that they could go to the shore of the Sea of Marmara and find Cunégonde, no matter how ugly she might be.

On the galley there were two conscripts who rowed very badly. The Levantine[129] ship owner periodically whipped their bare shoulders with a cat-o'-nine-tails. Candide responded to this in a perfectly natural fashion, and looked at them more closely than he looked at the other oarsmen, and

---

128. Francis Leopold Rakoczy, 1676–1735; in exile in Turkey, 1720–1735.

129. From the east, i.e., the Eastern Mediterranean.

was even moved by pity to approach them. Some features of their ravaged faces seemed to him to give them some slight resemblance to Pangloss and to the wretched Jesuit, the baron, the brother of Miss Cunégonde. This fancy moved him and saddened him. He looked at them even more closely. "In truth," he said to Cacambo, "if I hadn't seen Dr. Pangloss hanged, and if I hadn't had the misfortune to kill the baron, I would believe that it was they who are on the bench there, rowing this galley."

At the mention of the baron and of Pangloss, the two conscripts let out a loud cry, stopped rowing, and dropped their oars. The Levantine ship owner ran over to them, and the blows of the cat-o'-nine-tails fell faster than ever. "Stop, sir, stop!" cried Candide. "I'll give you as much money as you want." "What! It's Candide," said one of the conscripts. "What! It's Candide," said the other. "Is this a dream?" said Candide. "Am I awake? Am I really on this galley? Is that really His Honor the Baron, whom I killed? Is that really Dr. Pangloss whom I saw hanged?"

"It is we! It is we!" they replied. "What! Is that the great philosopher?" said Martin. "Eh! You, sir," said Candide to the Levantine ship owner, "how much money do you want for the ransom of His Honor the Baron of Thunder-ten-tronckh, one of the most important barons in the Holy Roman Empire, and for the ransom of Dr. Pangloss, the most profound metaphysician in Germany?" "Christian dog," said the Levantine ship owner, "since these two dogs, these Christian conscripts, are barons and metaphysicians, which must mean they are important people in their own countries, you will have to pay me fifty thousand sequins for them." "I'll pay, sir. Take me back as fast as possible to Constantinople and I'll pay you immediately. No, no! Take me to Miss Cunégonde." The Levantine ship owner, on hearing Candide's first offer, had already turned the prow toward the city, and he had his slaves row faster than a bird cuts through the air.

Candide hugged the baron and Pangloss a hundred times. "How on earth did I fail to kill you, my dearest baron? And my dearest Pangloss, how can you be alive when you were hanged? And why are you both rowing in a Turkish galley?" "Is it really true that my dearest sister is in this country?" asked the baron. "Yes," replied Cacambo. "So I see my dearest Candide again!" cried Pangloss. Candide introduced Martin and Cacambo to them. They all hugged each other, and all talked at once. The galley flew onward; before they knew it they were in the harbor. A Jew was fetched, and Candide sold a diamond worth a hundred thousand sequins to him for fifty thousand, after he had sworn by Abraham that he would make a loss if he paid more. At once he ransomed the baron and Pangloss. Pangloss threw himself at the feet of his liberator and washed them with his tears; the other thanked him with a slight nod of his head, and promised to repay him the money as soon as possible. "But is it really true that my sister is in Turkey?" he asked. "Nothing is more true," replied Cacambo, "for she is washing dishes in the household of a Transylvanian prince." At once two Jews were sent for. Candide sold more diamonds, and they all set out in another galley to go and rescue Cunégonde.

CHAPTER TWENTY-EIGHT: *What happened to Candide, Cunégonde, Pangloss, Martin, etc.*

"Forgive me, I beg you again," said Candide to the baron; "forgive me, Reverend Father, for having given you a violent thrust with a sword and pierced right through you." "Let's not mention it again," said the baron. "I was a little too sharp, I admit it. But since you want to know the sequence of events that ended with your seeing me rowing in a galley, I will tell you that, after my wound had been healed by the brother apothecary at the Jesuit college, I was attacked and taken prisoner by a Spanish raiding party. I was put into a prison in Buenos Aires around the same time as my sister was leaving. I asked to be returned to Rome, to the general of the order. From there I was assigned to go and serve as chaplain to the French ambassador in Constantinople. I had only been doing my new job for a week when one evening I came across a young icoglan[130] with an excellent physique. It was very hot. The young man wanted to go to the bathhouse. I took the opportunity to go to the bathhouse as well. I didn't realize that it was a capital crime for a Christian to be found completely naked in the company of a young Muslim. A judge ordered that I should be given a hundred blows of a cane on the soles of my feet, and also sentenced me to the galleys. I don't believe there has ever been a more dreadfully unjust sentence. But I would like someone to explain to me why my sister is working in the kitchen of a Transylvanian ruler in exile in Turkey?"

"But you, my dear Pangloss," said Candide, "how has it come about that we meet again?" "It is true," said Pangloss, "that you saw me hanged; properly speaking I ought to have been burned, but you will remember that it began to pour with rain just when they were going to cook me. The storm was so violent that they gave up trying to light the fire. I was hanged because they couldn't find anything better to do. A surgeon bought my body, took it back to his house, and dissected me. He first made an opening in the shape of a cross running from my navel to my throat. You couldn't be more incompetently hanged than I had been. The executioner who carried out the sacred instructions of the Holy Inquisition, who was a subdeacon, did a first-rate job of burning people, but he had no experience of hanging them. The rope was wet, which increased the friction; the

---

130. A young man brought up in the Sultan's seraglio and educated for high office.

running knot jammed. So I was still breathing. The cross-shaped incision made me emit such an enormous scream that the surgeon fell backwards, and, believing that he was cutting open a devil, he ran away, scared almost to death, and fell down the stairs in his haste to escape. His wife came running from a room nearby when she heard the noise. She saw me laid out on the table with my cross-shaped incision. She was even more frightened than her husband had been; ran away, and fell on top of him. When they had recovered their wits a bit, I heard the surgeon's wife say to the surgeon: 'My dear, what were you thinking of when you decided to dissect a heretic? Didn't you realize that there is always a devil in the body of one of those people? I am going to go quickly to find a priest to exorcise it.' I shuddered on hearing these words, and I summoned up what little strength I had left to cry out, 'Have pity on me.' Finally the Portuguese barber[131] took courage. He sewed up my skin. His wife looked after me herself. After two weeks I was back on my feet. The barber found me a job, and arranged for me to serve as the valet of a knight of the order of Malta who was going to Venice. But my master couldn't afford to pay my wages, and so I hired myself out to a Venetian merchant, and went with him to Constantinople.

"One day I thought it would be interesting to go into a mosque. The only people there were an elderly mullah and a very pretty young female worshipper who was saying her prayers. Her dress was low-cut; between her two bosoms she had a pretty bouquet of tulips, roses, anemones, buttercups, hyacinths, and primroses.[132] She dropped her bouquet on the floor; I picked it up, and I replaced it where it had come from eagerly but deferentially. I took such a long time to put it back in place that the mullah became angry, and, realizing that I was a Christian, he called for help. I was taken to the judge, who had me beaten a hundred times on the soles of my feet, and sent me to the galleys. I was chained up in the very same galley and on the very same bench as His Honor the Baron. In this galley there were four young men from Marseilles, five Neapolitan priests, and two monks from Corfu, who told us that this sort of thing happens all the time. His Honor the Baron claimed that he had suffered a greater injustice than I, while I claimed that it was much more acceptable to replace a bouquet between the breasts of a woman than to be completely naked with a young man. We argued without stopping, and we were given twenty lashes with the cat-o'-nine-tails a day, when the causal chain linking the events in this universe brought you to our galley, and you purchased our freedom."

---

131. In the eighteenth century doctors did not perform surgery, which was the province of barber-surgeons.

132. Voltaire is describing a woman in a Christian church, for a Muslim would not have been dressed like this, nor been alone in the company of men.

"Well, my dearest Pangloss," said Candide to him, "while you were being hanged, dissected, lashed, and were rowing in the galleys, did you continue to think that all went as well as could be?" "I still think as I always did," said Pangloss, "for, after all, I'm a philosopher, and it would be inappropriate for me to change my mind. Leibniz cannot have been wrong, and moreover the preestablished harmony is the most beautiful thing in the world, along with the plenum and subtle matter."[133]

CHAPTER TWENTY-NINE: *How Candide found Cunégonde and the old woman*

While Candide, the baron, Pangloss, Martin, and Cacambo were telling their adventures; while they were philosophizing about the events that occur in this universe, and whether they are contingent or not contingent; while they debated effects and causes, moral evil and physical evil, liberty and necessity, the consolations one can experience while one is a Turkish galley-slave, they approached the shores of the Sea of Marmara where the ruler of Transylvania had his house. The first things they saw were Cunégonde and the old woman, who were hanging out some napkins on the line to dry them.

The baron turned pale at this sight. Candide, the tender lover, on seeing his beautiful Cunégonde weather-beaten, her eyes bloodshot, her throat wizened, her cheeks lined, her arms red and chapped, was horror-struck and fell back three paces; then he advanced again in good order. She hugged Candide and her brother; they hugged the old woman; Candide bought both of them their freedom.

There was a small holding in the neighborhood; the old woman suggested to Candide that he should make himself at home there, at least until the whole group of them experienced an improvement in their fortunes. Cunégonde did not realize that she had become ugly, for no one had told her. She reminded Candide of his promises in a tone so peremptory that good Candide did not dare turn her down. He indicated therefore to the baron that he was going to marry his sister. "I will never permit," said the baron, "that she should act in so unbefitting a manner, or that you should behave in such an insolent fashion. No one will ever be able to reproach me for condoning this infamous behavior. The children of my sister would not be able to be received into aristocratic company in Germany. No: my sister will never marry anyone who is not a baron of the empire." Cunégonde threw herself at his feet and bathed them in tears; he was unyielding. "You're an absolute fool," Candide said to him. "I rescued you from the galleys; I paid for your freedom; I paid for your sister's freedom.

---

133. Leibniz denied the possibility of a vacuum.

She was here washing dishes; she is ugly; I have the generosity to make her my wife, and you still have the audacity to oppose it. I would kill you again if I allowed my fury to get the better of me." "You can kill me again," said the baron, "but you will never marry my sister while I am alive."

CHAPTER THIRTY: *Conclusion*

Deep down, Candide had no desire to marry Cunégonde. But the baron's outrageous impertinence decided him to go through with the marriage, and in any case Cunégonde was urging him so forcefully that he could not back out. He consulted Pangloss, Martin, and the faithful Cacambo. Pangloss wrote a fine dissertation, in the course of which he proved that the baron had no authority over his sister, and that all the laws of the empire permitted her to marry Candide with her left hand.[134] Martin recommended that they throw the baron into the sea. Cacambo was of the view that they should return him to the Levantine ship owner, and have him chained once more to the oar; after which he would be sent by the first available boat to Rome, to the father general of the order. Everyone thought this advice was excellent; the old woman approved; not a word was said to his sister; the plan was carried out with the help of some money, and they had the pleasure of capturing a Jesuit and of punishing a German baron for his pride.

It would be perfectly natural to imagine that, after so many disasters, Candide, now that he had married his mistress, and was living with the philosopher Pangloss, the philosopher Martin, the wise Cacambo, and the old woman, would live the most enjoyable life imaginable, particularly if one takes into account the fact that he had brought back so many diamonds from the original homeland of the Incas. But he had been so badly cheated by the Jews that he had nothing left but his little farm; his wife, who grew more ugly every day, had become shrewish and unbearable; the old woman was sick, and was even more ill tempered than Cunégonde. Cacambo, who worked the land, and who took vegetables to Constantinople to sell, was worn out by his labors, and cursed his fate. Pangloss was in despair because he did not have the chance to shine in some German university. As for Martin, he was convinced that one is equally badly off wherever one is, and he put up with everything patiently. Candide, Martin, and Pangloss sometimes debated questions of metaphysics and morality. Through the farmhouse windows one could often see boats passing, carrying nobles, governors, and judges who were being sent into exile at

---

134. This is termed a morganatic marriage. It would normally occur when a man was marrying beneath him, and his children were to be excluded from the succession to his title.

Lemnos, or Mytilene, or Erzeroum. One could see other judges, other governors, other lords on their way to take the place of those who had been sent into exile; and then one could see them go into exile in their turn. One could see severed heads, properly stuffed with straw, that were being taken to be presented to the sultan.[135] These sights made them argue ever more heatedly; and when they were not arguing the boredom was so dreadful that the old woman one day dared to say: "I would like to know which is worse, either to be raped a hundred times by Negro pirates, to have a buttock cut off, to run the gauntlet in the Bulgar army, to be whipped and hanged during an auto-da-fé, to be dissected, to be a galley slave—in short, to experience all the miseries added together that each one of us has gone through—or alternatively to stay here doing nothing?" "That's a tough question," said Candide.[136]

This speech gave rise to new reflections, and Martin in particular concluded that human beings are born to live either in convulsions of restlessness or in the lethargy of boredom. Candide did not agree, but he had no alternative to propose. Pangloss admitted that his life had been nothing but dreadful suffering; but having once maintained that everything was going well, he still did so, and didn't believe it for a moment.

Something happened that confirmed Martin in his detestable principles, that made Candide hesitate more than ever, and that embarrassed Pangloss. For one day they saw Paquette and brother Giroflée arrive on their farm. They were in the most absolute misery: they had quickly run through their three thousand piastres, parted, come back together, fallen out with each other, been thrown into prison, escaped, and finally brother Giroflée had converted to Islam. Paquette worked as a prostitute wherever she went, and no longer earned anything by it. "This is what I foresaw," said Martin to Candide, "I knew your gifts would soon be gone and would prove to have simply made them more miserable. You've spewed out millions of dollars, you and Cacambo, and you are no happier than brother Giroflée and Paquette." "Ah ha!" said Pangloss to Paquette, "heaven has brought you here among us, my poor child! Do you realize that you have cost me the end of my nose, an eye, and an ear? And look what's become of you! Ah, what a world this is!" This new event provoked them to philosophize more than ever.

In the neighborhood there was a very famous dervish who was thought to be the best philosopher in Turkey. They went to consult him. Pangloss

---

135. The heads of those executed at a distance were indeed brought to the sultan stuffed with straw: de Guer, *Moeurs et usages des Turcs* (1746).

136. Voltaire often expresses his horror of boredom—e.g., *Essai sur les moeurs*, ch. 193: "boredom which, throughout the world, is life's mortal enemy."

spoke for them and said, "Master, we come to beg you to tell us why such a strange creature as man was created?"

"What's it to do with you?" said the dervish. "Is it any business of yours?" "But, Reverend Father," said Candide, "there is a terrible amount of evil on earth." "What does it matter whether there is evil or good on earth? When His Highness sends a vessel to Egypt, does he worry whether the rats who are on the ship are comfortable or not?" "So what should one do?" asked Pangloss. "Keep quiet," said the dervish. "I was hoping," said Pangloss, "to philosophize a little with you about effects and causes, about the best of all possible worlds, about the origin of evil, about the nature of the soul, about the preestablished harmony." On hearing this the dervish closed his door in their faces.

While they were talking, news had got about that in Constantinople they had just strangled two members of the Supreme Court and the highest authority in matters of religion, and that they had impaled several of their allies. This catastrophe was much talked about everywhere, at least for a few hours. Pangloss, Candide, and Martin, on their way back to their small farm, met an old man who was catching the breeze, sitting outside his front door in the shade of some orange trees that had been trained into an arch. Pangloss, who was as inquisitive as he was argumentative, asked him the name of the religious leader who had just been strangled. "I have no idea," replied the good man, "and I have never known the name of a single religious leader, or a single member of the Supreme Court. I know nothing of the event you're talking about. I presume that, as a general principle, people who involve themselves in politics sometimes die miserably, and deserve to do so; but I never find out what is going on in Constantinople. I am content to send the fruits of the land I cultivate there for sale." Having said these words he invited the strangers into his house. His two daughters and his two sons served them a variety of flavors of homemade sorbet, Turkish delight studded with roasted pine nuts, oranges, lemons, limes, pineapples, Mocha coffee that was not adulterated with the inferior coffee from Indonesia and the East Indies. After which the two girls of this good Muslim scented the beards of Candide, Pangloss, and Martin.

"You must have," said Candide to the Turk, "a vast and magnificent estate?" "I only have twenty acres," replied the Turk. "I cultivate them with my children. Works keep at bay three dreadful evils: boredom, depravity, and poverty."

Candide, back on his little farm, thought hard about what the Turk had said. He said to Pangloss and to Martin: "That old man seems to me to have made for himself a destiny that is much better than that of the six kings with whom we had the honor of dining." "Titles," said Pangloss, "are very dangerous, as all philosophers agree. For consider, Eglon king of

the Moabites was assassinated by Ehud; Absalom was hanged by his hair
and stabbed with three javelins; King Nadab, son of Jeroboam, was killed
by Baasha; King Elah by Zimri; Ahaziah by Jehu; Athaliah by Jehoiada;
kings Jehoiakim, Jeconiah, Zedekiah were enslaved.[137] You know how
Croesus, Astyages, Darius, Dionysius of Syracuse, Pyrrhus, Perseus,
Hannibal, Jugurtha, Ariovistus, Caesar, Pompey, Nero, Otho, Vitellius,
Domitian,[138] Richard II of England, Edward II, Henry VI, Richard III,
Mary Stuart, Charles I,[139] the three Henris of France, the Emperor Henry
IV died? You know . . ." "I also know," said Candide, "that we must work
our land." "You are right," said Pangloss, "for when human beings were
placed in the Garden of Eden they were put there *ut operaretur eum*,[140] so
that they might work. Which proves that man is not born for a life of
leisure." "Let us work without philosophizing," said Martin, "it is the
only way to make life bearable."

All the members of the little community joined in this praiseworthy
plan; each one made an effort to make use of their abilities. The little farm
proved highly productive. Cunégonde was, in truth, very ugly; but she
became an excellent pastry chef; Paquette embroidered; the old woman
washed clothes. Everyone, even brother Giroflée, did something useful—
he was a very good carpenter, and even became a hard worker. Sometimes
Pangloss said to Candide, "All events are linked together in this, the best
of all possible worlds; for after all, if you had not been driven out of a
beautiful castle, with hefty kicks on your backside, because you loved Miss
Cunégonde, if you had not been arrested by the Inquisition, if you had not
crossed America on foot, if you had not thrust your sword through the
baron, if you had not lost all the sheep you had obtained in the good land
of El Dorado, you would not be sitting here eating roasted pine nuts and
pistachios." "That's well said," replied Candide, "but we must work our
land."[141]

CHAPTER TWENTY-TWO: *The first version (from the manuscript)*

Candide did not stay in Bordeaux any longer than was necessary to get
hold of a good two-seater for his philosopher Martin and himself. He was

---

137. These are all from the Old Testament.

138. These are from the history of Greece and Rome.

139. These are from English history.

140. Genesis 2:15.

141. "*Il faut cultiver notre jardin.*" The meaning of this phrase has been much
discussed. See in particular Murray, *Voltaire's "Candide,"* ch. 1; Patrick Henry,
"Sacred and Profane Gardens in *Candide,*" *SV* 176 (1979), 133–52; David Langdon, "On the Meanings of the Conclusion of *Candide, SV* 238 (1985), 397–432.

very distressed to have to part from his sheep, which he donated to the Scientific Academy of Bordeaux. However all the travelers that Candide met in the inns along the road said to him, "We're going to Paris." This general eagerness finally gave him a desire to see the capital himself; it didn't involve much of a detour from the road to Venice.

He entered by the suburb of Saint Marceau, and for all he could tell he was in one of the most poverty-stricken villages in Westphalia. A moment later he passed near to a cemetery. There were cries and horrible howlings; one would have thought that all the dead had been revived to play a part in this dreadful Sabbat. He saw little girls, abbots, traveling salesmen, sacristans, old women who howled, who gnashed their teeth, who rolled on the ground, who leaped in the air, who sang psalms, who shook, and who drooled while crying out: "A miracle! A miracle!"[142]

"Ah! Good God!" said Candide to Martin, "is this what the capital of a great kingdom is like? What a difference there is between this sewer and the city of El Dorado."

They had not walked a hundred yards when they were obstructed by a crowd of people who were crying out even more loudly than the first mob, surrounding a dozen biers each covered with black cloth, and each with a stoup of holy water at the foot. Candide and Martin asked what was the cause of this tumult. A respectable chap from the neighborhood said to them, "Gentlemen, do you not know about the tax that has recently been imposed upon the dead?" Candide swore to him that he knew nothing about the affairs of either the dead or the living in this wretched city; that he was a foreigner; that he had just arrived; and that he planned to leave without delay.

"Alas, sir," said the good man, "for some months now they have been giving to the dying certificates that must be handed in to the gatekeeper at the next world. Every person at the point of death must sign, and if they do not sign they are not buried. Here are twelve who are being refused burial. The result is going to be that plague will spread through the city."

The postilion who was driving the two travelers had great difficulty in getting through the crowds. He had scarcely reached a crossroads nearby, which stank a thousand times worse than all the local dead, when a shouting crowd suddenly appeared. People were running up from every direction without knowing where they were going. They were crying, "Catch the killer." Everybody came out of the houses. People screamed. A thousand voices asked Candide and Martin, "Have you come from the court? Is he arrested? Has he revealed his accomplices?" Candide and

---

142. The Jansenists claimed that miracles took place at the tomb of the archdeacon of Paris (d. 1727). In order to halt the "convulsions" of believers, access to the tomb was blocked after 1732, so at this point time appears to be telescoped.

Martin learned in the end, with much difficulty, that someone had just committed a shocking outrage, a crime unheard of in any one of twenty other countries, an assassination that made everyone shudder and weep.[143] A whole hour went by before they could reach a barely respectable hotel. There they were given dinner.

Seated with them was a little abbot from Périgord. He was one of those people who watch out for foreigners who are passing through, offer to show them around, and offer to run errands for them. This chap told them all the news. He advised them to stay in Paris for a long time; he told them about all the Parisian scandals, and finally he promised Candide he would get him the first actress who took his fancy.

Candide was appropriately grateful for these kind offers; but he confessed to him that he could not accept them because he had to go to Venice to meet Miss Cunégonde. The Périgordian was slippery and little by little persuaded him to tell the story of his adventures with this illustrious Westphalian. "I believe," said the abbot. . . .

VOLTAIRE'S LETTER OF 1 APRIL 1759 TO THE *JOURNAL ENCYCLOPÉDIQUE*[144]

Sirs,

You say in the issue of your journal for the month of March that some sort of little novel called *Optimism* or *Candide* is attributed to someone called M. de V. . . . I do not know which M. de V. . . . you have in mind, but I assure you that this little book is by my brother M. Démad, presently captain in the Brunswick Regiment; and with regard to the supposed kingdom of the Jesuits in Paraguay, which you describe as a miserable myth, I declare to you, with all Europe as my witness, that there is no room for doubt in this matter at all. I served on one of the Spanish ships sent to Buenos Aires in 1756 to subdue the neighboring colony of Sacramento; I spent three months at Asunción; the Jesuits have, to my personal knowledge, twenty-nine provinces, which they call their Reductions, and in them they are the absolute masters as a result of their paying the governor of Buenos Aires eight reales for the head of each family, and even then they only pay the tax on a third of their territories. They do not permit any Spaniard to remain more than three days in their Reductions. They have never permitted their subjects to learn Spanish. It is they alone who

---

143. I.e., Damiens' attempt on the life of Louis XV, 5 Jan. 1757.

144. Voltaire was replying to a review that had appeared on 15 March 1759. His response was not published until 15 July 1762, but was apparently written in the spring of 1759 (the date of 1 April identifies it as an April Fool).

instruct the Paraguayans in the bearing of arms, and they alone who provide their officers. The Jesuit Tomas Verle, a native of Bavaria, was killed in the attack on the town of Sacramento, in leading the assault at the head of a Paraguayan army. This was in 1737 and not 1735, as is claimed by the Jesuit author Charlevoix, an author as boring as he is ill informed.[145] It is generally known that they undertook a war against Don Antequera; everyone knows what it was that they were recently plotting against the crown of Portugal,[146] and that they have defied the order of the Council of Madrid.[147]

They are so powerful that they obtained from Philip V, in 1743, a confirmation of their powers that it has been impossible to take away from them. I know, of course, sirs, that they do not have the title of king, and you can take advantage of that fact to justify what you say about the miserable myth of the kingdom of Paraguay. But the dey of Algiers is not a king, and is nonetheless the ruler. I would not advise my brother the captain to travel to Paraguay unless he had the capacity to fight.

As for the rest, sirs, I have the honor to inform you that my brother the captain, who is the *loustik*[148] of the regiment, is a very good Christian, who wrote the novel Candide to amuse himself when the army was in its winter quarters. His main purpose was to convert the Socinians. These heretics do not think it sufficient to deny openly the Trinity and eternal damnation. They say that God has of necessity made our world the best of all possible worlds, and that all is well. This theory is manifestly contrary to the doctrine of original sin. These innovators forget that the serpent, who was the most subtle of beasts, seduced the woman, who had been made out of Adam's rib; that Adam ate the forbidden apple; that God cursed the earth that he had previously blessed: *Maledicta terra in opere tuo; in laboribus comedes.*[149] Do they not know that all the Church Fathers without a single exception based the Christian religion on this curse pronounced by God himself, a curse whose effects we feel at every moment? The Socinians pretend to have a more elevated conception of Providence, and they do not see that we are guilty and are tortured for it, and that we ought to acknowledge our sins and our punishment. Let these heretics take care not to appear in front of my brother the captain: he'll show them if everything is well.

---

145. Charlevoix, *Histoire du Paraguay* (1756).

146. The attempted assassination of 3 Sept. 1758.

147. Which was obliged, under a treaty with Portugal of 1750, to transfer part of Paraguay to the Portuguese.

148. A buffoon.

149. Genesis 3:17–9.

I am, sirs, your very humble and obedient servant,

Démad

From Zastrou, 1 April 1759

P.S. My brother the captain is a close friend of Mr. Ralph, a fairly well known professor in the Academy of Frankfurt-on-Oder. Mr. Ralph gave him a lot of help in writing this profound work of philosophy, and my brother was so modest as to entitle it a translation from the work of Mr. Ralph. Such modesty is rare among authors.

Leibniz, "Metaphysics Summarized"[1]

1. There is a reason in the nature of things why something exists rather than nothing. It is a consequence of that great principle that nothing occurs without a reason, and also of the principle that there must be a reason why one thing occurs rather than another.

2. That reason must be in some real entity or cause. For a cause is simply a real reason; and truths about possibilities and necessities (or of cases where the impossibility of the opposite has been demonstrated) would have no effect unless possibilities were grounded in something that actually exists.

3. This real entity must be necessary, otherwise yet another cause must be sought outside it to explain why it exists rather than does not exist, which is contrary to the hypothesis. This entity is the ultimate reason for the existence of things, and is usually referred to by a single word, "God."

4. There is therefore a cause that explains why existence occurs at the expense of nonexistence, which is to say that the necessary entity is existence creating.

5. But the cause that ensures that something exists, or that the possibility of existence must be realized, also ensures that everything that is possible seeks to come into existence, for no reason can be found why existence should be restricted to certain possibilities among all the possible existences.

6. And so it can be said that everything that can exist must exist, inasmuch as existence is grounded in a necessary entity that actually exists, without which there is no way in which the possible could become the actual.

7. But it does not follow from this that all possibilities must become realities, though this would follow if the existence of all possibilities were compatible with the existence of all other possibilities.

8. But since some things are incompatible with other things, it follows that certain possibilities cannot come into existence. Moreover it is not simply the case that there are certain things that cannot exist at the same time as certain other things, but that if certain things exist others cannot exist at any time, because future events are determined by present ones.

9. Meanwhile out of the conflict of all the possibilities that are seeking

---

1. Written c. 1697, this brief summary of Leibniz's metaphysics, here translated from the Latin, was first published in 1903. It summarizes the argument of his *Théodicée* (1710), the only work published during Leibniz's lifetime.

to come into existence this at least follows, that there comes into existence that series of things that enables the greatest number of things to exist, or the largest of all possible series.

10. This series is the only one that is determinate, just as among lines only the straight line is determinate, and among angles only the right angle is determinate, and among shapes only the most capacious is determinate, whether it be the circle or the sphere. And so just as we see liquids spontaneously and naturally collect into spherical drops, so it is in the nature of the universe that the most capacious series should exist.

11. That which exists, therefore, is that which is most perfect, since perfection is nothing other than the quantity of reality.

12. Moreover perfection is not to be located in matter alone—that is, in something that fills time and space—for the quantity of that would have been the same no matter what, but is to be located in form or variety.

13. So now it follows that matter is not everywhere alike, but is rendered dissimilar by its forms; otherwise it would not achieve as much variety as it could. I won't go into something that I have demonstrated elsewhere: that otherwise no diversity of phenomena would occur.

14. It also follows that that series has won out through which there occurs the greatest amount of that which is distinctly conceptualizable.

15. Distinct conceptualizability gives order to a thing and gives beauty to the thinker. For order is nothing other than a distinct relation of several things; and confusion exists when several things are present, but there is no logic for distinguishing them from each other.

16. This eliminates atoms, and all those bodies with regard to which there is no logic for distinguishing one part from another.

17. And it follows as a principle to which there can be no exceptions that the world is a *cosmos*, ornamented through and through; in other words that it is constructed in such a way as to give the maximum satisfaction to an intelligent being.

18. Pleasure for an intelligent being is nothing other than the perception of beauty, of order, of perfection. And all pain contains some element of disorder, though only relative to the being experiencing pain, for in absolute terms everything is ordered.

19. And so when something in the series of existing things displeases us, that occurs because of a defect in our understanding. For it is not possible that every mind should understand everything distinctly. Since we observe only some parts and not others, the harmony of the whole cannot be apparent to us.

20. From the above it follows that justice is observed in the universe, for justice is nothing other than order or perfection with regard to minds.

21. And priority is always given to minds, since through them one achieves the greatest variety in the smallest space.

22. So it can be said that minds are the primary existences in the universe, and most closely resemble the first Being, for they distinctly perceive necessary truths, that is, the reasons that must have acted on the first Being and shaped the universe.

23. Moreover the first cause is of the highest goodness, for at one and the same time it produces as much perfection as possible in things and it bestows as much pleasure as possible on minds, for pleasure consists in the perception of perfection.

24. So much so, that evils themselves serve the greater good, and minds only experience pain because it is necessary for them to do so if they are to attain greater pleasures.

POPE, *ESSAY ON MAN* (1733–34) [SELECTIONS]

Epistle I
[lines 1–172, 280–94]

Argument of the First Epistle:
Of the nature and state of man with
respect to the universe.

Of Man in the abstract. 1. That we can judge only with regard to our own system, being ignorant of the relations of systems and things, verse 17, etc. 2. That Man is not to be deemed imperfect, but a being suited to his place and rank in the creation, agreeable to the general order of things, and conformable to ends and relations to him unknown, verse 35, etc. 3. That it is partly upon his ignorance of future events, and partly upon the hope of a future state, that all his happiness in the present depends, verse 77, etc. 4. The pride of aiming at more knowledge, and pretending to more perfection, the cause of man's error and misery. The impiety of putting himself in the place of God, and judging of the fitness or unfitness, perfection or imperfection, justice or injustice of his dispensations, verse 113, etc. 5. The absurdity of conceiting himself the final cause of the creation, or expecting that perfection in the moral world, which is not in the natural, verse 131, etc. . . . 10. The consequence of all, the absolute submission due to Providence, both as to our present and future state, verse 281, etc. to the end.

Awake, my St. John![1] leave all meaner things
To low ambition and the pride of kings.
Let us (since life can little more supply

---

1. Henry Saint-John (pronounced "Singen"), Viscount Bolingbroke.

Than just to look about us, and to die)
Expatiate free o'er all this scene of man;
A mighty maze! but not without a plan:
A wild where weeds and flowers promiscuous shoot;
Or garden, tempting with forbidden fruit.
Together let us beat this ample field,
Try what the open, what the covert yield![2]
The latent tracts, the giddy heights explore
Of all who blindly creep, or sightless soar;
Eye Nature's walks, shoot folly as it flies,
And catch the manners living as they rise:
Laugh where we must, be candid where we can;
But vindicate the ways of God to man.

1. Say first, of God above, or man below,
What can we reason, but from what we know?
Of man, what see we but his station here,
From which to reason, or to which refer?
Through worlds unnumbered, though the God be known,
'Tis ours to trace Him only in our own.
He, who through vast immensity can pierce,
See worlds on worlds compose one universe,
Observe how system into system runs,
What other planets circle other suns,
What varied beings people every star,
May tell why Heaven has made us as we are.
But of this frame the bearings and the ties,
The strong connections, nice dependencies,
Gradations just, has thy pervading soul
Look'd through? or can a part contain the whole?
  Is the great chain, that draws all to agree,
And drawn, supports, upheld by God or thee?

2. Presumptuous man! the reason wouldst thou find,
Why form'd so weak, so little, and so blind?
First, if thou canst, the harder reason guess,
Why form'd no weaker, blinder, and no less?
Ask of thy mother earth, why oaks are made
Taller and stronger than the weeds they shade?
Or ask of yonder argent fields above,
Why Jove's satellites are less than Jove?
  Of systems possible, if 'tis confess'd,

---

2. I.e., go through the woods and fields driving game into the open.

That Wisdom infinite must form the best,
Where all must fall, or not coherent be,
And all that rises, rise in due degree;
Then in the scale of reas'ning life, 'tis plain,
There must be, somewhere, such a rank as man:
And all the question (wrangle e'er so long)
Is only this, if God has placed him wrong?
    Respecting man, whatever wrong we call,
May, must be right, as relative to all.
In human works, though labor'd on with pain,
A thousand movements scarce one purpose gain;
In God's, one single can its end produce;
Yet serves to second too, some other use.
So man, who here seems principal alone,
Perhaps acts second to some sphere unknown,
Touches some wheel, or verges to some goal;
'Tis but a part we see, and not a whole.
    When the proud steed shall know why man restrains
His fiery course, or drives him o'er the plains;
When the dull ox, why now he breaks the clod,
Is now a victim, and now Egypt's god:
Then shall man's pride and dullness comprehend
His actions', passions', being's use and end;
Why doing, suff'ring, check'd, impell'd; and why
This hour a slave, the next a deity.
    Then say not man's imperfect, Heaven in fault;
Say rather, man's as perfect as he ought:
His knowledge measured to his state and place;
His time a moment, and a point his space.
If to be perfect in a certain sphere,
What matter, soon or late, or here or there?
The blest today is as completely so,
As who began a thousand years ago.
3.   Heaven from all creatures hides the book of Fate,
All but the page prescribed, their present state:
From brutes what men, from men what spirits know:
Or who could suffer being here below?
The lamb thy riot dooms to bleed to-day,
Had he thy reason, would he skip and play?
Pleased to the last, he crops the flowery food,
And licks the hand just raised to shed his blood.
Oh blindness to the future! kindly given,

That each may fill the circle mark'd by Heaven:
Who sees with equal eye, as God of all,
A hero perish, or a sparrow fall,
Atoms or systems into ruin hurl'd,
And now a bubble burst, and now a world.
   Hope humbly then; with trembling pinions soar;
Wait the great teacher, Death; and God adore.
What future bliss, He gives not thee to know,
But gives that hope to be thy blessing now.
Hope springs eternal in the human breast:
Man never Is, but always To Be blest.
The soul, uneasy and confined from home,
Rests and expatiates in a life to come.
   Lo, the poor Indian! whose untutor'd mind
Sees God in clouds, or hears Him in the wind;
His soul, proud Science never taught to stray
Far as the solar-walk or milky-way;
Yet simple Nature to his hope has given,
Behind the cloud-topp'd hill, and humbler Heaven,
Some safer world in depth of woods embraced,
Some happier island in the watery waste,
Where slaves once more their native land behold,
No fiends torment, no Christians thirst for gold.
To Be, contents his natural desire,
He asks no angel's wings, no seraph's fire;
But thinks, admitted to that equal sky,
His faithful dog shall bear him company.
4.   Go, wiser thou! and in thy scale of sense,
Weigh thy opinion against Providence;
Call imperfection what thou fanciest such,
Say, here He gives too little, there too much:
Destroy all creatures for thy sport or gust,
Yet cry, "If man's unhappy, God's unjust";
If man alone engross not Heaven's high care,
Alone made perfect here, immortal there:
Snatch from His hand the balance and the rod,
Re-judge His justice, be the god of God.
   In pride, in reas'ning pride, our error lies;
All quit their sphere, and rush into the skies.
Pride still is aiming at the blest abodes,
Men would be angels, angels would be gods.
Aspiring to be gods, if angels fell,

Aspiring to be angels, men rebel:
And who but wishes to invert the law
Of Order, sins against the Eternal Cause.

5.   Ask for what end the Heavenly bodies shine—
Earth for whose use? Pride answers, "'Tis for mine:
For me kind Nature wakes her genial power,
Suckles each herb, and spreads out ev'ry flower;
Annual for me, the grape, the rose renew,
The juice nectareous, and the balmy dew;
For me, the mine a thousand treasures brings;
For me, health gushes from a thousand springs;
Seas roll to waft me, suns to light me rise;
My footstool earth, my canopy the skies."
      But errs not Nature from this gracious end,
From burning suns when livid deaths descend,
When earthquakes swallow, or when tempests sweep
Towns to one grave, whole nations to the deep?
"No," 'tis replied, "the first Almighty Cause
Acts not by partial, but by gen'ral laws;
The exceptions few: some change since all began:
And what created perfect?"—Why then man?
If the great end be human happiness,
Then Nature deviates; and can man do less?
As much that end a constant course requires
Of showers and sunshine, as of man's desires;
As much eternal springs and cloudless skies,
As men for ever temperate, calm, and wise.
If plagues or earthquakes break not Heaven's design,
Why then a Borgia, or a Catiline?[3]
Who knows but He, whose hand the lightning forms,
Who heaves old Ocean, and who wings the storms;
Pours fierce ambition in a Caesar's mind,
Or turns young Ammon[4] loose to scourge mankind?
From pride, from pride, our very reas'ning springs;
Account for moral as for natural things:
Why charge we Heaven in those, in these acquit?
In both, to reason right, is to submit.

---

3. Cesare Borgia, a papal nephew and military adventurer of the early sixteenth
century, was praised by Machiavelli; Catiline led an attempted rebellion in classical
Rome and was prosecuted by Cicero. They serve as exemplars of unscrupulous and
bloodthirsty evil in politics.

4. Alexander the Great, who claimed to be the son of the God Ammon.

Better for us, perhaps, it might appear,
Were there all harmony, all virtue here;
That never air or ocean felt the wind,
That never passion discomposed the mind.
But all subsists by elemental strife;
And passions are the elements of life.
The general order, since the whole began,
Is kept by Nature, and is kept in man.
10.   Cease then, nor order imperfection name:
Our proper bliss depends on what we blame.
Know thy own point: this kind, this due degree
Of blindness, weakness, Heaven bestows on thee.
Submit, in this, or any other sphere,
Secure to be as blest as thou canst bear:
Safe in the hand of one Disposing Power,
Or in the natal, or the mortal hour.
All Nature is but art, unknown to thee
All chance, direction, which thou canst not see;
All discord, harmony not understood;
All partial evil, universal good:
And, spite of pride, in erring reason's spite,
One truth is clear, Whatever is, is right.

Epistle IV
[lines 111–204]

Argument of the Fourth Epistle:
Of the nature and state of Man,
with respect to happiness.

. . . 4. The folly of expecting that God should alter his general laws in favor of particulars, verse 111, etc. 5. That we are not judges who are good; but whoever they are, they must be happiest, verse 131, etc. 6. That external goods are not the proper rewards, but often inconsistent with, or destructive of virtue, verse 167. That even these can make no man happy without virtue: Instanced in riches, verse 185; honors, verse 193. . .

   . . .

4.   What makes all physical or moral ill?
There deviates nature, and here wanders will.
God sends not ill, if rightly understood;
Or partial ill is universal good,
Or change admits, or nature lets it fall,
Short, and but rare, 'till man improved it all.
We just as wisely might of heaven complain

That righteous Abel was destroy'd by Cain,
As that the virtuous son is ill at ease
When his lewd father gave the dire disease.
Think we, like some weak prince, the Eternal Cause
Prone for His favorites to reverse His laws?
    Shall burning Ætna, if a sage requires,
Forget to thunder, and recall her fires?
On air or sea new motions be impress'd,
Oh blameless Bethel! to relieve thy breast?[5]
When the loose mountain trembles from on high,
Shall gravitation cease if you go by?
Or some old temple, nodding to its fall,
For Chartres' head reserve the hanging wall?
5.   But still this world (so fitted for the knave)
Contents us not. A better shall we have?
A kingdom of the just then let it be:
But first consider how those just agree.
The good must merit God's peculiar care!
But who but God can tell us who they are?
One thinks on Calvin Heaven's own spirit fell,
Another deems him instrument of hell;
If Calvin feel Heaven's blessing, or its rod,
This cries, "There is", and that "There is no God."
What shocks one part will edify the rest,
Nor with one system can they all be blest.
The very best will variously incline,
And what rewards your virtue, punish mine.
"Whatever is, is right."—This world, 'tis true,
Was made for Caesar—but for Titus too;[6]
And which more blest? who chain'd his country, say,
Or he whose virtue sigh'd to lose a day?
    "But sometimes virtue starves, while vice is fed."
What then? is the reward of virtue bread?
That, vice may merit, 'tis the price of toil;
The knave deserves it, when he tills the soil,
The knave deserves it, when he tempts the main,[7]
Where folly fights for kings, or dives for gain.
The good man may be weak, be indolent;
Nor is his claim to plenty, but content.

---

5. Hugh Bethel, a friend of Pope's, suffered from asthma.

6. Titus, emperor of Rome, who stands as an exemplar of virtue.

7. When he braves the ocean . . .

But grant him riches, your demand is o'er?
"No—shall the good want health, the good want power?"
Add health and power, and every earthly thing,
"Why bounded power? why private? why no king?"
Nay, why external for internal given?
Why is not man a god, and earth a heaven?
Who ask and reason thus will scarce conceive
God gives enough while He has more to give;
Immense the power, immense were the demand;
Say, at what part of nature will they stand?

6. What nothing earthly gives, or can destroy,
The soul's calm sunshine, and the heartfelt joy,
Is virtue's prize: a better would you fix?
Then give humility a coach and six,
Justice a conqueror's sword, or truth a gown,
Or public spirit its great cure, a crown.
Well, foolish man! Will Heaven reward us there
With the same trash mad mortals wish for here?
The boy and man an individual makes,
Yet sighs't thou now for apples and for cakes?
Go, like the Indian, in another life,
Expect thy dog, thy bottle, and thy wife;
As well as dream such trifles are assign'd,
As toys and empires, for a godlike mind.
Rewards, that either would to virtue bring
No joy, or be destructive of the thing:
How oft by these at sixty are undone
The virtues of a saint at twenty-one!

  To whom can riches give repute, or trust,
Content, or pleasure, but the good and just?
Judges and senates have been bought for gold,
Esteem and love were never to be sold.
O fool! to think God hates the worthy mind,
The lover and the love of human kind,
Whose life is healthful, and whose conscience clear,
Because he wants a thousand pounds a year.

  Honor and shame from no condition rise:
Act well your part; there all the honor lies.
Fortune in men has some small difference made,
One flaunts in rags, one flutters in brocade;
The cobbler apron'd, and the parson gown'd,
The friar hooded, and the monarch crown'd.
"What differs more," you cry, "than crown and cowl?"

I'll tell you, friend! a wise man and a fool.
You'll find, if once the monarch acts the monk,
Or, cobbler-like the parson will be drunk,
Worth makes the man, and want of it the fellow:
The rest is all but leather or prunella.[8]

8. A strong fabric used to make shoes.

The Lisbon Earthquake:
Rousseau versus Voltaire

Preface to the "Poem on the Lisbon Disaster" (1756)[1]

If the question of physical evil has ever deserved the attention of all human beings, it is when these dreadful events occur, events that call us back to the contemplation of our feeble nature, events like the great plagues that killed off one quarter of the population of the known world, the earthquake that swallowed up four hundred thousand people in China in 1699, those that happened in Lima and in Callao, and finally the earthquake in Portugal and in the kingdom of Fez. The axiom that "All is well" seems a little odd to those who witness these disasters. All is arranged, all is organized, doubtless, by Providence; but it is only too apparent that All, for a long time now, is not arranged for our present welfare.

When the illustrious Pope published his *Essay on Man,* and developed in poetry that will endure forever the systems of Leibniz, of Lord Shaftesbury,* and of Lord Bolingbroke, a crowd of theologians from every

---

1. The footnote marked by an asterisk is Voltaire's own. In this note I have substituted Shaftesbury's own words for Voltaire's translation of Shaftesbury. The same passage recurs below, p. 140.

*This is perhaps the first time that anyone has said that Pope's system was the same as Lord Shaftesbury's, yet this is an indisputable truth. The whole of the discussion of physical nature is drawn almost word for word from the chapter entitled "The Moralists," section 3: "Much is alleged in answer to show why Nature errs, and how she came thus impotent and erring from an unerring hand. But I deny she errs. . . . the world's beauty [is] founded thus on contrarieties, whilst from such various and disagreeing principles a universal concord is established. Thus in the several orders of terrestrial forms a resignation is required, a sacrifice and mutual yielding of natures one to another. The vegetables by their death sustain the animals, and animal bodies dissolved enrich the earth, and raise again the vegetable world. . . . The central powers, which hold the lasting orbs in their just poise and movement, must not be controlled to save a fleeting form, and rescue from the precipice a puny animal, whose brittle frame, however protected, must of itself so soon dissolve."

This is admirably said; but that doesn't mean the illustrious Dr. Clarke, in his treatise on the existence of God, can't write that "the human race finds itself in a situation where the natural order of things in this world is manifestly turned upside down" (2nd ed., vol. 2, p. 10, translated by M. Ricotier). That doesn't mean human beings can't say, "I, a thinking and feeling creature, ought to be as dear to my master as the planets, who in all probability have no feelings." That doesn't mean that it would be impossible for this world to be different, for we are taught that the natural order has been perverted, and that it will be reestablished; that doesn't mean that physical evil and moral evil are things that cannot be understood by the human intellect; that doesn't mean that we cannot question the saying that "All is well," while showing respect for Shaftesbury and Pope, whose system was at first attacked as being tainted with

type of Christianity attacked his system. There was a revolt against this new principle that "All is well," that "Man enjoys all the happiness of which his constitution is capable," etc. There is always a way of reading a book that justifies condemning it, and another way of reading it that justifies defending it. It would be much more reasonable to pay attention

---

atheism, and nowadays is canonized.

The whole of the discussion of morality in Pope's *Essay on Man* is also in Shaftesbury, in the chapter on the quest for virtue, in the second volume of the *Characteristics*. It is there that the author says that the interest of the individual, properly understood, coincides with the public interest: "To be well affected toward the public interest and one's own, is not only consistent but inseparable." That's what he proves throughout his book, and that's the basis of the section on morality in Pope's *Essay on Man*. That's why Pope finishes with the lines:

That reason, passion, answer one great aim,
That true self-love and social be the same.

Such a fine moral theory, which is much better developed in Pope than it is in Shaftesbury, has always been attractive to the author of the poems "On Lisbon" and "On the Law of Nature" [i.e., Voltaire]. That's why he says [in the poem "On the Law of Nature"], "But Pope develops the arguments they sketched, and in his work man learns to know himself." Lord Shaftesbury also proves that "perfection of virtue must be owing to the belief of a God."

It is apparently on the basis of these words that some people have accused Shaftesbury of being an atheist. If they had read his book with care, they would not have made this accusation, which brings shame on the memory of an English Lord, of a philosopher who was educated by the wise Locke.

This is how Father Hardouin manages to accuse Pascal, Malebranche, and Arnauld of atheism; this is how Dr. Lange manages to accuse the respectable Wolff of atheism because he praised the moral philosophy of the Chinese; and when Wolff appealed to the testimony of the Jesuit missionaries in China, the doctor replied, "Doesn't he realize that the Jesuits are atheists?" Those who expressed horror at the whole story of the Devils of Loudun, which was so humiliating for anyone who takes pride in mankind's rational capacities, those who thought it was wrong for a friar, while taking Urbain Grandier to be executed, to strike him in the face with a metal crucifix, were called atheists by the friars. The Jansenists who had convulsions have said in print that those who mocked their convulsions were atheists; and the followers of Molina have called the Jansenists atheists on a hundred occasions.

When a man who is now well known [i.e., Voltaire himself] was the first to write in France, more than thirty years ago, on the subject of inoculation against smallpox, an unknown author wrote, "Only an atheist who has been led astray by English nonsense could propose that our nation should do certain harm in the hope of an uncertain benefit."

The author of the *Nouvelles ecclésiastiques,* who has been calmly writing for so long in opposition to law and reason, has devoted a series of pages to proving that M. de Montesquieu was an atheist, and another series of pages to proving that he was a deist.

Saint-Sorlin Desmarets, known in his own day for his poem *Clovis* and for his religious fanaticism, one day saw La-Mothe-Le-Vayer, councilor of state and tutor to the king's eldest son, pass by in the Louvre's gallery. "There," he said, "is a man who

only to the useful beauties to be found in a book than to try and find in it an objectionable meaning; but it is one of the imperfections of human nature that we put an unfavorable interpretation on anything that is open to such a reading, and that we want to attack anything that has met with success.

So people thought they could discover in the proposition that "All is well" a direct attack on a number of accepted beliefs. "If all is well," they said, "then it is false that human nature has been corrupted by sin. If the general order of things requires that everything should be as it is, then human nature has not been corrupted; and it follows that we are not in need of a redeemer. If this world, just as it is, is the best of all possible worlds, then one cannot hope for a better in the future. If all the ills that trouble us are aspects of a general good, then all civilized societies have been mistaken when they have sought the origins of physical evil and of moral evil. If a person who is eaten by savage beasts brings about the welfare of these beasts and contributes to the ordering of the world, if the miseries of individuals are nothing but the consequence of this general and necessary order, then we are nothing but cogs that make a great machine work; we are no more precious in the eyes of God than the animals that eat us."

These are the conclusions that people drew from Mr. Pope's poem; and these very conclusions increased the notoriety and the sales of his book. But he ought to have been read in a different way. People ought to have considered that the very heart of this excellent book lay in its emphasis on the respect we owe to God, on the resignation we should show in face of his supreme commands, on a healthy morality, on tolerance. This is how the public read it; and this work, having been translated by men worthy of their undertaking, triumphed over its critics, and its triumph was the greater the more they raised delicate issues.

It is the characteristic of violent attacks that they give credibility to the opinions that they seek to destroy. People protest against a book because it is successful; they claim that it contains false teachings. What happens? People revolt against these protests, and decide to accept as truths the very errors that the critics claimed to be able to identify. Critics conjure up

---

has no religion." La-Mothe-Le-Vayer turned back to him and condescended to say to him, "My friend, I have enough religious conviction to ensure that your religion isn't mine."

In general, this ridiculous and abominable mania for accusing of atheism without rhyme or reason all those who do not think as we do has contributed more than anything else to the development, from one end of Europe to another, of the profound contempt that the whole reading public has these days for books of [religious] controversy.

phantoms in order to attack them, and readers, indignant at these attacks, embrace these phantoms with open arms.

The critics said, "Leibniz and Pope teach fatalism"; and the supporters of Leibniz and Pope reply, "If Leibniz and Pope teach fatalism, then they must be right, and we must believe that our destiny is unalterable."

Pope said, "All is well," giving the phrase a meaning that was entirely acceptable; and his supporters now say it, giving it a meaning that deserves to be attacked.

The author of the "Poem on the Lisbon Disaster"[2] is not attacking the illustrious Mr. Pope, whom he has always loved and admired.[3] He agrees with him on almost every question; but, acutely aware of the miseries of humankind, he raises his voice against the improper use to which this ancient axiom, "All is well," can be put. He makes his own that dreadful and even more ancient truth, acknowledged by all human beings, that "Evil is loose on the earth." He maintains that the saying "All is well," taken in an absolute sense and without any hope for a future life, is nothing but an insult to the sufferings of our lives.

If, when Lisbon, Mesquinez, Tetuan, and so many other towns were swallowed up in the month of November 1755, philosophers had called out to the miserable individuals who barely managed to pull themselves out of the ruins, "All is well. The heirs of the dead will get rich; the construction workers will make money rebuilding houses; animals will fatten themselves on the bodies buried under the rubble. This is the necessary consequence of inevitable causes; your personal ill fortune is of no account, for you contribute to the overall well-being," such a speech would certainly have been as cruel as the earthquake was destructive. And that's what the author of the "Poem on the Lisbon Disaster" is saying.

He admits, as everyone does, that there is evil to be found on earth as well as good; he admits that no philosopher has ever been able to explain the origins of moral evil and of physical evil; he admits that Bayle, the greatest dialectician who has ever written, has taught us only how to doubt, and that he attacks the very views that he defends; he admits that there are as many weaknesses in our understanding as there are miseries in our lives. He gives an account of all the different systems in the space of a few words. He says that revelation alone is capable of untying this tangled knot, which all the philosophers have only managed to make harder to unpick. He says that the hope of a development of our being within a new order of things[4] can alone provide a consolation for our present miseries, and that the goodness of Providence is the only asylum to which human

2. Voltaire himself.

3. They had, in fact, been friends.

4. I.e., a life after death.

beings can turn for shelter when they stumble through the darkness cast by their reasonings, and are caught up in the calamities of our feeble and mortal nature.

P.S. Unfortunately it is always necessary to warn one's readers that they must distinguish between the objections that an author makes to his own arguments and his replies to those objections, for otherwise they will mistake the views he refutes for the views he holds.

POEM ON THE LISBON DISASTER[5]

An Inquiry into the Maxim,
"Whatever is, is right."

Oh wretched man, earth-fated to be cursed;
Abyss of plagues and miseries the worst!
Horrors on horrors, griefs on griefs must show,
That man's the victim of unceasing woe,
And lamentations which inspire my strain,
Prove that philosophy is false and vain.
Approach in crowds, and meditate awhile
Yon shattered walls, and view each ruined pile,
Women and children heaped up mountain high,
Limbs crushed which under ponderous marble lie;
Wretches unnumbered in the pangs of death,
Who mangled, torn, and panting for their breath,
Buried beneath their sinking roofs expire,
And end their wretched lives in torments dire.
Say, when you hear their piteous, half-formed cries,
Or from their ashes see the smoke arise,
Say, will you the eternal laws maintain,
Which God to cruelties like these constrain?
Whilst you these facts replete with horror view,
Will you maintain death to their crimes was due?
And can you then impute a sinful deed
To babes who on their mothers' bosoms bleed?
Was then more vice in fallen Lisbon found,
Than Paris, where voluptuous joys abound?

5. For the poem I reproduce the translation in Voltaire, *Works*, translated by Tobias Smollett and others (25 vols., London: J. Newbery, 1761–5); the preface and notes are translated by the present editor. Notes marked by asterisks and other symbols are Voltaire's own.

Was less debauchery to London known,
Where opulence luxurious holds her throne?
Earth Lisbon swallows; the light sons of France
Protract the feast, or lead the sprightly dance.
Spectators who undaunted courage show,
While you behold your dying brethren's woe;
With stoical tranquility of mind
You seek the causes of these ills to find;
But when like us Fate's rigors you have felt,
Become humane, like us you'll learn to melt.
When the earth gapes my body to entomb,
I justly may complain of such a doom.
Hemmed round on every side by cruel fate,
The snares of death, the wicked's furious hate,
Preyed on by pain and by corroding grief
Suffer me from complaint to find relief.
'Tis pride, you cry, seditious pride that still
Asserts mankind should be exempt from ill.
The awful truth on Tagus' banks explore,[6]
Rummage the ruins on that bloody shore,
Wretches interred alive in direful grave
Ask if pride cries, "Good Heaven, thy creatures save."[7]
If 'tis presumption that makes mortals cry,
"Heav'n, on our sufferings cast a pitying eye."
All's right, you answer, the eternal cause
Rules not by partial, but by general laws.
Say what advantage can result to all,
From wretched Lisbon's lamentable fall?
Are you then sure, the power which could create
The universe and fix the laws of fate,
Could not have found for man a proper place,
But earthquakes must destroy the human race?
Will you thus limit the eternal mind?
Should not our God to mercy be inclined?
Cannot then God direct all nature's course?
Can power almighty be without resource?
Humbly the great Creator I entreat,
This gulf with sulfur and with fire replete,
Might on the deserts spend its raging flame,
God my respect, my love weak mortals claim;

---

6. The Tagus is the river running through Lisbon.

7. See the references to pride in Pope's *Essay on Man,* above, pp. 88–90.

When man groans under such a load of woe,
He is not proud, he only feels the blow.
Would words like these to peace of mind restore
The natives sad of that disastrous shore?
Grieve not, that others' bliss may overflow,
Your sumptuous palaces are laid thus low;
Your toppled towers shall other hands rebuild;
With multitudes your walls one day be filled;
Your ruin on the North shall wealth bestow,
For general good from partial ills must flow;
You seem as abject to the sovereign power,
As worms which shall your carcasses devour.
No comfort should such shocking words impart,
But deeper wound the sad, afflicted heart.
When I lament my present wretched state,
Allege not the unchanging laws of fate;
Urge not the links of the eternal chain,
'Tis false philosophy and wisdom vain.
The God who holds the chain can't be enchained;*

---

*The great chain of being is not, as has been claimed, an unbroken series that links together all beings. There is probably an immense distance between human beings and animals; between human beings and the creatures superior to them; there is an infinite gap between God and all creatures. The spheres that circle around our sun do not form such an unbroken series, not in their size, nor in their distances, nor in their satellites.

Pope says that human beings cannot know why the moons of Jupiter are smaller than Jupiter herself. On this he is wrong—it's an excusable mistake, an oversight that does not detract from his fine genius. Any mathematician could have explained to Lord Bolingbroke and Mr. Pope that if Jupiter were smaller than its satellites then they would be unable to rotate around it; but there is no mathematician who can discover an unbroken series in the fabric of the solar system.

It is not true that if one removed a single atom from the world, the world could no longer survive; and that's what M. de Crousaz, a distinguished geometer, very acutely pointed out in his book against Mr. Pope. It seems that on this question he was in the right, although on other matters he has been uncontestably refuted by Mr. Warburton and M. Silhouette.

This chain of events has been accepted and very ingeniously defended by a great philosopher, Leibniz. It deserves to be clarified. Every object, every event depends on other objects and other events. That's true. But every object is not necessary to the conservation of the universe, and every event is not necessary to the series of events. A drop of water, a grain of sand more or less can change nothing in the overall scheme of things. Nature is not obliged to respect any particular, exact quantity, nor does matter have to be distributed in any particular, precise form. No planet moves in an orbit that can be perfectly described mathematically; no known object has a shape that corresponds exactly to a mathematical design; no particular, exact quantity is required for any chemical reaction. Nature never depends on absolute precision. So

By His blest will are all events ordained:
He's just, nor easily to wrath gives way,
Why suffer we beneath so mild a sway:†
This is the fatal knot you should untie,
Our evils do you cure when you deny?
Men ever strove into the source to pry,
Of evil, whose existence you deny.
If he whose hand the elements can wield,
To the winds' force makes rocky mountains yield;
If thunder lays oaks level with the plain,
From the bolts' strokes they never suffer pain.
But I can feel, my heart oppressed demands
Aid of that God who formed me with His hands.
Sons of the God supreme to suffer all

---

there's no reason at all to claim that if there was one less atom on earth the whole earth would be destroyed.

It is the same with events. Each of them has its cause in the event which preceded it; this is something that no philosopher has ever questioned. If Caesar's mother hadn't undergone a Caesarian operation, Caesar would not have destroyed the republic, he would not have adopted Octavius, and Octavius would not have left the empire to Tiberius. Maximilian [I, 1459–1519] married the heiress to Burgundy and the Low Countries [in 1477], and this marriage gave rise to two centuries of warfare. But if Caesar had spat to his left or his right; if the heiress of Burgundy had done her hair according to one style or according to another, that would certainly have made no difference to the overall course of events.

Thus there are events that have effects, and others that do not. The chain of events is rather like a genealogical tree; one sees branches that die out after one generation, and others that continue the family. Many events have no descendants. In the same way in any machine there are some effects that are necessary to its functioning, and other effects that are without significance. They are the consequence of the machine's operation, and have no consequences themselves. The wheels of a cart are necessary to make it run; but whether they throw up a bit less or a bit more dust makes no difference to the completion of the journey. The general construction of the world is such that the links in the chain will not be broken if there is a little bit more or less matter, a little bit more or less irregularity.

The chain is not in a space that is entirely filled with matter. It has been demonstrated that the celestial bodies travel through a space that offers no resistance. All of space is not full, and consequently there is not an unbroken succession of bodies from an atom here to the most distant of the stars. Thus there can be immense voids between creatures capable of sensation, as there are between insensible objects. One cannot therefore conclude that human beings are necessarily placed in a chain of causation that connects one to another by a series of links that are unbroken. "Everything is linked in a chain" means only that everything forms part of a pattern. God is the cause and the master of this pattern. Homer's Jupiter was the slave of the fates; but in a more sophisticated philosophy God is master of the fates. See Clarke, *Treatise on the Existence of God* [i.e., The Boyle Lectures of 1704–5].

†"Under a just God, no one suffers unless he deserves to": Saint Augustine.

Fated alike; we on our Father call.
No vessel of the potter asks, we know,
Why it was made so brittle, vile, and low?
Vessels of speech as well as thought are void;
The urn this moment formed and that destroyed,
The potter never could with sense inspire,
Devoid of thought it nothing can desire.
The moralist still obstinate replies,
Others' enjoyments from your woes arise,
To numerous insects shall my corpse give birth,
When once it mixes with its mother earth:[8]
Small comfort 'tis that when Death's ruthless power
Closes my life, worms shall my flesh devour.
Remembrances of misery refrain
From consolation, you increase my pain:
Complaint, I see, you have with care repressed,
And proudly hid your sorrows in your breast.
But a small part I no importance claim
In this vast universe, this general frame;
All other beings in this world below
Condemned like me to lead a life of woe,
Subject to laws as rigorous as I,
Like me in anguish live and like me die.
The vulture urged by an insatiate maw,
Its trembling prey tears with relentless claw:
This it finds right, endowed with greater powers
The bird of Jove[9] the vulture's self devours.
Man lifts his tube, he aims the fatal ball
And makes to earth the towering eagle fall;
Man in the field with wounds covered o'er,
Midst heaps of dead lies weltering in his gore,
While birds of prey the mangled limbs devour,
Of Nature's Lord who boasts his mighty power.
Thus the world's members equal ills sustain,
And perish by each other born to pain:
Yet in this direful chaos you'd compose
A general bliss from individuals' woes?
Oh worthless bliss! in injured reason's sight,
With faltering voice you cry, "What is, is right"?
The universe confutes your boasting vain,

---

8. See the passage from Shaftesbury quoted by Voltaire above, p. 95.
9. The eagle.

Your heart retracts the error you maintain.
Men, beasts, and elements know no repose
From dire contention; earth's the seat of woes:
We strive in vain its secret source to find.
Is ill the gift of our Creator kind?
Do then fell Typhon's* cursed laws ordain
Our ill, or Arimanius† doom to pain?
Shocked at such dire chimeras, I reject
Monsters which fear could into gods erect.
But how conceive a God, the source of love,
Who on man lavished blessings from above,
Then would the race with various plagues confound
Can mortals penetrate his views profound?
Ill could not from a perfect being spring,
Nor from another,‡ since God's sovereign king;
And yet, sad truth! in this our world 'tis found,
What contradictions here my soul confound!
A God once dwelt on earth amongst mankind,
Yet vice still lays waste the human mind;§
He could not do it, this proud sophist cries,
He could, but he declined it, that replies;[10]
He surely will, ere these disputes have end,
Lisbon's foundations hidden thunders rend,
And thirty cities' shattered remnants fly,
With ruin and combustion through the sky,
From dismal Tagus' ensanguined shore,
To where of Cadiz' sea the billows roar.
Or man's a sinful creature from his birth,
And God to woe condemns the sons of earth;[11]
Or else the God who being rules and space,
Untouched with pity for the human race,
Indifferent, both from love and anger free,
Still acts consistent to His first decree:[12]
Or matter has defects which still oppose

---

*The name given by the Egyptians to the principle of evil.

†The name given by the Persians to the principle of evil.

‡That is to say, not from any other being.

§An English philosopher has claimed that the physical world ought to have been transformed at the Incarnation, as the moral world was.

10. See the quotation from Lactantius, below, p. 138.

11. The doctrine of original sin.

12. A version of Leibniz's argument.

God's will, and thence all human evil flows;[13]
Or else this transient world by mortals trod,
Is but a passage that conducts to God.
Our transient sufferings here shall soon be o'er,
And death will land us on a happier shore.
But when we rise from this accursed abyss,
Who by his merit can lay claim to bliss?
Dangers and difficulties man surround,
Doubts and perplexities his mind confound.
To nature we apply for truth in vain,
God should His will to human kind explain.
He only can illume the human soul,
Instruct the wise man, and the weak console.
Without him man of error still the sport,
Thinks from each broken reed to find support.
Leibniz can't tell me from what secret cause
In a world governed by the wisest laws,
Lasting disorders, woes that never end
With our vain pleasures real sufferings blend;
Why ill the virtuous with the vicious shares?
Why neither good nor bad misfortunes spares?
I can't conceive that "what is, ought to be,"
In this each doctor knows as much as me.
We're told by Plato, that man, in times of yore,
Wings gorgeous to his glorious body wore,
That all attacks he could unhurt sustain,
By death ne'er conquered, ne'er approached by pain.
Alas, how changed from such a brilliant state!
He crawls 'twixt heaven and earth, then yields to fate.
Look round this sublunary world, you'll find
That nature to destruction is consigned.
Our system weak which nerves and bones compose,
Cannot the shock of elements oppose;
This mass of fluids mixed with tempered clay,
To dissolution quickly must give way.
Their quick sensations can't unhurt sustain
The attacks of death and of tormenting pain,
This is the nature of the human frame,
Plato and Epicurus I disclaim.[14]

---

13. A view said to have been held by the ancient Greek philosopher Xenophanes, and discussed in Bayle's *Dictionary,* art. "Xenophanes," remark D.

14. Epicurus argued one should be indifferent to pain.

Nature was more to Bayle than either known:
What do I learn from Bayle, to doubt alone?*
Bayle, great and wise, all systems overthrows,
Then his own tenets labors to oppose.
Like the blind slave[15] to Delilah's commands,
Crushed by the pile demolished by his hands.
Mysteries like these can no man penetrate,
Hid from his view remains the book of fate.
Man his own nature never yet could sound,
He knows not whence he is nor whither bound.†

---

*A hundred remarks scattered through Bayle's *Dictionary* have won him an immortal reputation. He has left the outcome of the dispute over the origins of evil unclear. In his works he presents all the differing points of view; all the arguments that support a point of view and all the arguments that undermine it are equally carefully explored; he is like a lawyer who is prepared to represent any philosopher who becomes his client, but he never tells us what his own views are. In this he is like Cicero, who often, in his philosophical works, plays the part of an undecided skeptic, as the wise and judicious abbot d'Olivet has pointed out.

I think it is my duty to try here to mollify those who for some years now have been attacking Bayle with so much violence and with so little effect. I should not say with little effect, but the only effect they have is to make more people eager to read his books. They ought to learn from him how to argue and how to remain calm. Moreover Bayle, as a philosopher, has never denied the existence of Providence, nor the immortality of the soul. People translate Cicero, they comment on him, they use him in the education of princes; but what does one find on almost every page of Cicero, in among much that is admirable? One finds that "If there is a Providence, it is at fault for having given men an intelligence which it knew they would misuse" (*De natura deorum,* bk. 3, ch. 31). "No one has ever believed that virtue comes from the gods, and they are right" (ibid., ch. 36). "If a criminal dies unpunished you say that the gods will punish his descendants. Would a town put up with a legislator who wanted to punish the grandchildren for their grandfather's crimes?" (ibid., ch. 38). And what's even stranger is that Cicero finishes his book on *The Nature of the Gods* without refuting such statements. In a hundred places in the *Tusculanes* he maintains that the soul is mortal after having claimed that it is immortal.

There's more. He was speaking to the whole Roman senate when he said, in his defense of Cluentius, "What harm has death done him? We reject all the ridiculous stories of hell. What then has death taken away from him, other than the experience of pain?" (ibid., ch. 61).

Finally, in his letters, where he speaks his private thoughts, doesn't he say "When I cease to exist all sensation will die with me" (*Epistolae familiares,* bk. 6, letter 3).

Bayle never said anything that comes close to this. Yet we give Cicero to our young people to read, and everyone attacks Bayle. Why? It is because people are inconsistent, it is because they are unjust.

15. Samson.

†It is clear that mankind on its own cannot find the answer to these questions. The human intellect cannot form any ideas except on the basis of experience; and there is no experience that can teach us either what happened to us before we came into

Atoms tormented on this earthly ball,
The sport of fate, by death soon swallowed all,
But thinking atoms, who with piercing eyes
Have measured the whole circuit of the skies;
We rise in thought up to the heavenly throne,
But our own nature still remains unknown.
This world which error and o'erweening pride,
Rulers accursed between them still divide,
Where wretches overwhelmed with lasting woe,
Talk of a happiness they never know,
Is with complaining filled, all are forlorn
In seeking bliss; none would again be born.* [16]
If in a life midst sorrows past and fears,
With pleasure's hand we wipe away our tears,
Pleasure his light wings spreads, and quickly flies,
Losses on losses, griefs on griefs arise.
The mind with sad remembrance of the past,
Is with black melancholy overcast;
Sad is the present if no future state,
No blissful retribution mortals wait,
If fate's decrees the thinking being doom
To lose existence in the silent tomb.
All may be well; that hope can man sustain,
All now is well; 'tis an illusion vain.
The sages hold me forth delusive light,
Divine instructions only can be right.
Humbly I sigh, submissive suffer pain,
Nor more the ways of Providence arraign.

---

existence or what will happen to us after we cease to exist. Nor can experience teach us what it is that gives us life in our present existence. How were we given life? What mechanism maintains it? How does our brain come to have ideas and memory? How do our limbs come to obey our wishes instantaneously? etc. We haven't any idea. Is this world the only one that is inhabited? Was it made after other worlds, or in the same instant of time? Does each species of plants descend from one original ancestor of the whole species? Does each species of animals descend from two original ancestors of the whole species? The greatest philosophers are no better placed to answer these questions than the most ignorant and uneducated. We have to go back to the popular proverb: "Which came first, the chicken or the egg?" The proverb is unsophisticated, but it befuddles the wisest of men, who know nothing about the origins of the world except through supernatural assistance.

*It is difficult to find anyone willing to live the same life over again, and experience again everything they experienced the first time.

16. A claim made by Erasmus (1466–1535) in the *Colloquies* and repeated by Bayle in "Xenophanes." For Rousseau's response, see below, p. 112.

In youthful prime I sung in strains more gay,
Soft pleasure's laws which lead mankind astray.[17]
But times change manners; taught by age and care
Whilst I mistaken mortals' weakness share,
The light of truth I seek in this dark state,
And without murmuring submit to fate.[18]
A caliph once when his last hour drew nigh,
Prayed in such terms as these to the most high:
"Being supreme, whose greatness knows no bound,
I bring thee all that can't in Thee be found;
Defects and sorrows, ignorance and woe."
Hope he omitted, man's sole bliss below.*

JEAN-JACQUES ROUSSEAU, "LETTER TO VOLTAIRE ON OPTIMISM," 18 AUGUST 1756[19]

Your last two poems, sir, have reached me in my solitude.[20] And although all my friends know that I love your writings, still I don't know who could have sent them to me, if not you.[21] They gave me pleasure and I learned from them; and I could tell they were written by no lesser person than

---

17. Voltaire is referring to his poem *Le Mondain*.

18. The first, prepublication versions of the poem ended here, and were attacked because they appeared to offer no hope of immortality.

*Most human beings have had this hope [of immortality], even before revelation came to their assistance. The hope of surviving after death is grounded in the love we have for living while we are alive. It is grounded in the probability that what thinks will continue to think. It is not supported by any demonstrative proof, for something can only be demonstrated if the opposite to it involves self-contradiction, and once a truth has been demonstrated that puts an end to all argument about it. Lucretius, in order to destroy this hope, constructs, in his third book, a set of arguments so strong that they give pain; but all he does is use plausible arguments to attack plausible arguments that are more convincing. Quite a few Romans agreed with Lucretius, and they cried out in the Roman theater "After death there is nothing!" But instinct, reason, the need to be comforted, the welfare of society, won out, and human beings have always hoped for a life to come—a hope, it must be said, often tinged with doubt. Revelation destroys this doubt, and puts certainty in its place.

19. First published (without Rousseau's permission or knowledge) in 1759, perhaps in response to the publication of *Candide*. In his *Confessions* Rousseau claims both that *Candide* was Voltaire's reply to this letter, and that he himself has never read *Candide*.

20. The "Poem on the Lisbon Disaster" and the "Poem on Natural Religion," which had been published together in March.

21. Rousseau was correct to think that Voltaire had arranged for him to receive a copy.

yourself. So I think I am under an obligation to thank you at the same time both for the printed copies and the texts. I won't tell you that every part of them seemed to me equally good; but the things that displeased me only inspired me with more confidence in the things that swept me away. It is not without difficulty, on occasion, that I defend my reason against the charms of your poetry; but it is in order to make my admiration more worthy of your works that I struggle not to admire every part of them.

I will do more, sir; I will tell you straight, not the beauties that I believed I experienced reading these two poems, for such an undertaking is too daunting for someone as lazy as I, nor the faults that cleverer people than I will perhaps discover in them, but the displeasures that disturb at this moment the pleasure that I have been taking in learning from you; and I will describe them to you while I am still moved by my first reading, during which my heart listened eagerly to yours, loving you like a brother, honoring you as my master. I flatter myself that you will recognize in my intentions the frankness of an honest spirit, and in my words the tone of a lover of the truth who speaks to a true philosopher. Moreover, the more your second poem enchants me, the more I feel free to criticize your first, for since you were not frightened of being at odds with yourself, why should I be frightened of agreeing with you? I'm bound to believe that you are not really attached to views that you refute so effectively.

All my criticisms, then, are aimed at your "Poem on the Lisbon Disaster," for I expected it would have an effect on me that was worthier of the concern for the welfare of others, which seems to have inspired you to write it. You reproach Pope and Leibniz with showing contempt for the evils we suffer when they claim that all is well, and you portray such a vast extent of misery that you make us more miserable than before. In place of the consolations that I hoped to find, all you do is weigh me down; one might think that you fear that I am insufficiently aware of how unhappy I am, and it seems as though you may believe that you reassure me by proving to me that all is ill.

Don't be misled, sir. The result is exactly the opposite of what you intend. This optimism that you find so cruel consoles me while I suffer the very pains that you describe to me as being insupportable. Pope's poem alleviates my sufferings and encourages me to be patient; yours increases my sufferings, incites me to complain, and, taking from me everything but a shattered hope, it reduces me to despair. In this strange conflict, which occurs between what you prove to be the case and what I experience to be the case, I beg you to calm the perplexity that agitates me and tell me which is wrong, the viewpoint of sentiment or that of reason.

"Humans, be patient," Pope and Leibniz say to me; "your ills are a necessary consequence of your nature and of the design of this universe. The eternal and benevolent Being who governs it would have wished to have protected you from them. Of all the possible economies, he chose the one that combined the least evil with the most good; or, to say the same thing even more bluntly if needs must, if he has not made a better universe it is because he could not."

Now what does your poem say to me? "Suffer without respite, unhappy human. If there is a God who has created you, then he is surely all-powerful, and could have prevented your sufferings. So you have no ground for hoping they will ever end, for there's no conceivable reason why you exist, if it is not to suffer and to die." I can't see what would make such a doctrine more consoling than optimism, or even than fatalism. As far as I'm concerned, I confess that it seems to me even more cruel than Manicheism. If the little difficulty of the entry of evil into the world requires that you vary one of God's perfect qualities, why defend his power at the expense of his goodness? If one must choose between two untruths, I would prefer the opposite choice.

You do not want us, sir, to think of your work as a poem against Providence, and I will take care not to call it this, although you have described a work I wrote in which I defended humanity against its own accusations as a book against the human species.[22] I know the distinction that must be drawn between an author's intentions and the consequences that can be drawn from his teaching. But my obligation to defend myself against false charges merely requires me to point out to you that in portraying the miseries of human existence, my purpose was one that can be excused and perhaps should even be praised for all that I can tell: for I showed human beings how their sufferings were of their own making, and consequently how they could avoid them.

I do not see that one can look for the origins of moral evil anywhere except in human nature: free, as far as it could be, yet corrupted. As for physical suffering, if a type of matter that feels but cannot suffer is a contradiction in terms, as it seems to me to be, then such suffering is inevitable in any universe that contains human beings; in which case the question is not why are human beings not perfectly happy, but why do they exist? Moreover, I believe I have shown that, with the exception of death, which is scarcely to be counted as an evil except for the antechambers one is made to pass through to reach it, most of the physical evils we experience are likewise of our own making. Without leaving your chosen subject of Lisbon, you must acknowledge, for example, that it was not nature that piled up there twenty thousand houses of six or seven floors each; and that if the inhabitants of this great city had been spread out more evenly and had lived in less massive buildings, the destruction would have been a lot

---

22. This is how Voltaire described Rousseau's *Discourse on the Origins of Inequality* (1755) in a letter to Rousseau (30 Aug. 1755, D6451).

less, and perhaps insignificant. Everyone would have run away at the first shock, and one would have found them the next day fifty miles away and just as happy as if nothing had happened. But they had to stay put, stubbornly remain on the Mazures, expose themselves to new shocks because what they would be leaving behind was worth far more than what they could carry away with them. How many poor creatures died in this disaster because one wanted to go back for his clothes, another for his papers, a third for his money? Can't you see that the physical existence of a human being has become the least important part of themselves, and that it seems to be scarcely worth saving it when one has lost all the rest?

You would have wanted the earthquake to occur in the distant reaches of some desert rather than in Lisbon. Is there any reason to think earthquakes don't occur in deserts? But we don't discuss them, because they do no harm to the city dwellers, the only human beings to whom we attribute any significance. It's true they don't do much harm to the animals and the savages who live scattered through those inaccessible zones, and who don't worry about their roofs falling in or their houses being undermined. But supposing you had your wish, what would it imply? Would it mean that the order of nature must change to suit our fancies, that nature must submit herself to our laws, and that, to forbid the occurrence of an earthquake in any particular place, all that would be necessary would be to build a town there?

There are some events that often seem to be more or less striking according to the point of view from which one considers them, and that lose much of the horror that they inspire when first one catches sight of them when one comes to examine them from closer up. I learned from *Zadig*,[23] and day after day nature provides confirmation, that an early death is not always a real evil, and that it can sometimes be regarded as a relative good. Of all the human beings crushed under the ruins of Lisbon, several, we can be sure, escaped even greater sufferings, and, notwithstanding how touching a description of their sufferings may be, and what good poetry may be written about them, it is not certain that a single one of these unfortunates suffered more than they would have done if, as happens to most of us, they had gone through long agonies while waiting for death to carry them away. Was their death worse than that of someone who is mortally ill, who is nursed when no good can come of it, who is pestered by his lawyer and his heirs, who is killed little by little in his own bed by his own doctors, and whom barbarous priests employ every sophisticated technique to terrify with the fear of death? In my view, it's apparent over and over again that the sufferings nature imposes on us are less cruel than those we add on ourselves.

---

23. A story by Voltaire (1748).

But no matter how ingenious we may be at increasing our miseries through the fine institutions we construct, we haven't (at least so far) been so successful that we have turned life into a source of unhappiness for most of us, and have made death preferable to survival. Otherwise depression and despair would quickly have seized the majority, and the human species would not have been able to continue existing for long. Now if it is better for us to live than not to live, then that's enough to justify our existence, even if we have no compensation to receive in the future for the ills that we have suffered, and even if these ills are as bad as you portray them. But it is difficult to find good faith among human beings and good arithmetic among philosophers when it comes to this question; for philosophers, when they are comparing the good they have experienced with the evil, always forget the sweet experience of being alive, quite apart from any sensation we may have while alive; while human beings are so proud of their capacity to treat death with contempt that they find themselves obliged to dismiss life as worthless, rather like those women who, if they have a dress with a stain and a pair of scissors, pretend that they prefer holes to stains.

You agree with Erasmus, who held that few people would want to be reborn if they had to live their lives over again. We all know there are people who try and strike a hard bargain, but who would be ready to settle for much less if they thought the deal would go through. Moreover, who am I to take it that you have consulted on this question? Some rich people perhaps? Caught up in false pleasures, but with no experience of true delights; always bored with life, and always afraid of losing it. Perhaps some writers, of all types of human being the most sedentary, the most unhealthy, the most introspective, and consequently the most unhappy? Do you want to find some people whose state of mind is better, or who at least are generally more honest? Who are much more numerous and who, if only for that reason, ought to be listened to with care? Ask an honest businessman who has lived a life that is obscure and peaceful, without plans and without ambition; or a good craftsman who gets a decent living from his trade; or even a laborer, not in France where they take the view that laborers must be starved so that we can get fat, but in the country where you live, for example,[24] or indeed any country that is free from despotism. I dare to suggest that in the high alps there may not be a single mountain dweller who is fed up with his life, even though it is that of an automaton; not a single one who would not happily accept, instead of the paradise he expects and that he has earned, the offer of being perpetually reborn to the same life, so that he can vegetate interminably. These differences make me think that it is often the misuse we make of our lives

---

24. I.e., Switzerland.

that makes them onerous to us, and I have a much less good opinion of those who are fed up with having lived than with those who can echo what Cato said: "I do not regret having lived the life I have, for this is the life I have had, and I would not want to think that it would have been better for me if I had not been born."[25] This does not mean that a wise man may not on occasion decide of his own free will to end his life, without complaint or despair, when either nature or fate brings him an unambiguous order to move on. But in the ordinary course of events, no matter what evils are scattered through our lives, life is not, all in all, a bad thing to be given; and if it isn't always an evil to die, still it is very rarely an evil to have to live.

Our different ways of thinking on all these questions provide an explanation as to why several of your arguments are far from convincing for me. For I am well aware of the extent to which human reason finds it easier to mold itself to our opinions than to shape itself to the truth; and realize that between two people of conflicting opinions, an argument that one thinks has been proved conclusively is often dismissed by the other as a piece of sophistry.

When you attack, for example, the chain of being so well described by Pope, you say that it is not true that if one removed one atom from the world the world could no longer continue to exist. On this question you cite M. de Crousaz, and then you add that nature is not restricted to any exact measurement that must remain constant, nor obliged to preserve any particular shape; that no planet moves in an orbit that repeats itself absolutely perfectly; that no being in nature has a shape that is mathematically exact; that no fixed quantity is required for any chemical reaction; that nature never acts inflexibly; that thus there is no reason to assert that one atom more or less on earth would bring about the world's destruction. I confess that as far as all that is concerned, sir, I am more impressed by the force with which you assert your views than with the strength of your reasoning, and that on this occasion I am happier to give way to your authority than to your arguments.

As far as M. Crouzas is concerned, I have not read his book against Pope,[26] and I might well not be capable of understanding it if I did; but one thing is absolutely certain, and that is that I would not concede to him ground that I am willing to hold against you, and that I have no more confidence in his proofs than I have respect for his authority. Far from thinking that nature is not restricted to precise quantities and to geometrical shapes, I would be prepared to believe quite the opposite: that she

---

25. Cicero, *De senectute*, 84.

26. Jean-Pierre de Crousaz, *Commentaire sur la traduction en vers, de M. l'abbé du Resnel, de l'Essai de M. Pope sur l'homme* (Geneva, 1738).

inflexibly operates with such precision because she alone knows exactly how to make means correspond to ends and to ensure that the energy employed corresponds exactly to the resistance to be overcome. As for these supposed irregularities, they are the result, no doubt, of laws that are unknown to us, laws that nature follows as exactly as she follows the laws that are known to us; they are the consequence of some force that we do not perceive and whose resistance or assistance operates in all circumstances according to fixed principles; otherwise we would be obliged to say plainly that there are events that are not law-governed and effects without causes, which is unacceptable in any philosophy.

Let us suppose there are two weights hanging from a balance; they are in equilibrium and yet they are unequal. Add to the smaller weight the amount required to make them equal; either the two weights will stay in equilibrium, and we will have a cause without an effect, or the equilibrium will be broken, and we will have an effect without a cause. But if the two weights were made of iron, and there was a fragment of magnet hidden under one of them, the precision with which nature operates would then deprive the balance of the appearance of precision, and, because of her exact working, she would appear to work inexactly. There isn't a shape, a reaction, a law of nature for which one could not construct some example comparable to the one I have just offered you with regard to weight.

You say that no object in existence has a shape that can be precisely defined in mathematical terms. I ask you, sir, if there is any shape that cannot? Cannot the most peculiar curve be as mathematically exact in the eyes of nature as a perfect circle is in ours? I imagine, moreover, that if any figure could have this regularity from our point of view it would only be that of the universe itself, if we may suppose it is full and delimited. For mathematical figures are only abstractions, and relate only to themselves, while the figures of natural bodies are interrelated with those of other bodies and with movements that modify them; thus this would prove nothing against the precision of nature, assuming we could agree on the meaning you want to give to this word "precision."

You distinguish events that have effects from those that do not; I'm not convinced that this distinction is well founded. It seems to me that every event must of necessity have some effect, whether moral, or physical, or a mixture of the two; but we don't always perceive these effects because the chain of events is even more difficult to follow than the genealogy of human beings. Since, in general, one should not look for effects more significant than the causes that produce them, miniscule causes often render the search for effects ridiculous, although it is certain that there are effects, and sometimes moreover several almost imperceptible effects join together to produce a significant event. Let me add that this effect does not cease to occur even if it operates outside the body that produced it.

Thus the dust that is thrown up by a passing carriage may have no effect on the carriage, but may have an effect elsewhere in the world. But, as there is nothing that is not part of the universe, everything that happens necessarily acts upon the universe itself.

Thus, sir, your examples seem to me more ingenious than convincing. I can see a thousand credible reasons why it was not without significance for Europe that on a particular day the next in line to the throne of Burgundy was well or badly dressed, nor to the destiny of Rome that Caesar turned his eyes to the left or the right and spat on one side or the other on his way to the senate the day that he met his just deserts there. In a word, in recalling the grain of sand that Pascal refers to,[27] I am in certain respects of the same opinion as your Brahmin;[28] and, however one looks at matters, if all events do not have effects that can be identified, still it seems to me beyond question that all of them have real effects; even if our human intelligence easily loses track of them, nature never does.

You say that it has been demonstrated that the celestial bodies travel on their orbits through a space that offers no resistance; this would be quite something to prove, but, as is normally the case with people who know very little, I have very little confidence in demonstrations I cannot follow. I would imagine that in order to construct this proof one would have to reason roughly as follows: such a force, acting according to such a law, ought to give the heavenly bodies such and such a movement in a space which offers no resistance; and the heavenly bodies have exactly the predicted movement; therefore they pass through a space that offers no resistance. But who can know if there are not, perhaps, a million other possible laws, not to mention the authentic law, according to which the same movement could be better explained as taking place within a fluid rather than by your law governing movement in a vacuum? Wasn't nature's horror of a vacuum for a long time used to explain most of the effects that are now explained by atmospheric pressure? Other experiments having later served to destroy the idea of the horror of a vacuum, wasn't it taken to follow that a vacuum was impossible? Was the idea of vacuum not then reestablished on the basis of new calculations? How can we know that a yet more powerful theory will not destroy it once again? Let us leave aside the innumerable difficulties that a natural scientist might make when it comes to the nature of light and its passage through space;[29] but do you honestly think that Bayle, whom I agree with you in admiring for his wisdom and his grasp when it comes to matters in dispute, would have found your case

---

27. Pascal, *Pensées* (Brunschvicg, 176).

28. See Voltaire's "Dialogue entre un Brachmane et un Jésuite" (1756).

29. There was no satisfactory explanation of how light (unlike sound) could travel through a vacuum.

so completely convincing? In general it seems that skeptics forget their principles a bit as soon as they begin to speak at all dogmatically; they of all people ought to be careful how they use the word "demonstrate." How do you expect to be believed when you take pride in knowing nothing and assert so much?

As for the rest, you have made a very sensible corrective to Pope's system when you remark that there is no graduated proportion between the creatures and their creator, and that if the chain of created beings stops at God it is because he holds the end of it, not because he is the last link in it.

On the idea that the good of the whole system is preferable to the good of a part, you make mankind say, "I ought to be as important to my master—I who am a creature that thinks and feels—as the planets, which are probably insensible." Doubtless this material universe ought to be less important to its creator than even one creature that thinks and feels; but the system of this universe—which produces, sustains, and perpetuates all the creatures that think and feel—ought to be more important to him than a single one of these creatures; he therefore can, despite his goodness, or rather by reason of his goodness, sacrifice some part of the happiness of some individuals in order to preserve the whole. I believe, I hope that I am worth more in the eyes of God than the earth that makes up some planet; but if the planets are inhabited, as seems likely, then why should I be worth more in his eyes than all the inhabitants of Saturn? It's all very well to laugh at these ideas, for it is certain that every argument from analogy is in favor of life on other worlds, and only human pride opposes the idea. But once we concede the existence of such life, then the conservation of the universe surely is a moral obligation for God himself, one that increases with every additional inhabited world.

The fact that a human being's corpse provides nourishment for worms, or wolves, or plants is not, I must admit, any compensation to them for their death; but if, in the overall system of this universe, it is necessary for the conservation of the human species that there should be a circulation of matter between human beings, animals, and vegetables, then the harm suffered by one individual contributes to the good of all. I die, I am eaten by worms, but my children, my brothers will live as I have lived; my body manures the earth whose produce they will eat; and I do, according to nature's laws and to the benefit of mankind in general, what Codrus, Curtius, the Decies, the Philenes, and a thousand others voluntarily did for a small group of men.

Let us go back, sir, to the system that you attack. I believe one cannot properly examine it without distinguishing with care harm suffered by an individual, the reality of which has been denied by no philosophical system, from evil in general, whose existence is denied by optimism. It is not a question of knowing whether each one of us suffers or not, but of knowing whether it is good that the universe exists, and whether our sufferings were inevitable aspects of its existence. Thus the addition of a definite article would make the proposition more accurate, and instead of saying "All is well," it would perhaps be better to say "The whole is well," or "All is well from the point of view of the whole." At once it is apparent that nobody could produce direct proofs either for or against this proposition, for such proofs would depend on a perfect knowledge of the construction of the universe and the purposes of its author, and this knowledge is unquestionably outside the grasp of a merely human intelligence. The true principles of optimism cannot be derived either from the properties of matter or from the mechanical ordering of the universe, but can only be deduced from the perfections of God, who has charge of the whole. Thus one cannot prove the existence of God from Pope's account of the universe, but one can prove the truth of Pope's account of the universe on the basis of the existence of God. And no one denies that the question of the origin of evil is subsidiary to the question of Providential design. If these two questions have been equally badly handled it is because the standard of argument with regard to Providence has been so poor that the nonsense said about it has completely messed up all the conclusions that one ought to be able to derive from this great and reassuring doctrine.

The first who made a mess of the case for God are the priests and the faithful, who can't tolerate the idea that anything happens according to the natural order of events, but keep making God's justice intervene in purely natural processes. In order to be sure that God's handiwork is visible, they have him punish and injure the wicked, and either test or reward the good, claiming that he has chosen to treat them either well or ill (it doesn't matter which) depending on what happens to them. Personally, I don't know whether this is good theology; but I do know that it is a bad way to argue, to ground the evidence for the action of Providence equally on the good and the ill that happens, and to attribute to Providence without hesitation all that would happen equally without it.

The philosophers in their turn hardly seem any more reasonable to me when I hear them complain to the heavens that they are not more insensitive to their own suffering, cry out that all is lost when they have toothache, or when they are poor, or when they are robbed; and hold God responsible, as Seneca puts it, for the safe keeping of their wallets.[30] If some tragic accident had made Cartouche or Caesar perish in their childhood, the philosophers would have asked, "What crime did they commit?" These two robbers lived, and we ask, "Why did God allow them to stay

---

30. Seneca, *De providentia*, vi.i.

alive?" A committed Christian would approach the matter differently. In the first case they would say that God wished to punish a father by taking his child from him; in the second that God preserved the child in order to punish the nation. Thus whatever nature might do, Providence is always in the right as far as the faithful are concerned and always in the wrong according to the philosophers. Perhaps in the scheme of human life Providence is neither right nor wrong because everything derives from the common law of nature and no exceptions are made for anyone. We can reasonably believe that particular events are insignificant in the eyes of the master of the universe; that his providence is confined to universal laws; that he is content to confine himself to conserving varieties and species and to preside over the whole without worrying himself about the way in which each individual lives out this short life. A wise king, who wants everyone to live happily in his kingdom, does he have to concern himself whether the hotels are good or not? The traveler complains for an evening if they are bad, and spends the rest of his life laughing at his own misplaced impatience: "The world is a hotel in which we stay for a few nights; we have no permanent residence here."[31]

In order to think straight on this matter it seems that we have to think relatively when it comes to questions of physics, and absolutely when it comes to questions of morality. The finest idea that I can construct of Providence is that each material being is placed in the best possible relationship to the whole and each intelligent and sensitive being is placed in the best possible relationship to himself. What I mean, to put it differently, is that for any creature that is aware of its own existence it is better to exist than not to exist. But we have to apply this rule to the whole period of the life of each sensitive being, and not to some particular moment in its existence, such as its life as a human being: which shows just how closely the question of Providence is linked to that of the immortality of the soul, in which I have the good fortune to believe even though I realize that there are rational grounds for questioning it; and to that of the doctrine of eternal damnation, which neither you, nor I, nor ever any man who thought well of God would believe for a moment.

If I take these different questions back to their common origin, it seems to me that they all relate to that of the existence of God. If God exists he is perfect; if he is perfect he is wise, strong, and powerful; if he is wise and strong all is well; if he is just and powerful my soul is immortal; if my soul is immortal, thirty years on earth have no importance to me and are perhaps necessary to the functioning of the universe. If you concede the first principle then you will never unpick those that follow from it; if you deny it, then there's no point in arguing about the consequences.

---

31. Cicero, *De senectute*, 84.

Neither of us denies the key premise. At least it would seem that I had no grounds for imagining that you might deny it as I read through the volumes of your works. Most of them present me with ideas of the divinity that are exceptionally noble, sweet, reassuring, and I much prefer a Christianity like yours to that of the Sorbonne.

As for me, I will openly admit to you that in this matter neither the argument for nor the argument against seem to me demonstrated conclusively in rational terms; if the theist grounds his opinion, in the end, on probabilities, the atheist is even further from conclusive proof, and seems to me to rely on the possibility that the opposite is true. Moreover the objections that each side makes against the other can never be refuted because they depend on matters about which human beings have no real idea. I admit all that, and yet I believe in God as strongly as I believe any other truth, because believing and not believing are, of all that is, the things over which I have least control. Moreover, being in a state of doubt is far too stressful for my spirit. When my reason floats free, my faith is incapable of remaining for long in suspense and anchors itself on its own. Finally there are a thousand factors that induce me to adopt the opinion that is the most comforting; and the weight of experience tips the balance of reason.

Here then, there is a truth from which we both take our point of departure, and, with it to fall back on, you must recognize how easy it is to defend optimism and justify Providence. I don't have to repeat to you the arguments (which may be commonplace but are nevertheless sound) that have been so frequently produced on this subject. As far as philosophers who do not accept our first principle are concerned, one should not enter into arguments with them about these questions, for what is for us only an argument grounded in our feelings cannot become a logical demonstration, which is what they require; and it isn't reasonable to say to someone, "You must believe this because I do." They on their side should equally refrain from arguing with us about these matters, for they are nothing but conclusions drawn from the key premise, which is one that a respectable opponent will scarcely dare call into question; and they in their turn would be wrong to require that we prove the conclusions independently of the proposition from which they are derived. I think there is a further reason why they ought not to dispute about these questions: for there is something cruel about disturbing the spirits of those who mean you no harm, about driving people to despair without them gaining anything in return when what you want to teach them is neither certain nor useful. I think, in a word, that, following your own example, one cannot attack too strongly the superstitious beliefs that cause distress, nor show too much respect for the religious faith that holds society together.

But, like you, I am indignant that each individual is not perfectly free to decide for themselves what they wish to believe, and outraged that there are people who dare to claim authority over our conscientious convictions, to which we alone have access, as if we had a choice as to whether to believe or not to believe with regard to questions that are not susceptible to demonstration, and as if reason could ever be enslaved by authority. Do the rulers of this world have some jurisdiction in the next? Do they have the right to torture their subjects down here in order to force them to go to paradise? No, all earthly government is by its nature restricted to our civil obligations, and, no matter what that sophist Hobbes may have claimed,[32] as long as a person is a good servant of the state they are under no obligation to account to anyone for the manner in which they serve God.

I can't know whether a just God will one day punish every act of tyranny carried out in his name, but I can at least be confident that he will not make himself a party to it, and that he will never refuse eternal happiness to any unbeliever who is virtuous and sincere. Can I, without attacking his goodness and even his justice, suppose that an honest intent will not be sufficient to excuse an involuntary error, and that irreproachable conduct will not be held to be much more important than a thousand bizarre acts of worship that are required by authority and are denounced by reason? I will go further: if I could choose to improve my behavior at the price of giving up my faith, if I could compensate by my virtuous life for my hypothetical unbelief, I wouldn't hesitate a moment. I would prefer to be able to say to God, "I have done without thinking of you the good of which you approve, and my spirit obeyed your commands without knowing them" than to have to say to him, as I will one day have to do, "I loved you, and never ceased to disobey you; I knew you, and did nothing to please you."

There is, I confess, a type of declaration of religious faith that the laws can require, but, aside from the principles of morality and natural justice, it ought to be purely negative; for religions that attack the foundations of society can exist, and it is necessary to begin by exterminating these religions in order to ensure peace in the state. Of these doctrines that should be proscribed, intolerance is without doubt the most hateful, but it is necessary to grasp it by the root, for the most bloody fanatics change their language according to their circumstances, and preach nothing but patience and gentleness when their opponents are stronger than they are. Thus I call intolerant in his principles any person who imagines that one cannot be a good person without believing everything they believe, and damns without pity those who do not believe as they do. Actually, believers are rarely in a mood to leave the damned alone in this world, and a saint who believes that they are living in the midst of condemned souls is

---

32. *Leviathan* (1651).

only too willing to make a beginning of the devil's work. If there were intolerant unbelievers who wanted to force people to believe nothing, I would banish them just as severely as those who want to force people to believe whatever they choose. For one can tell from the force with which they express their convictions, the bitterness with which they argue for their nonsense, that they only await the moment when they are in charge to begin persecuting believers as cruelly as they are themselves persecuted by other fanatics. Where is the man who is peaceful and gentle and who thinks it is fine for someone to disagree with him? You certainly won't ever find such a person among the devout, and I'm still looking for him among the philosophers.

So I would like there to be a moral code in every state, or a type of declaration of civic religion, which provides a positive declaration of the social principles that everybody would be required to accept, and a negative statement of the fanatical principles that everybody would be required to reject, not on the grounds that they were heretical, but that they were seditious. Thus any religion that could bring itself into line with the code would be permitted, and any religion that would not bring itself into line would be banned; and everyone would be free to have no religion beyond the code itself. This text, if constructed with care, would be, I think, the most useful that has ever been written, and perhaps the only one that anyone need ever read.[33] There, sir, is a task for you to undertake! It is my passionate desire that you might wish to undertake the writing of this work, and that you might beautify it with your poetry so that everybody could learn it easily. If everyone committed it to memory, every heart would contain from childhood those sentiments of gentleness and kindness that shine from your writings and that the devout Christians will always lack. I urge you to give consideration to this project, which must give pleasure to all that is best in you. You have given us in your poem on natural religion the catechism of humanity; now give us in the poem I am proposing to you the catechism of the citizen.[34] This is a task that deserves years of contemplation, and that perhaps should be held back to be the last of your publications so that you may complete with an act of charity toward the whole human species the most brilliant career that any man of letters has ever had.

I cannot prevent myself, sir, from remarking in this context a striking disagreement that exists between you and me with regard to the subject of this letter. Surfeited in glory and having learned to see through false marks of status, you live a free man surrounded by wealth. Confident of your

---

33. Rousseau had been at work for some time on his *Social Contract* (1762).

34. There is some evidence that Rousseau himself composed such a catechism; see also the final chapter of Rousseau's *Social Contract,* "On Civic Religion."

place in history, you sit and philosophize in peace on the nature of the soul. If your body or your heart trouble you, you have Tronchin as your doctor and as your friend. And yet you see nothing but evil loose on the earth! While I, a man of no standing, poor, and tormented by an illness that cannot be cured, I meditate with pleasure in my retreat and find that all is well. Where do these seeming contradictions come from? You have given the explanation yourself: you experience pleasure, while I live in hope, and hope makes everything beautiful.

I find it as difficult to stop writing this tedious letter as you will find it hard-going to make it to the end. Forgive me, oh great man, my zeal, which is perhaps out of order, but I would not pour out my views to you if I did not have such a high opinion of you. I pray that I may not give offense to the one person alive for whose abilities I have the highest admiration, and whose writings speak most directly to my heart. But I write in defense of the Providence that holds me in its hands. After having drawn for so long lessons of comfort and of courage from your teachings, I find it hard that you now deprive me of what I cared for most, and offer me only an uncertain and ill-defined hope, as if it was rather a medicine to ease my suffering than a promise of good to come. No, I have suffered too much in this life not to look forward to another. All the fine arguments of the metaphysicians will not make me doubt for a moment that the soul is immortal and that Providence is benevolent. I feel it, I believe it, I wish it, I hope it, I will defend it until I draw my final breath; and this will be, of all the disputes in which I have engaged myself, the only one where my own selfish interest will never be out of my mind.

I am, with respect, sir . . .

Toward *Candide*

The History of the Travels of Scarmentado, Written by Himself (1756)[1]

I was born in the town of Candia,[2] in 1600. My father was the governor; and I remember that a second-rate poet, who was second to none in his cynicism, called Iro,[3] wrote some bad verses in praise of me, in which he described me as a direct descendant of Minos.[4] But, when my father fell into disgrace and was recalled, he wrote another poem in which I was only a descendant of Pasiphae and her lover.[5] He was a really wicked man, that Iro, and the most irritating bastard in the whole island.

When I was fifteen my father sent me to study in Rome. I arrived hoping to learn the truth about everything, for up until then they had taught me everything but that, as is customary in this wretched world wherever one goes from the Alps to China. Monsignor Profondo,[6] to whom I was entrusted, was a man out of the ordinary, and one of the most terrifying scholars in the whole world. He wanted to teach me the categories of Aristotelian philosophy, and was on the point of placing me into the category of his catamites: I escaped by the skin of my teeth. I saw processions, exorcisms, and a few rapes. It was said, entirely falsely, that Lady

---

1. The name Scarmentado is from the Spanish *escarmentar*, v. intr., "to be tutored by experience"; v. tr., "to inflict an exemplary punishment." Although first published in the *Complete Works* of 1756, this story was probably written in 1753–4, when Voltaire was recovering from his conflict with Frederick the Great. Having fled to Alsace, Voltaire was unable to obtain permission to return to France. At the time Voltaire was working on his *Essai sur les moeurs*, which had reached the early seventeenth century. The historical moment that interests Voltaire is described in ch. 191 (ed. Pomeau, 2 vols., Paris: Classiques Garnier, 1990), vol. 2, pp. 756–7: "The beginning of the seventeenth century was the age of usurpers from almost one end of the earth to the other . . . If one surveys the history of the world, one sees weakness punished, while tyrants are successful, and the whole universe is a vast panorama of brigandage abandoned to fortune." The table of contents says simply: "The whole world suffered. As is often the case."

2. The capital of Crete, then under Venetian control.

3. This is a veiled attack on an enemy of Voltaire's named Roy.

4. The legendary king of Crete, son of Zeus and Europa.

5. Pasiphae was Minos' wife; her lover was a bull; their offspring was the Minotaur.

6. The name means "deep" or "profound."

Olimpia, a very wise lady, sold many things that one ought not to sell.[7] I was at an age when all that seemed very amusing. A young lady with very charming ways called Lady Do-It decided to love me. She was courted by the Reverend Father Poignardini and the Reverend Father Aconiti,[8] young members of a religious order that no longer exists. She settled their differences by being generous to me; but at the same time I ran the risk of being excommunicated, not to mention poisoned. I left Rome very pleased with the architecture of St. Peter's.

I traveled in France. King Louis the Just was on the throne.[9] The first thing they asked me was whether I would like to have a little bit of Marshal d'Ancre with my dinner. The common people had roasted his body and were selling bits of it for next to nothing to those who wanted a taste.[10]

This state was continually torn apart by civil wars, which were sometimes fought so that someone could claim a seat at the council table, and sometimes over a couple of pages of controversial theology. For more than sixty years this fire, sometimes damped down and smoking, and sometimes with flames licking high, had been destroying this beautiful country. "Alas," I said. "The people of this nation are in fact born peaceable; who can have led them so far from their true character? They tell jokes, and they massacre. Happy day when they settle for just telling jokes."

I went on to England. The same conflicts were exciting the same violent clashes there. Some Catholic saints had resolved, for the good of the Church, to blow up the king, the royal family, and the whole of Parliament with gunpowder, and so to rescue England from these heretics.[11] I was shown the place where the blessed Queen Mary, daughter of Henry VIII, had had more than five hundred of her subjects burned. A Scottish priest assured me that this had been a very good thing to do: firstly, because those who had been burned were English, and secondly because they never used holy water and did not believe in St. Patrick's hole.[12] He was particularly surprised that Queen Mary had not yet been canonized, but

---

7. Olimpia Maldacchini, sister-in-law to Pope Innocent X (d. 1655), who traded in ecclesiastical benefices.

8. The two fathers apparently represent two forms of death: death by stabbing and death by poison.

9. Louis XIII (1601–43), called The Just from childhood, a title he never deserved. *Essai sur les moeurs*, ch. 175

10. An actual event, reported in Voltaire's *Essai sur les moeurs*, which happened in 1617. D'Ancre had been chief minister, and his assassination marked the end of the regency and the beginning of Louis's personal rule.

11. The Gunpowder Plot of 1605. *Essai sur les moeurs*, ch. 179.

12. St. Patrick's hole, in Ireland, was supposed to be the gateway to hell.

he hoped that she would be soon, as soon as the pope's nephew was not too busy.

I went to Holland, where I hoped I would find more tranquillity in the company of a more phlegmatic people. They were cutting the head off a respectable old man when I arrived at The Hague.[13] It was the bald head of the prime minister, Barneveldt, the man who had done more than any other to advance the republic's interests. Moved by pity, I asked what his crime had been, and whether he had committed treason. "He has done much worse," a preacher wearing a black coat replied; "this was a man who believed that one can save oneself by good works just as effectively as by faith. You surely understand that if opinions of this sort became commonplace no republic could survive, and that we must have strict laws to root out such scandalous horrors." A deep-thinking Dutch politician said to me with a sigh, "Alas, sir, the good times won't last forever; it's only by chance that this people are so zealous; their deep-seated instincts really tend toward the execrable doctrine of toleration. One day it will come to that: the thought makes me shudder." As for me, while I was waiting for the dreadful day of moderation and toleration to dawn, I quickly left a country where bigotry wasn't sweetened by any form of pleasure, and boarded a ship bound for Spain.

The court was in residence at Seville. The galleons bearing gold from the New World had arrived. Everything had an air of abundance and of joy and it was the most delightful season of the year. I saw, at the end of a driveway of orange and apple trees, a sort of immense arena surrounded by steps covered in precious fabrics. The king, the queen, the princes, the princesses were on a lofty dias. Opposite this eminent family there was another throne, but higher still. I said to one of my traveling companions: "Unless this throne is reserved for God, I can't see what its purpose can be." These indiscreet words were overheard by a solemn Spaniard and were to cost me dear. However, I was imagining we were going to see some sort of tournament or bullfight when the Grand Inquisitor appeared on this throne and gave his blessing to the king and to the populace.

After him there came an army of monks marching two by two—white monks, black monks, gray monks; barefoot monks and monks with shoes; bearded monks and clean-shaven monks; with pointed hoods and without hoods. After them marched the executioner; then one caught sight, among the sergeants-at-arms and the members of the nobility, of a group of about forty people, enveloped in sacks on which devils and flames had been painted. These were Jews who had not wanted completely to renounce

13. Part of the conflict between Gomarists (advocates of a strict Calvinist theory of predestination) and Arminians (who recognized a limited freedom of the will). *Essai sur les moeurs*, ch. 187.

Moses, Christians who had married their godparents or who had not worshiped at the shrine of Our Lady of Atocha, or who had not been willing to hand over their change to the Franciscans. Beautiful prayers were sung with devotion, after which all the convicts were burned over a slow fire. The entire royal family seemed to find the whole business enlightening.

In the evening, when I was about to go to bed, two employees of the Inquisition accompanied by the police came to see me. They embraced me affectionately and took me, without saying so much as a word, to a very clean dungeon, furnished with a straw mattress and a beautiful crucifix. I stayed there for six weeks, at the end of which the Reverend Father Inquisitor sent someone to invite me to come and talk to him. He hugged me for a while, displaying a fatherly affection for me. He told me he was sincerely distressed to have learned how dreadful my accommodation was, but that all their guest rooms were full, and that next time he hoped they would make me more comfortable. Then he asked me in the most friendly fashion if I didn't happen to know why I was there. I told the Reverend Father that I assumed it was for my sins. "Well, my dear child, for which of your sins? Speak frankly to me." I guessed as best I could, but I didn't get the right answer. He was so kind as to give me some hints.

Finally I remembered my indiscreet words. They let me go with a flogging and a fine of thirty thousand reales. They took me to pay my respects to the Chief Inquisitor. He was well mannered, and asked me whether I had enjoyed the little show he had put on for the public. I told him that it was exquisite, and I went off to urge my traveling companions to leave this country, beautiful though it is. They had had enough time to learn about all the important things that the Spanish have done for Christianity. They had read the memoirs of the famous bishop of Chiapa,[14] from which they had learned that ten million unbelievers in America had had their throats cut or had been burned in order to convert them. I believe that this bishop was exaggerating the number of those sacrificed, but even if one halves his figures, and concludes there were five million victims, this would still be a significant number.

Still the desire to travel nagged at me. I had planned to finish my tour of Europe by going to Turkey, and so we set out for there. I mentally resolved not to tell anyone I met what I thought of any public spectacles I might see. "These Turks," I said to my companions, "are infidels who haven't been baptized, and will consequently be much more cruel than the Reverend Fathers Inquisitors. Let's keep silent while we are in a Muslim country."

---

14. Barthélemy de Las Casas, *Brevissima relación de la destrucción de las Indias* (1552). *Essai sur les moeurs*, ch. 148.

So we went there. I was taken aback to find many more Christian churches in Turkey than there were in Candia. I saw large groups of monks who were left free to pray to the Virgin Mary, and to speak ill of Mohammed, which they did in the language of their choice, some in Greek, some in Latin, some in Armenian. "What good chaps the Turks are!" I cried out. The Greek Orthodox Christians and the Roman Catholic Christians were at daggers drawn in Constantinople. These slaves persecuted each other, like dogs who fight in the street and have to be hit with sticks by their masters in order to separate them. At that time the grand vizir favored the Greeks. The Greek patriarch accused me of having had dinner with the Roman patriarch, and I was condemned in open court to one hundred blows of a cane on the soles of my feet, or a fine of five hundred sequins. The next day the grand vizir was executed by strangulation; the day after, his successor, who favored the Roman faction, and who wasn't strangled until a month later, condemned me to the same punishment as before for having had dinner with the Greek patriarch. I was placed in the unfortunate position of being no longer able to attend either the Greek or the Latin churches. To cheer myself up I rented a very beautiful Circassian girl who made love tenderly and who was devoted to the mosque. One night, in the sweet transports of love, she cried out as she held me, "Alla, Illa, Alla."[15] Now these are holy words in the Turkish liturgy; but I thought they were sacred words of love. I also cried out as sweetly as could be, "Alla, Illa, Alla." "Ah!" she said to me, "merciful God be praised, you're a Turk." I told her that I blessed her for having given me the strength, and that I couldn't be happier. That morning the imam came to circumcise me; and, as I expressed unwillingness, the local judge, a reliable fellow, proposed to have me impaled. I saved my foreskin and my behind with a thousand sequins, and I quickly fled to Persia, resolved that I would never again listen to either a Greek Orthodox or a Roman Catholic mass in Turkey, and that I would never again cry "Alla, Illa, Alla" in the transports of passion.

When I arrived at Ispahan I was asked if I preferred the white sheep or the black sheep. I replied that I really didn't mind, so long as it was tender. One needs to know that at that time the Persians were divided into two factions, named the White Sheep and the Black Sheep. It was assumed that I was ridiculing both factions, with the result that I found myself in physical danger before I had even passed through the gates of the city. Yet again I had to spend a large number of sequins, this time to escape from questions about sheep.

---

15. "God is great."

I traveled as far as China with an interpreter who assured me that in that country people enjoyed freedom and lived a merry life. The Tartars had seized control, after having put the whole country to fire and sword; and both the reverend fathers of the Jesuit order and their competitors, the reverend fathers of the Dominican order, claimed to be converting people to Christianity, although there was no independent evidence to support their rival claims.[16] There have never been more zealous missionaries, for they took turns to persecute each other. Each side wrote whole volumes of libels to Rome attacking the other. They accused each other of being pagans, and of sacrificing the truth in order to gain converts. Worst was a dreadful quarrel between them on the correct manner in which two people should greet each other. The Jesuits wanted the Chinese to greet their mothers and fathers according to the Chinese custom, and the Dominicans wanted them to adopt the Roman custom. It so happened that the Jesuits took me for a Dominican. They assured His Tartar Majesty that I was a papal spy. The supreme council instructed a senior bureaucrat, who gave instructions to a sergeant-at-arms, who gave orders to four local guards that I should be ceremoniously arrested and bound. After four hundred genuflections I found myself in front of His Majesty. He asked me whether I was the pope's spy, and whether it was true that this ruler was planning to come in person to seize his throne. I replied that the pope was a priest aged seventy; that he lived four thousand leagues away from His Tartaro-Chinese Sacred Majesty; that he had about two thousand soldiers who sheltered under parasols while on guard; that he was not going to seize anyone's throne and that His Majesty could sleep in peace. Of all my adventures, this was the least awful. They sent me to Macao,[17] and from there I took a ship for Europe.

My ship had to be placed in dry dock near the coast of Golconda.[18] I took the opportunity to go and see the court of the great Aureng-Zeb,[19] about whom marvelous things were being said all round the world. At that time he was in Delhi. I had the pleasure of seeing him on the day of the elaborate ceremony in the course of which he received the heavenly present that had been sent him by the governor of Mecca. It was the broom with which the Holy House, the Kabbah, the Beth Allah, had been cleaned. Symbolically, this broom sweeps out all the muck that pollutes

---

16. *Essai sur les moeurs*, ch. 195; *Siècle de Louis XIV,* ch. 39.

17. A Portuguese colony in China.

18. The coast of the Bay of Bengal between the Indian rivers of Krishna and Mahanadi.

19. 1619–1707. *Essai sur les moeurs*, ch. 194.

the soul. Aureng-Zeb appeared to have no need of it. He was the most pious man in all Hindustan. It is true that he had cut the throat of one of his brothers and strangled his father. Twenty rajahs and as many omrahs had been tortured to death; but that doesn't count, and everyone spoke only of his religious devotion. The only person thought to be comparable to him was his Sacred Majesty the most Serene Emperor of Morocco, Muley-Ismaël, who cut off heads every Friday after prayers.

I didn't say a word. My travels had educated me, and I felt that it wasn't my business to decide on the relative merits of these two august sovereigns. A young Frenchman with whom I was staying lacked, I must admit, proper respect for the emperors of India and of Morocco. He took it upon himself to say, very indiscreetly, that in Europe there were some very pious sovereigns who governed their states very well, and even went regularly to church, but who did not kill their brothers and their fathers and cut off their subjects' heads. Our interpreter reported in Hindu the disrespectful speech of this young man. Having learned from experience, I quickly had my camels saddled up: we left, I and the Frenchman. Later I learned that that very night the police officers of the great Aureng-Zeb came to seize us. The only person they found was the interpreter, who was executed in a city square, and all the courtiers declared without the slightest hypocrisy that he deserved to die.

I was left with Africa to visit before I could enjoy all the sweet pleasures of Europe. And see it I did. My ship was captured by black pirates. Our captain complained bitterly to them. He asked them why they violated the law of nations in this way. The African captain replied, "You have long noses, and we have flat noses. You have straight hair and we have curly hair. You have skin that is the color of ash, and we have skin the color of ebony. As a consequence my people and your people must, according to the sacred laws of nature, always be enemies. You buy us at markets on the Guinea coast as if we were beasts of burden, and make us do any work that is both backbreaking and humiliating. You have us beaten with whips in the mountains in order to force us to extract a type of yellow earth, which in itself is useless and which isn't worth anything like as much as a good Egyptian onion. So, when we meet up with you and find ourselves the stronger, we enslave you, we make you labor in our fields, and if you don't we slice off your noses and your ears."

There was nothing I could say in reply to so wise a speech. I went and labored in the fields of an old African woman in order to preserve my nose and ears. After a year my freedom was purchased. I had seen everything that is beautiful, good, and admirable on the face of the earth. I resolved to travel no more. I married in my hometown. I was cuckolded. And I realized that there was no situation in life preferable to mine.

The Comforter Comforted (1756)[20]

One day the great philosopher Citophile[21] said to a woman who was in despair, and had every reason to be so: "Madame, the queen of England,[22] the daughter of Henri IV, has been as unhappy as you. She was driven out of her kingdoms. She very nearly died at sea in a storm. She watched her husband the king die on the scaffold." "That was hard on her," said the lady, and she set to crying about her own misfortunes.

"But," said Citophile, "do you remember Mary Stuart?[23] She had an honorable love for a handsome musician who had a very beautiful lower back. Her husband killed her musician in front of her; and later her good friend and close relative Elizabeth, who claimed to be a virgin, had her head cut off on a scaffold draped in black, after having held her in prison for eighteen years." "That was very cruel," said the woman, and sank back into melancholy.

"Perhaps you have heard speak," said the comforter, "of the beautiful Joanna of Naples, who was seized and strangled."[24] "I have a vague memory of her," said the one in need of comforting.

"Then I must tell you about the adventures," said the other, "of a head of state who was overthrown after supper and during my lifetime, and who died on a desert island." "I already know the whole story," said the woman.

"All right. I will tell you about what happened to another powerful princess to whom I taught philosophy. She had a lover, as all powerful and beautiful princesses have. Her father came into her bedroom and took her lover, whose face was all flushed and whose eyes were sparkling like carbuncles, by surprise. The princess was also glowing a bright pink. The look on the face of the young man so displeased the princess's father that he struck him the hardest blow that anyone in the whole of his realm had ever received. The lover took up a pair of tongs and smashed the head of his lover's father—he barely recovered from it, and he still bears the scar left by this wound. The princess, horrified, leaped out of the window and twisted her ankle, so that she still limps noticeably, although in every other respect she has a very attractive body. Her lover was condemned to death

---

20. Possibly written in response to the death of the son of the Duchess of Saxe-Gotha (June 1756; D6905): Voltaire's friend persisted in Leibnizian optimism no matter how dreadful her experiences.

21. Someone who is keen on citations or on lists of examples.

22. Henrietta Maria, wife of Charles I. See *Essai sur les moeurs*, chs. 179, 180.

23. Mary Queen of Scots (d. 1587). See *Essai sur les moeurs*, ch. 169.

24. Joanna I (c. 1324–1382), queen of Naples. She is discussed at length in Bayle's *Dictionary*, art. "Naples."

for having smashed the head of a very powerful prince. You can imagine the state the princess was in when her lover was taken off to be hanged. I used to spend a lot of time with her when she was in prison. The only subject she ever spoke of was that of her misfortunes."

"Well then, why don't you want me to dwell on mine?" the woman asked him. "Because," said the philosopher, "it's wrong to dwell on them, and because, since so many great ladies have been so unfortunate, it's not appropriate for you to give way to despair. Think of Hecuba. Think of Niobe."[25] "Ah," said the woman, "if I had lived when they did, or when so many beautiful princesses were alive, and if, in order to comfort them, you had told them the story of my misfortunes, do you think they would have listened to you?"

The next day the philosopher lost his only son, and came close to dying of grief. The woman had a list drawn up of all the kings who had lost their children and took it to the philosopher. He read it, he found it very well researched, and he didn't stop crying for all that. Three months later they met up again and were astonished to find each other in the best of spirits. They had a beautiful statue erected to Time, with this inscription: "To the great healer."

---

25. Hecuba and Niobe both symbolize grief. Hecuba was the wife of Priam, king of Troy at the time of its destruction. Niobe saw all her many children killed.

Voltaire's Correspondence

Letter to Jean-Robert Tronchin, 24 November [1755][1]

Well, sir, physics can be a cruel science. It would really be quite difficult to work out how the laws of physics create such horrendous disasters in the best of all possible worlds. One hundred thousand ants, our neighbors, crushed all of a sudden in our ant heap, and half of them doubtless dying in indescribable torments in the midst of the debris from which it was impossible to extricate them. Families all across Europe ruined. The wealth of a hundred thousand businessmen from your homeland destroyed in the ruins of Lisbon. What a miserable game of chance is the game of human life! What will the preachers say if the palace of the Inquisition has survived? I reassure myself that at least the reverend fathers the inquisitors will have been crushed along with everyone else. That ought to teach people not to persecute other people, for just when some holy idiots are burning some fanatics the earth opens up and swallows both together!

I have already seen our friend Gauffecourt. I will go to Montriond as late as I can. I believe our mountains are protecting us from the earthquakes. Goodbye, my dear correspondent, tell me, I beg you, the latest news regarding this dreadful event.

Letter to François-Louis Allamand, 16 December 1755[2]

I have come, sir, to Montriond to turn myself into a squirrel for the winter, after having undergone my own little earthquake[3] like everyone else. The best of all possible worlds seems to me to be a bomb. Like you, I mourn the Portuguese; but human beings do more harm to each other on their little mole hill than nature does harm to them. Our wars murder more people than are swallowed up in earthquakes. If there was nothing in this world to fear but the Lisbon disaster, we would be in a reasonably good situation. Moreover we are now told that half that city is still standing. At first both the good and the bad are always exaggerated. I believe that Lisbon still looks less turned over than the cliffs and rocks where you are. If you could leave your lair to join me in my squirrel hole, we could argue back and forth about physical and moral evil during the periods when my physical pains occasionally let up. I would be delighted to see how an imagination

---

1. D6597.
2. D6629.
3. 9 Dec. 1755.

as brilliant as yours has been able to keep its fire in the land of frost. You seem to me to be like a champagne, which is all the better for being on ice. I embrace you, one philosopher to another, without ceremony, as usual.

LETTER TO ELIE BERTRAND, 18 FEBRUARY 1756[4]

I was in the middle, my dear philosopher, of a vicious recurrence of my stomachache when I received your letter. I can console myself, therefore, with the thought that I won't have stomachache in the next world. Indeed, I very much hope so, and I say a little word about it in my sermon.[5] The question at issue is not this one of hope. The sole question concerns the axiom, or rather the joke, that all is well as it is, everything is as it ought to be, and universal happiness here and now is the consequence of the miseries suffered right now by each creature. But in truth, this is as ridiculous as that fine saying of Posidonius,[6] who said to his gout, "You won't force me to admit that you are painful."

Men of all times and of all religions have so sharply felt the miserable condition of human beings that they have all said that God's handiwork has been changed. Egyptians, Greeks, Persians, Romans: all have imagined that something comparable to the fall of the first man had taken place. One must admit that Pope's work is an attack on this truth, and that my little speech defends it. For if all is well, if all has been as it ought to be, then there is no fallen nature. But on the other hand if there is evil in the world, then this evil indicates that nature has been corrupted in the past and will be mended in the future. That's the natural conclusion to draw. You will say to me that I don't draw this conclusion, that I abandon the reader in depression and in doubt.[7] All right. All one need do is add the word "hope" to the word "adore" so that it reads:

> mortals, you must suffer,
> Submit, adore, hope, and die.

But the heart of the work remains unhappily the presentation of an uncontestable truth. There is evil on earth. And you're laughing at me if you say that a thousand miserable lives are the embodiment of happiness. Yes, there is evil, and few people would want to start their lives over again, perhaps not one in a hundred thousand. And when people tell me it could

---

4. D6738.

5. I.e., the "Poem on the Lisbon Disaster."

6. A Stoic philosopher of the first century B.C.E.

7. This was a common criticism of the first version of the poem, and resulted in a substantial revision.

not be otherwise, they attack my reason and show contempt for my sufferings. A workman who has bad raw materials and bad tools is allowed to say, "I could not do better." But my poor Pope, my poor hunchback, whom I knew, whom I loved, who told you that God could not make you without a hunchback? You are making a mockery of the story of the apple. It is still (speaking on the basis of natural reason, and leaving sacred truths to one side) a more convincing account than the optimism of Leibniz; it explains why you are hunchbacked, sick, and a little malicious.

We need a God who speaks to the human species. Optimism leads to despair. It is a cruel philosophy hiding under a reassuring name. Alas, if all is well while everyone is suffering, then we could travel to a thousand different worlds whose creatures suffered and where all was well. One could travel from misery to misery, looking for a world better than the one before. And if all is well, how can the followers of Leibniz admit that one world could be better than another? This idea of a better world, is it not proof in itself that all is not well? Ah! How do we know that Leibniz did not live in hope of a better world? Between us, dear sir, Leibniz, and Shaftesbury, and Bolingbroke, and Pope were only trying to be clever. As for me, I suffer, and I say as much; and I speak as truly when I say that I very much want to go to Berne to thank you for your kindnesses and for those of M. de Freydenreik. You know all the news: all is well in France; Mme. de Pompadour has joined the religious faction, and has taken a Jesuit for her confessor.

Letter to Marie Ursule de Klinglin, Countess of Lutzelbourg, 4 June [1757][8]

May God protect Marie[9] and return sister Broumath[10] safe to you. Don't be surprised, madame, that Frederick had the better of the Irishman Brown,[11] and of Prince Charles.[12] The convention of rats is broken up by the cat Raminagrobis.[13] If the marshal d'Estrées[14] doesn't block the duke of Cumberland you can be sure that Raminagrobis will send twenty thou-

---

8. D7280.

9. The empress Maria-Theresa of Austria. The Austrian army was trapped in Prague.

10. Frau Zuckmantel de Brumath, sister of the Prussian ambassador to Mannheim.

11. Count Ulysses Maximilian von Brown, an Austrian general.

12. The Emperor Joseph's brother.

13. A reference to a story from La Fontaine's *Fables*. The cat is Frederick II.

14. The general commanding the French army on the Rhine, who was seeking to invade Hanover.

sand of his big bastards who fire seven shots in a minute, and who, being taller, stronger, and better trained than our little soldiers, and moreover having longer rifles, will have as much superiority when using the bayonet as when firing volleys.

What's one to do about all this, madame? Cultivate one's fields and vineyards; walk in the arbors that one has planted; live in a fine house, have good furniture, drive an elegant carriage, eat the best food, read good books, live in the company of decent people from day to day; don't think of death or of the evil deeds of the living. Mad men enter into the employment of kings; wise men enjoy the most precious peace and quiet.

A thousand tender respects.

Letter to Louisa Dorothea, Duchess of Saxe-Gotha, 24 June [1757][15]

Madame,

It is the letters that Your Most Serene Highness honors me with that are the charming ones. You resemble the goddesses of Homer who, according to Madame Dacier, "sweetened the harsh atmosphere of the wars." It seems to me that your mood is like your estates, tranquil in the midst of public conflicts. The best of all possible worlds has been pretty horrible for the last two years. But it's been that way for ages. The latest catastrophe doesn't yet equal those in previous centuries. But with a little time we may manage to equal all the miseries and all the horrors of the most heroic epochs.

People will be pretty disappointed if the armies of Prussia, Austria, Russia, Hanover, France, etc., do not destroy at least a hundred or so cities, do not reduce to penury some fifty thousand families, and do not kill four or five hundred thousand men. Look, already one quarter of Prague has been reduced to ashes. One cannot yet say that "All is well," but things aren't going badly; and in time the truth of optimism will be demonstrated.

I do not know, however, madame, whether I should offer more hearty congratulations to those who are crushed by bombs, with their wives and children, or to those whom nature condemns to suffer all their life long, and who are entrusted to the doctors so that they can fulfill their fine destiny. I have the honor to be one of these, and but for that I would have the honor to write more often to Your Highness.

I have some desire, madame, to live long enough to see the outcome of this great tragedy, which is still only in its second act. But I wish to live above all so that I can place myself at your feet. For even if this world is not

---

15. D7297.

the best of all worlds, your court is assuredly for me the best of all possible courts. No news reaches me, madame, in my place of retreat. All the better when there is no news, for most of the news about public events is bad news. I am still living in this house in the country to which I have a sentimental attachment because of the name of the prince who once lived here. Here I pray for the prosperity of Your Most Serene Highness, and for all your noble household. I often think of the great mistress who rules our hearts, and, as I am running out of paper, I finish with my profound respects.

Letter [in English] to George Keith, 4 October [November] 1758[16]

My Lord,

When I ran last year into prophecies, like Isaiah and Jeremiah, I did not think I should weep this year over your worthy brother. I learned his death and that of the king's sister at a time. Nature and war work on together your king's calamities. The loss of Marshal Keith is a great one. All your philosophy cannot remove your grief. Philosophy assuages the wound and leaves the heart wounded. This present war is the most hellish that was ever fought. Your lordship saw formerly one battle a year at the most. But nowadays the earth is covered with blood and mangled carcasses, almost every month. Let the happy madmen who say that all what is, is well, be confounded. 'Tis not so indeed with twenty provinces exhausted and with three hundred thousand men murdered.

I wish your lordship the peace of mind necessary in this lasting hurricane of horror. I enjoy a calm and delightful life, that Frederick will never taste of. But the more happy I am, the more I pity kings. I hope you were as happy as I am, were you not tender brother![17] Preserve your goodwill, my lord, for a country philosopher who will always have, through and through, the most tender respect for you.

---

16. D7931. All but the last sentence is in Voltaire's English, with modernized spelling and revised punctuation.

17. I.e., "I would wish that you were as happy as I am, but I realize that the death of your brother makes this impossible."

"WELL (ALL IS)" FROM THE *PORTABLE PHILOSOPHICAL DICTIONARY* (1764)

There was quite a fuss in the universities, and even among those who think for themselves, when Leibniz, while paraphrasing Plato, constructed his theory of the best of all possible worlds, where he imagined that everything is for the best. Even while living in the north of Germany,[1] he maintained that there was only one world that God could make. Plato had at least left God free to make five worlds on the grounds that there are only five regular solids: the tetrahedron (a pyramid with three faces and sides of equal length), the cube, the hexahedron, the dodecahedron, the icosahedron. But since our world isn't shaped like any of Plato's five solids he evidently ought to have allowed God a sixth type of construction.

Let's leave the divine Plato there. Leibniz, who was certainly a better geometer than Plato, and a profounder metaphysician, thus did the human species the kindness of making us see that we ought to be entirely satisfied, and that there was nothing more that God could do for us, for he had no choice but to choose, among all the possible worlds, the one that was unquestionably the best.

"What will become of original sin?" was the question on everyone's lips. "It will have to look after itself," said Leibniz among his friends; but in public he wrote that original sin entered of necessity into the best of all possible worlds.

What! To be driven out of a garden of delights where one would have lived forever if one had not eaten an apple! What! To engender in misery miserable children who will experience every possible form of suffering and will make others suffer all there is to suffer! What! To suffer every type of disease, to face every sort of disappointment, to die in pain, and to be cheered up by being burned throughout eternity! Is this fate really the best there could be? It certainly isn't *good* from our point of view, and how can it be good from God's?

Leibniz realized that there was no reply to such questions; so he wrote fat books in which he contradicted himself.

One can laughingly deny there is evil in the world if one is a Lucullus who is in good health and who is having a good dinner with his friends and his mistress in the hall of Apollo;[2] but if he puts his head out the window

---

1. In Voltaire's view more or less the worst of all possible worlds.

2. Licinius Lucullus (d. 56 B.C.E.) was a Roman noble famous for living in luxury. His dining hall was called the hall of Apollo; Apollo being a god particularly interested in music and poetry.

he'll see people who are unhappy; if he gets a fever he will be unhappy himself.

I don't like quoting; it's usually hard work and the rewards are very uncertain. You have to leave out what precedes and what follows the passage you quote, and you expose yourself to a thousand different criticisms. But I am nevertheless obliged to quote Lactantius, one of the Church Fathers,[3] who in chapter 13 of his book *On God's Anger* has Epicurus speak as follows:

> Either God wants to eliminate evil from this world, and is unable to do so; or he is able to do so, and doesn't want to; or he is neither able to do it nor wants to do it; or finally he wants to do it and he can do it. If he wants to do it and can't, then he is not omnipotent, which would be contrary to the nature of God; if he can do it and doesn't want to, then he is wicked, which is equally contrary to his nature; if he is neither able nor willing, then he is not omnipotent and he is wicked; if he is willing and able (which is the only option which is worthy of the divine nature), then why is there evil on earth?[4]

This is a strong argument, and Lactantius replies to it very poorly, saying that God wishes for evil to exist, but that he has given us the wisdom required to acquire good. One must admit that this reply is very weak when compared to the difficulty it is supposed to resolve, for it supposes that God could not give us wisdom without being the author of evil; and if that's the case wisdom isn't very attractive!

The origin of evil has always been an abyss the bottom of which no one has been able to see. This is what forced so many ancient philosophers and legislators to have recourse to two divine principles, one good, the other evil. The Egyptians called the evil principle Typhon, while the Persians called him Ahriman. As is well known, the Manicheans adopted this theology; but as no Manichean had ever spoken to either the good or the evil principle, we shouldn't regard their word as sufficient proof of their existence.

Among the absurdities with which our world is stuffed, among those that are themselves harmful, one must include as a far-from-insignificant absurdity the supposition that there are two all-powerful beings who are at war over which of the two will have the greater influence on this world, and who reach mutual understandings like the two doctors in Molière: "Pass me the emetic, and I'll pass you the leeches."

---

3. Writing c. 300 C.E.

4. Voltaire's source is probably the article "Paulicians," remark E, in Bayle's *Dictionary*.

Basilides, a Platonist who lived in the first century of organized Christianity,[5] claimed that God had given the task of making our world to the lowest angels, and that they, not being very skillful, made the world as we see it. This theological fairytale crumbles into dust when it meets the fatal objection that it would not be in the nature of a God who is both all-powerful and perfectly wise to have a world constructed by a team of architects who were completely incompetent.

Simon,[6] who foresaw this line of argument, sought to block it by saying that the angel who was in charge of the works was sent to hell for having done such a lousy job; but burning this angel doesn't relieve us from our pains and sufferings.

The myth of Pandora, as told by the Greeks, does not provide any more satisfactory a response to my objection. The box in which all the world's evils are to be found, and at the bottom of which, when everything else has escaped, hope remains, is certainly a delightful allegory; but this Pandora was only made by Vulcan so that he could have his revenge on Prometheus, who had made a man out of mud.

The Indians have come no closer to success. According to them, God created man and then gave him a drug that would guarantee him permanent good health. Man loaded the drug onto the back of his donkey; the donkey grew thirsty; the serpent showed him a spring, and while the donkey was drinking the serpent took the drug for himself.

The Syrians imagined that man and woman, having been created in the fourth heaven, took it into their heads to eat a cake instead of the ambrosia that was their natural diet. The waste products of ambrosia were breathed out through their pores; but, now they had eaten cake, they needed to go to the toilet. The man and the woman asked an angel where they could find a restroom. "Do you see," said the angel to them, "that little planet, absolutely minuscule, which is about sixty million leagues from here? That's the toilet for the whole universe. Go there as quickly as you can." They went there; they were left there; and since then our world has been what it is.

One's bound to ask the Syrians why God let man eat cake, and allowed this action to unleash such a horde of absolutely dreadful consequences for the human race.

Leaving this fourth heaven behind, I move quickly to Lord Bolingbroke, in order to ensure that I don't become bored.[7] This man,

---

5. A Gnostic of the second century C.E. Gnosticism was influenced by Manicheism.

6. Simon of Gitta.

7. Bolingbroke's "Fragments or Minutes of Essays" were published in his posthumous *Works* (5 vols., London: D. Mallett, 1754).

who was without doubt of extraordinary ability, gave the famous Pope the outline of his "All is well," an expression that one finds more or less word for word in the posthumous works of Lord Bolingbroke, and one that Lord Shaftesbury had already formulated in his *Characteristics*. Read Shaftesbury's chapter on the moralists, and you will find the following words:

> It is easy to reply to these complaints regarding the supposed defects of nature. How has nature emerged so defective and imperfect from the hands of a perfect being? But I deny that she is imperfect. . . Her beauty is the result of contrasts, and the universal harmony is the product of a perpetual conflict. . . It is necessary for each species to be sacrificed for the good of others: vegetables provide food for animals, and animals die, rot, and fertilize the soil . . . ; and the laws of the central power and of gravitation, which give to the celestial bodies their weight and their movement, will never be disturbed for the benefit of a feeble animal whose existence is protected by these same laws, but who will soon be reduced to dust by them.[8]

Bolingbroke, Shaftesbury, and Pope (who worked up their ideas) are no better at solving the problem than everyone else. Their "All is well" amounts to nothing more than that everything is under the control of unalterable laws. Is this news to anyone? They aren't teaching us anything when, like generations of children, they announce that flies are born in order to be eaten by spiders; spiders in order to be eaten by swallows; swallows in order to be eaten by hawks; hawks in order to be eaten by eagles; eagles in order to be killed by men; men in order to kill each other, and in order to be eaten by worms (and then, in the case of at least nine hundred and ninety-nine out of a thousand, by devils).

Thus you can see an order which is clear-cut and unchanging between all the different species; there is order everywhere you look. When a stone forms in my bladder the mechanism involved is wonderful. Juices rich in minerals pass little by little into my blood; the minerals are filtered out by the kidneys; the waste products pass through the urethra, and are deposited in my bladder; there they form into a sphere by the working of a fine example of the Newtonian principle of attraction; the stone forms and grows; I suffer pains a thousand times worse than death itself as a result of this admirable mechanism that is second to none; a surgeon, having per-

---

8. This is a translation of Voltaire's rather loose translation: the original text is to be found in Shaftesbury, "The Moralists" pt. 1, sect. 3, in *Characteristics* (1711; ed. Cambridge, 1999), pp. 244–5. See above, p. 95.

fected the technique invented by Tubalcaïn,[9] comes and sticks an implement with a fine point and sharp sides into my perineum and seizes my stone with his pincers. The laws of mechanics ensure that the force he applies to the stone breaks it. And the same laws ensure that I die in the most terrible torment. "All this is good," all this is the inevitable consequence of unalterable physical laws. I won't argue with you, and I knew it every bit as well as you do.

If we were incapable of sensation there would be no problem with these mechanisms. But the mechanisms aren't the point at issue, for the real question is whether there are bad experiences, and if so where they come from. "There are no evils," says Pope in his fourth letter on "All is well"; "or, if there are any particular instances of evil, they form part of the overall good."

There's something remarkable about the overall good, when it is made up of the stone, of gout, of all the crimes men perform, of all the pain they suffer, of death, and of damnation.

The Fall is the bandage that we put over all the particular diseases of the body and of the soul, diseases that we call "overall health." But Shaftesbury and Bolingbroke laugh at the idea of original sin, and Pope doesn't mention it. It is evident that their theory undermines the foundations of the Christian religion, while explaining nothing whatsoever.

Nevertheless, this system has recently met with the approval of many theologians who are happy to reconcile the irreconcilable. Frankly, we shouldn't begrudge anyone the comfort to be derived from putting up the best arguments one can to explain the great flood of evils under which we are drowning. It is only right to allow people suffering from a fatal illness to eat whatever takes their fancy. It has even been claimed that this argument itself alleviates suffering.[10] "God," says Pope, "has the same feelings at the death of a great man as at the death of a sparrow; he is as affected by the destruction of one atom as by that of a thousand planets; he takes the same pleasure in the formation of a soap bubble and of an entire world."[11]

Well, I must admit, this is a pleasant way of alleviating our suffering. Don't you find yourself feeling much better as a result of Lord Shaftesbury's decree, which states that God will not make exceptions to his eternal laws for the sake of an animal as feeble as man? One must admit, at least, that this feeble little creature is entitled to whimper humbly, and to seek to understand, while whimpering, why these eternal laws are not made for the well-being of each individual.

---

9. The descendant of Cain and the first blacksmith (Genesis 4:22).

10. See Rousseau, above, p. 109.

11. Voltaire's version of *Essay on Man*, i.87–90.

This system of "All is well" represents the author of the universe as a king who is both powerful and ill intentioned, who isn't the slightest bit upset if four or five hundred thousand men have to lose their lives, and the rest of the population live out their days in hunger and tears, provided he achieves his goals.

Far then from the belief that this is the best of all possible worlds being a source of consolation, it is enough to drive the philosophers who adopt it to despair. The question of good and evil remains a trackless wasteland for those who seek an answer in good faith; it offers opportunities to show off for those who like to argue—they are like convicts making music with their chains. As for those who don't think at all, they remind me of fish who have been moved from a river into a reservoir. The fish don't suspect for a moment that they are there to be eaten during Lent. Like them, we know, through our own capacities, nothing at all about the factors determining our destiny.

Let us place at the end of almost all the chapters on metaphysics the two letters the Roman judges employed when they did not understand a lawsuit: *N.L., non liquet;* this isn't clear.

Voltaire's Feminism

Wives Obey Your Husbands[1]

One day the abbot of Châteauneuf[2] told me that madame the wife of the marshal de Grancey[3] was very overbearing; and that she had some very fine qualities. Above all she took pride in her own self-respect, so she never did anything that would make her feel guilty, even in secret; she never demeaned herself to tell a lie: she preferred to speak a truth that might prove harmful to her rather than conceal the truth to her own benefit. She said that dissimulation is always a sign of cowardice. A thousand generous deeds adorned her life, but when she was praised for them she thought she was being insulted. She said, "Am I to take it you think that behaving properly required an effort on my part?" Her lovers adored her; her friends cherished her; and her husband respected her.

Forty years went by, devoted to pleasure and to the cycle of amusements that are the serious business of women; during this period she never read a word except when she read letters addressed to her; she thought about nothing except political gossip, the idiocies of her neighbors, and the affections of her heart. Finally, when she found herself at the age at which, as they say, women who have both beauty and brains begin to rely on their brains rather than their beauty, she decided to start reading. She began with the tragedies of Racine, and was astonished to find that she enjoyed reading them even more than she had enjoyed seeing them performed. The good taste with which she was gifted enabled her to recognize that this was an author who could never be boring or untruthful; that he had an unerring sense of form; that he was plain-speaking and noble, avoiding anything artificial or rhetorical, and not interested in showing off; that the details of his plots, and the thoughts of his characters were taken from nature. She rediscovered in her reading the story of her own emotions, and found her own life portrayed.

She was encouraged to read Montaigne. She was charmed by an author who entered into a conversation with her and who had no certainties. Then she was given Plutarch's *Great Men*. She asked why he hadn't written the lives of great women.

---

1. Probably written c. 1764, when Voltaire was much impressed with Catherine the Great, empress of Russia, who had recently come to the throne. First published in the *Mélanges* (1765).
2. d. 1709.
3. d. 1694.

One day the abbot of Châteauneuf happened to meet her. She was red with anger. "What's the matter, madame?" he asked her.

"I happened to open a book that was lying around in my study. It is, I think, a collection of letters. In it I caught sight of these words: 'Wives, obey your husbands.' I threw the book on the floor."

"What, madame! Don't you realize that those were the epistles of St. Paul?"

"I don't care who wrote them. The author is downright rude. Monsieur the marshal never ever wrote to me in that tone. I'm sure that it can't have been easy to put up with your St. Paul. Was he married?"

"Yes, madame."

"Well his wife must have been a very good-natured person. If I had been married to someone like that I would have sent him packing. *Wives obey your husbands!* It wouldn't have been so bad if he had said, 'Be sweet, amenable, attentive, economical.' Then I would have said, 'Here's someone who knows how to live the good life!' And why should we obey, I ask you? When I married M. de Grancey we promised each other to be faithful. I haven't exactly kept my word, and neither has he; but neither he nor I promised to obey.[4] Are we supposed to be slaves? Isn't it bad enough that a man, after he has married me, has the right to make me ill for nine months, at the end of which I may die? Isn't it bad enough that I give birth, in great pain, to a child who will be able to take me to court when he is of age? Isn't it bad enough that every month I suffer from an inconvenience that is very disagreeable for a woman of rank, and that, to make matters worse, if I miss one of these twelve medical conditions that I should have each year I may die of it? Why, on top of everything else, tell me to *obey?*

"Certainly, nature doesn't tell us to obey. She makes us physically different from men, but makes us necessary to men as they are to us. She doesn't maintain that one of us should be enslaved to the other! I remember Molière saying, 'Those who have beards have all the power.' But that's scarcely a sensible reason for imposing a master on me! What! Because a man has his chin covered in nasty coarse fur, which he has to cut as close to the skin as possible, while my chin is smooth from birth, does this mean I should humbly obey him? I know that in general men have muscles that are stronger than ours, and that they can give you a more effective blow with their fists. I rather fear that that may be the basis of their superiority.

"They also claim that they are better at thinking straight, and as a consequence they boast that they are better able to rule over others; but I could easily show them some queens who are worth more than most kings. Someone was telling me just recently about a German princess who gets

---

4. This was part of Protestant but not Catholic wedding ceremonies.

up at five every morning in order to work at making her subjects happy.[5] She manages all the business, answers all the letters, sponsors all the arts, and is as generous with her good deeds as she is enlightened in her understanding; and she is as brave as she is well informed. Moreover, she wasn't educated in a convent by idiots who teach us things we would be better off not knowing and make no attempt to teach us the things we need to know. As for me, if I had a state to govern, I believe I have what it would take to imitate this fine example."

The abbot of Châteauneuf, whose manners were excellent, was careful not to contradict madame.

"While we're on the subject," she said, "is it true that Mohammed had such contempt for us that he maintained that we are not worthy to enter into paradise, and that we would only be allowed into the forecourt?"

"If that's the case," said the abbot, "the men will be kept waiting at the gate; but let me reassure you, there isn't a single word of truth in what people say here about the Muslim religion. Our ignorant and wicked monks have completely misled us, as my brother, who for twelve years was our ambassador in Constantinople, told me."

"What! Are you telling me that it isn't true, monsieur, that Mohammed invented polygamy in order to win the support of men? Isn't it true that women are slaves in Turkey, and that they are forbidden to pray to God in a mosque?"

"That's all untrue, madame. Mohammed, far from having invented polygamy, censured it and restricted it. King Solomon the wise had seven hundred wives. Mohammed reduced the permitted number to no more than four. He taught that women go to paradise just as men do; and no doubt men and women will make love there, though in a different way from the way in which they do here, for you know very well that our experience of love in this world is very defective."

"Alas, you're quite right," said madame the marshal's wife; "men aren't up to much. But, tell me, your Mohammed, did he command wives to obey their husbands?"

"No, madame, that command is not to be found in the Koran."

"Then why are women slaves in Turkey?"

"They aren't slaves: they own property; they can testify; they can, under the appropriate circumstances, insist on a divorce; they go to the mosque at set times, and go out to meet friends at other times. You see them in the streets, with the lower half of their faces veiled, just as a few years ago fashionable women here wore a mask in public. It's true that women aren't to be seen at the opera or the theater; but that's because neither exist. Do you imagine that if there was ever an opera house in

---

5. Catherine the Great of Russia was born in Germany.

Constantinople, which is the birthplace of Orpheus,[6] the Turkish women would not fill the best boxes?"

"Wives obey your husbands," muttered the marshal's wife over and over again. "This chap Paul was a savage."

"He was a bit tough," replied the abbot; "and he very much liked to be the master. He treated St. Peter, who was quite a decent chap, as if he were his inferior. Moreover you mustn't take everything he says literally. People criticize him for having had more than a tendency toward Jansenism."[7]

"Ah, well I suspected he was a heretic," said the marshal's wife, and settled down to beautifying herself.

---

6. Orpheus was the son of Apollo and, according to Greek myth, the greatest of all singers.

7. The followers of Cornelius Jansen (1585–1638) were Catholics who followed Augustine and St. Paul in denying that we can contribute to our salvation by good deeds. Jansen's teaching was condemned by Urban VIII in the bull *In Eminente* (1642), but sustained persecution of his followers began with the bull *Unigenitus* (1713).